A Girl From Oz

Lyndall Hobbs

hardie grant books

Published in 2016 by Hardie Grant Books

Hardie Grant Books (Australia)
Ground Floor, Building 1
658 Church Street
Richmond, Victoria 3121
www.hardiegrant.com.au

Hardie Grant Books (UK)
5th & 6th Floor
52–54 Southwark Street
London SE1 1UN
www.hardiegrant.co.uk

A Cataloguing-in-Publication entry is available from the catalogue of the
National Library of Australia at www.nla.gov.au
A Girl from Oz
ISBN 978 1 74270 866 9

Cover design by Mark Campbell
Text design and typesetting by Patrick Cannon

Colour reproduction by Splitting Image Colour Studio
Printed in China by 1010 Printing International Limited

Contents

This book is dedicated to my exceptionally wonderful mum and dad, Pauline and Norman Hobbs, who loved me unconditionally. It is also dedicated to the two wonderful kids I'm lucky enough to have, Lola and Nick, who I likewise love and adore unconditionally.

My parents were so staggeringly good-natured, kind, supportive and selfless that not once, by word or deed, did they make me feel guilty for leaving home, never to return. (They didn't have to—I have enough guilt for a large village.) I, on the other hand, must warn my kids that I am not that selfless and if they stray too far, I will most definitely attempt to guilt-trip them into a swift return.

Royal Encounter

H E DINED OUT on the story for years, which was wildly unfair as it made me out to be an absolute floozy. But when Michael White, theatre producer, glamorous *Rocky Horror Show* impresario and man-about-town, swung into 'raconteur' mode, folks tended to sit up, listen and roar appreciatively—ignoring my noisy protests. Michael, my boyfriend, was probably the most prolific party-giver in London and a big deal, and thus very few would contradict him to defend me. I just had to grin and bear it.

The occasion for said tale was Michael's big West End premiere of *Ain't Misbehavin'* in 1979—which Prince Charles was to attend—and it was the epitome of a full-on day of fun and excitement that, looking back, I can only marvel at. I worked at Thames TV's *Today Show* as an on-camera reporter and host, and I'd already pitched an idea at the morning meeting that had received a speedy 'green light'. Andy Warhol had just arrived in London for an exhibition at a gallery on South Molton Street, and I would attempt to get an interview.

Frantic phone calls and a mad dash to the library to retrieve a file of Warhol newspaper cuttings followed. No Google or Wikipedia to help you back then. This was *before* computers! I wrote a piece-to-camera and worked on questions that might get the famously

Smiling with grim determination as I wait for the Thames TV crew to arrive and set up, having finally gotten the shy, tight-lipped Andy Warhol to agree to an interview before a gallery opening on London's South Molton Street.

tight-lipped Andy to open up. I called Michael to ask a quick question about a Warhol show we'd seen in New York, but he was in meetings planning the big night ahead. No mobile phones in those days so I was truly flying solo. I sped off in my yellow Volkswagen Bug and parked illegally as close as I could to South Molton Street, with the interview still unconfirmed. But I'd been told that Andy might be hanging pictures and it was worth a shot. Lying, I called the boss from a phone box to say it was a 'go' and to send a crew in an hour.

Well I found Andy, he of the ghostly eyes, and reminded him we'd met several times in New York at parties and at The Factory. His vague monotone responses just trailed off, but as soon as the crew arrived, my terror at failing to deliver was transformed into what I now think of as 'Manic Hyper Focus Mode' and I did manage to wrangle him for a few amusing minutes. It was like getting blood out of a stone, but

I'd paid the little dog he was holding a lot of attention and, perfectly amiably, he mumbled his answers like someone who'd very recently swallowed twenty-two Valium.

Interview over, the union crew was ready for lunch. They were always insisting on a bloody lunch break at some random time of their choosing, dependent on when they had clocked in for the day. It was only 11.30 am, for crying out loud. I begged them to come inside to shoot some cutaways (shots to cut to during the interview) of the art.

'Not enough light, love,' they happily insisted.

'But it's an exhibition. We need to show some of the art,' I pleaded. Stupid bastards, I wanted to say, but I knew well they didn't much like the idea of 'a woman reporter' and could make life difficult for me. However, by hovering close and smiling nonstop, I usually got my way. Eventually, lights were slowly retrieved from the van after a long, leisurely 'tea' break, and my cutaways were obtained. Then it was back to the Thames TV studios to wait for the film to be processed—the miracle of instantaneous video playback still a long way off in what I now realise are almost prehistoric times—and to nervously field calls from a few after-show dinner guests who were asking, in a roundabout way, about our royal seating arrangements. At least no one then could hound you with texts or emails!

After I cautiously told the boss that it was a 'decent' interview—not wanting to oversell it but I had to ensure it made its way onto the show's running order—the film was brought up from the basement labs and wheeled into a stuffy room where the editor seemed to work in slow motion as he methodically threaded the film through the Steenbeck (an ancient machine used in the '70s, kids, to edit actual film). Finally, we had a pretty good four-minute piece completed but, moments later, were told the running order was very full and that it had to be cut back by a minute. By the time we trimmed it down to three minutes, it was 4 pm already. No time to even hit the dry-cleaners to pick up the dress I wanted to wear. I'd have to squeeze into the gorgeous but very tight black velvet Bruce Oldfield strapless dress with a matching short jacket—and hair washing was probably out.

Luckily, I was not needed in the studio that night for any on-air interviews and I finally made it out, driving like a bat out of hell to Egerton Crescent, where Michael and I lived, right next door to the famous British TV interviewer David Frost, in a fabulous white five-storey house. (Egerton Crescent is still one of the most beautiful streets in London—with its curved row of gorgeous, identical all-white houses—just between Knightsbridge and Fulham Road.) Shortly after arriving in London with only two friends to look up, I was living an incredibly glamorous life with a sweet, kind but quite distant man, who never wanted to spend a night in with me but instead thrived on going out or entertaining virtually seven nights a week.

Michael, chic, handsome and dressed in a black velvet double-breasted jacket, was livid I was late. Nothing new. Definitely no time for a shower. I resorted to lifting my fringe and patting on some baby powder. Some mascara, lipstick and a squirt of Joy and it was back downstairs to the dining room for a gulp of Michael's vodka tonic as I breathed in so he could zip up my dress. Truly, it was a bloody tight squeeze.

'You've put on weight,' he said.

'Big rib cage,' I retorted as we scanned the freshly laid table and the seating plan sketch. We made the fateful decision that Sabrina Guinness (now deliriously happily married and more correctly known as Lady Tom Stoppard) should be on the Prince's right. Me on his left.

Then it was off to the theatre. We had to be there in time to greet the Prince. Bows, curtsies, the whole nine yards. The show, with its original all-black Broadway cast, was a gem and His Royal Highness seemed to be thoroughly entertained as my sideways glances at his twinkly-eyed countenance confirmed. I could barely think straight, I was so uncomfortable in my frock. It dawned on me that perhaps I had packed on a few pounds. Shit.

Outside, a very polite version of today's paparazzi, relatively well behaved and firmly ensconced behind a barrier, greeted our exit from Her Majesty's Theatre with shouts of, 'Your Highness. Over here!' Fortunately for Michael, the presence of royals always ensured plenty of press the next day. Then we made the mad scramble back to Egerton Crescent to make sure the champagne was chilled and the waiters ready to pour. Michael asked me to promise I wouldn't whip out my camera and take any photos. He knew that I couldn't give a stuff about what was and wasn't the 'done thing', but this was different so I promised. Well, half-promised. After all, for strictly sentimental reasons I loved the royals, having grown up in a country where 'God Save the Queen' was played every morning as we girls all stood to attention in school assembly, not to mention before the start of the movies at every single cinema in the country.

In 1974, Michael and I moved into a fabulous house on what I consider to be one of the most beautiful streets in London: the curved Egerton Crescent, Knightsbridge, a stone's throw from Harrod's. Our next-door neighbour was the very jolly and extremely bright TV interviewer David Frost. Twice he complimented me on 'splendid interviews' I'd done on Thames TV and I was thrilled.

Once home, I bolted up to the bedroom to change into a less suffocating one-shouldered leopard-skin leotard under a tight black skirt. I hot-footed it back downstairs in time to greet the Prince, but somehow had been unable to relinquish my camera and so, as a smiling Prince Charles strode through the front door with a friendly wave, I just had to snap one of him approaching—before Michael gave me a very stern look. (Oh—and one or two as he was leaving. No biggie!) I was suddenly aware that unlike for an interview, where I was always overprepared, I hadn't thought up a single witty conversational gambit.

No need. Our intimate dinner went very smoothly—it was a breeze in fact. There was me and Michael, aristocrats Nicholas Soames and Henry Pembroke (the Earl of Pembroke), Annabel (sister of Camilla Parker-Bowles) and Simon Eliot, Iman the model and His Royal Highness, who was incredibly charming and chatty. A brilliant conversationalist, with that lovely voice I found very sexy, he was suave, smiley and charismatic to boot. I instantly adored him! And so my nervous tension dissolved over smoked salmon and champagne as we discussed his vegie garden, my childhood Down Under and Andy Warhol. And yes, he did chat Sabrina up quite enthusiastically.

In fact, our inviting Sabrina truly did change the course of her life. The next day, a royal equerry, given Sabrina's number by Henry Pembroke, called her and said, 'Would you like to speak to the Prince of Wales?' Sabrina gave her assent and he was put through. Very jolly, he asked if she would like to go to the polo on Sunday and come back to meet his mum for tea. Sabrina said yes but then could not remember what time she was expected at Windsor Castle and called back a couple of days later to check the time. Prince Charles got on the phone laughing, clearly stunned that someone would forget the time they were meant to show up for a royal rendezvous. The trip was all meant to be under wraps but then Prince Charles put her next to Lord Mountbatten at the polo, the press picked up the story and Sabrina became tabloid fodder for many years. She subsequently stayed at Balmoral and at a house belonging to one of the Prince's friends in Sussex, but given that she already had such a colourful past—with the likes of Mick Jagger and David Bowie—this was not considered a match made in heaven.

Around midnight, with no rest for the wicked in the '70s, we belted back to the West End for the third time that day for a nightcap at the club Annabel's. The Prince was gracious enough to ask me to dance. On our way to the dance floor, as everyone stared, I remember thinking, Blimey, if Ma and Pa could see me now! Pretty much everything I did was to impress my parents and make them proud.

Alas, I don't remember all the songs we danced to but the last one was 'YMCA' by the Village People. Being a former athlete I may have been more manic than was strictly necessary. Prince Charles was in great high-spirited form and the British throne's heir had excellent rhythm. With elbows flying and a winning grin, he seemed determined to match my energy beat by beat. And then it happened. The elastic in my one-shouldered leopard-skin leotard, which did not cater for a brassiere, apparently snapped—because I was suddenly dancing with my right breast exposed for all and sundry, especially the Prince, to see. I say 'apparently' because I didn't feel a thing and only realised something was amiss when I noticed His Royal Highness gazing at my chest, grinning. I looked down, spotted the malfunction and nearly *died* on the spot. I may have prided myself on my rebellious scofflaw streak, but since the Prince had begun laying on the charm at the dinner table I would now be a staunchly devoted royalist till the end of time, and dancing half-naked in front of my future King was simply not on! Indeed, in my rather prudish book, it was verging on being dead common.

Covering the offending bare bosom with my hands, I broke with protocol and left him stranded on the dance floor as I wailed, 'So sorry, Sir!' and ran like greased lightning to the ladies room where a prim attendant parted with a giant safety pin. I remember starting to feel a bit woozy—as the hectic work day and the equally intense evening caught up with me. Feelings of mortification mixed with exhausted delirium started to set in. I had to be up at the crack of dawn to get a train to Cornwall for a story …

According to Sabrina, the Prince was highly entertained by the faulty leotard, or so he told everyone, including the Queen, as they took tea at Windsor a few days later.

Now Michael, in his delighted retelling of the story, always insisted to everyone that I had gotten up from the dinner table at one point and asked him the whereabouts of the bathroom so as to suggest to Prince Charles that I was unattached—totally apocryphal of course! In his relentless teasing that went on for months, he also implied that his devious seductress of a girlfriend had deliberately flashed the Prince, cutting the elastic to ensure that aforementioned breast would indeed be bared. Absolute codswallop! Truth be told, and I can prove it with photos, the leotard had doubled as a swimsuit the previous summer and Aussie saltwater had clearly weakened the elastic.

Posing (in a hideous, huge, grey flannel Kenzo dress) alongside Muhammad Ali after a studio interview I'd done with him for the Today Show *at Thames TV. Knowing bugger all about sport, I really had to cram and search the cuttings library to prepare for an interview that my dear old dad, a former boxer and avid fan, was very sorry he never saw back in Melbourne.*

As for being a devious seductress … not remotely. I was devoted to Michael but even more devoted to my career. I had to be. Having become the youngest-ever reporter on British TV, and being a female without a university degree, one could almost hear the knives being sharpened at every turn. There were no female colleagues, no women editors, perhaps just one or two producers and certainly no women on camera or sound. My fellow male reporters, some of the producers and a few of the crew members didn't like the fact that I attracted publicity and were convinced that I had screwed my way into a job. But finding no evidence of same, they simply resorted to mocking my story ideas in the morning meetings or interrupting me to ask if I was pregnant under one of the incredibly unflattering voluminous Kenzo dresses I favoured. When Muhammad Ali asked me, after a studio interview, what I was hiding under a particularly drab, billowing grey number, I was teased for days. It was a phase when I thought if I dressed very unsexily, wore glasses and no makeup, they would take me more seriously. But I tried hard not to be fazed by their sabotage attempts. I had a crack job and was wildly grateful for this fantastic, if gruelling, life. A life I could document with my cheap cameras and thus send a set of snaps back to the folks Down Under every few weeks.

I lived the 'life of Riley' in London at an early age. It was a preposterously wonderful time of fun, glamour, career excitement and excess. It finally ended. I later got a spot of cancer. Life goes on and I'm still a ridiculously lucky girl from Oz.

I have recurring nightmares now where I'm being chased but can hardly run at all—but back in the day I could beat anyone in my age group and above. Dad was very supportive and drove me to all the meets—but as soon as Geoff introduced me to my own comic strip in Go Set, *I decided my thighs were getting too muscly and Olympic sprinting was not in my future.*

CHAPTER 1

Warrior Woman
Gets the News

S O THERE I AM in the doctor's office about five years ago, the gung-ho TV reporter who once swam with sharks in order to get a story on air. An invincible, vitamin-popping health nut who prided herself on having never spent a single night in hospital. An ex-sprinter who did the gym, not drugs. A pregnant Aussie warrior woman who so dreaded the idea of interfering, by-the-book doctors that I decided to shun them completely and give birth to my daughter, Lola, squatting on the bedroom floor.

Foolish, most certainly, but not a complete fool. Having grown up with an ailing, overweight, depressed, cigarette-smoking, asthmatic mother, I've always understood that you have to *work* at staying healthy.

My dad understood it, up to a point, and way back in the 1950s in Melbourne, he would forgo a pub lunch of beer and a meat pie after a morning tramping the city streets and stop at a health food shop for a lunch of yoghurt, honey, wheatgerm and prunes. Alas, my pa suffered constant pain from knee injuries sustained while a Japanese prisoner of war on the Burma railroad and thus resorted to painkillers, which made him tired and irritable. Then, yoghurt and prunes notwithstanding, he would often drink too much at weekends, especially at Sunday barbecues at Uncle Ab and Aunty Pat's, as an unsuccessful rag trade salesman is wont to do.

But somehow, despite knowing that life isn't fair, I was convinced that looking after myself would pay off. I've always felt 'fit as a mallee bull' as the Australian expression goes.

So, a year after returning to Los Angeles from a four-year stint caring for my dad in Melbourne, it hardly seems reasonable that after many decades of taking excellent care of myself, to the point of pampering some might say—including many dollars spent on vitamins, juices, nutritionists, acupuncturists, massage, anti-ageing doctors, meditation, Korean spas, organic food, yoga, aerobics and B12 shots—should lead to me sitting here like an idiot, blubbering into a tissue, moments after being told by the young, exceptionally attractive breast surgeon Dr Peg that after a biopsy she did with something akin to a nail gun last week, I have breast cancer. A 1.2-centimetre tumour with nothing in the lymph nodes. Knowing what I now know, I would have done myself a gigantic, life-altering favour by simply having the lumpectomy to remove the tumour, avoiding the subsequent horrors—but read on.

This doctor, a serious glamour puss, leans in to pat my hand. She's a foot away. I know she's only forty but her skin is utterly dewy, poreless and flawless. Botox? Some genius retinol cream I should know about? It has the look of that spray-on airbrushed makeup. I'm dying to ask her for more details and have a nice soothing skin-care natter but it's hardly the time. I've suddenly joined the ranks of those poor souls with crappy defective genes who got *cancer*. I have actually become a stupid bloody sick person. Well, this is going to screw up my chances of getting a date, good and proper. Damn, why did I bother to renew that stupid internet-dating site membership last week?

Utterly gobsmacked and also ashamed, I've become an 'untouchable', someone who's failed one of life's big survival tests. Dr Peg is sweetly telling me to find an oncologist and to come back soon to discuss the lumpectomy.

As I drive away, desperately grabbing the old cigarette that's been in my car's dusty side pocket for months, I dread telling my children—22-year-old Lola and thirteen-year-old Nick. I call Lola right away and despite my resolve not to weep, as I say, 'Darling, I have cancer,' my voice breaks and there's a big silence. I can tell she doesn't know what to say after the initial, 'Mummy, you'll be okay …' I don't really know what to say either. Darling daughters trying to make their way in the world don't deserve this. Nor does my angel of a son.

I tell Nick later that night over dinner, playing it right on down with, 'It's just a teeny tiny lump that has to come out.' He's terribly sweet and actually stops eating his meatloaf and mashed potatoes to jump up and give me one of his divine long bear hugs, before seizing the loving moment to announce that he's just remembered he has a science quiz tomorrow on top of the Spanish quiz and massive amounts of maths homework. It's 8.05 pm. We'll be burning the midnight oil, just for a change.

At about 10.45 pm, my eyes burn from studying Nick's Algebra 1 textbook as I try with all my might to work out linear functions. Nick, on the other hand, is happily checking his Facebook. Since my body is apparently failing me, I take the maths on as a personal challenge to gauge whether I still have any semblance of brain power. The challenge is not going well. Out of the blue, the teen suddenly asks, 'How do you think you got the lump, Mum?' A fierce pang of guilt. I tell him I have no idea but, in fact, it occurs to me that it may well be the result of my putting my mobile phone in my bra—always on the left-hand side—during virtually the whole four years Down Under, looking after my dad.

The next day I feel compelled to call my former beau Al Pacino and tell him. I guess I'm looking for comfort but the quest is not successful. He's certainly pleasant but his overriding instruction is not to tell anyone. He elaborates by giving voice to my darkest fears and effectively says, though not in these exact words, that people in this town will be repelled, horrified, nauseated and afraid if they discover I have cancer. (And no, he doesn't suggest getting together for a comforting natter over lunch or dinner. Months later, when I take off my hat at lunch, revealing my bald head, he practically chokes on his pasta, demanding I put it straight on again.)

Alrighty then. I certainly know what he means and he's probably right, but it's confronting to hear it told so bluntly. I take his advice to heart and vow to soldier on, keeping my big trap shut. It lasts a day—just twenty-four hours where I avoid all calls and don't return any messages.

Alas, I'm a flawed, needy human who could use a tiny bit of support—and by the second day I've fessed up to just two pals, begging them to keep it secret. But it's impossible to even begin to articulate the shame and embarrassment that might convince them to respect my wishes and so they don't, and within days I'm getting the sympathy calls I'll come to dread. They start with the hushed voice as if I'm already on my way out, then swiftly segue to the obvious but annoying question, 'How did you find the lump?'

'Well, it's a pretty grim saga,' I tell the first couple of people before I learn that my natural tendency to be utterly candid is tiring and not necessarily the way to go.

The 'saga' begins two months earlier in December 2008 when I realise that as I've finally met my insurance excess, I should get my annual pap smear and breast exam done before the financial year ends. So I drag myself in to see the short, balding Beverly Hills gynecologist. Although I give it no credence, I've noticed a small but obvious lump on my left breast—very close to the surface. It's hard to miss but a similar lump last year turned out to be benign so I'm not worried.

So in comes the tiny doc—we'll call him Dr Tiny. He no longer bothers with a white coat, opting instead for a V-necked cashmere (today it's bright orange) to reveal his wildly hirsute chest. Despite fifteen years of loyal patronage, he doesn't remember my name, though he remembers that I dated a famous movie star and does manage to always ask, 'How's that movie star pal of yours? Al? How is Al?'

'Oh, we broke up a long time ago,' I tell him irritably. But I'm conscientiously upbeat and tell him how well he looks. He invites me to punch his stomach to feel how strong and taut it's become from upping his daily dose of Human Growth Hormone injections. Then, remembering how lucky I am to get even five minutes of his time, I say, 'You know, I really wish I didn't feel so unwell and tired all the time.'

'You know, I really wish I wasn't so short!' he shoots right back, laughing hysterically at his own joke. Unamused, I scoot down on the bastard examination table to have that most hideously humiliating exam called a pap smear. Guys, imagine having an ice-cold whacking great stainless steel speculum inserted, twisted and turned, and then another contraption sent down and tissue removed. It's why I decided to give birth at home—I'm not fond of authority or interference by strangers.

After that, feeling violated and sad, I stand up and submit to the breast exam. I mention the fatigue again. He tells me to get more sleep. He cops a good feel but doesn't notice the lump in my left breast. I'm exhausted and just don't have the energy to point it out. What the hell, I figure. I'm due to have that equally torturous procedure known as a mammogram next week. They'll see it. I'm sure it's nothing.

Cut to … a week later, I am heading into a very posh Beverly Hills mammogram joint. Now bear in mind that I am talking about seven years ago—and it was nine months before the startling *New York Times* headlines stating that a task force had recommended against routinely providing mammograms to women under fifty. (The task force was an independent panel of experts in prevention and primary care appointed by the US Department of Health and Human Services. While many women don't think a screening test can be harmful, these medical experts say the risks are real. A test can trigger unnecessary further tests, like biopsies, which can create extreme anxiety. And mammograms can find cancers that grow so slowly that they never would be noticed in a woman's lifetime, resulting in unnecessary treatment. Food for thought indeed—and mammograms, like so much in medicine, are big business and make many rich.) But still an obedient 'innocent' at this time, I slip my breasts between two big metal tit squashers and try to be extra nice to the female technician who must deal with cranky chicks and their bosoms all day. She slips out of the room and returns, inviting me to follow her to a consulting room. I'm now told to lie on an examination bed to wait for the radiologist. Well here we go, I think. They've seen the lump in the left tit and it doesn't look good.

The radiologist appears and I remember the same overweight red-faced gentleman from my last appointment a year ago. He studies the X-rays on a light box, gives my right breast a quick grope and tells me, 'It's fine. There's still a small mass there. Same size. Hasn't grown. See you in a year.' And he's off.

I breathe a huge sigh of relief. Then I remember the new lump is in my *left* breast. 'Uh, excuse me,' I call out and he pokes his head back in the room.

'What about the lump in my left breast?'

Clearly not amused, his smile vanishes and he comes back in, seemingly angry to have missed what he now so clearly notices. I'm expecting him to suggest a biopsy right away. Instead, he suggests that with Christmas coming, perhaps I'd rather 'enjoy the holidays without any bad news …'

Let's think—would I rather put it off, fret and worry right through Christmas and then get bad news? I think not, but he insists he's busy, must dash and he's gone! I call the next day and make an appointment for four days hence, irritated that it's now two tedious trips and not just the one.

The same radiologist does the biopsy. He appears with a scary, colossally huge needle and seems to be in a foul mood, barely greeting me as the nurse rubs a little numbing cream onto my left breast. About seven seconds later he jabs the needle in and I nearly hit the roof as a searing pain, unlike anything I've ever felt, makes me sit bolt upright. I'm afraid I scream, 'Fuck!' way louder than I intended. He looks appalled and shouts, 'I will not tolerate that kind of language! Do you want to continue or not?' Flabbergasted that he would shout at me so angrily, I splutter that I'm truly sorry and that I have a very high tolerance to pain but that was seriously painful.

'Well, you obviously don't have a high tolerance,' he retorts and I feel obliged to say that I put up with nineteen hours of drug-free childbirth.

'Perhaps we could please just wait a minute for the numbing cream to take effect,' I add plaintively.

Unsympathetic, he demands to know again if I want to continue or not. 'I'm busy,' he shouts.

Tears are springing to my eyes but I put on a brave front and say, 'Fine, let's continue.'

He performs the biopsy in dead silence as I hold my breath, and it hurts almost as much as the first needle and seems to last an eon. As he strides off, I sit up and say, 'Why are you being so unpleasant?'

He gives me one of the dirtiest looks I've had in a while and shouts, 'I don't put up with rude patients like you. Get out of here!'

'Get out?' I'm on my feet, whipping the robe around me to cover my bare tits. 'You're the rude one. Are you angry because you didn't even notice the lump last week?'

He turns on his heel and starts screaming, 'I am ordering you to get out of this building now. Get out!' and he thunders off down the corridor.

I'm not proud to say that I take off after him shouting, 'You are insane. You're rude and incompetent. Fuck you!' as robed, cowering women sitting in chairs in the corridor look on in horror.

I dash to the cubicle to dress and storm off through the foyer, pointedly staring at the women who take your credit card and hoping in vain that someone will try to make me pay so I can categorically refuse.

Ten days later I email my gyno—Dr Tiny—asking if there are any results. No response until four days later when I get a message from a nurse. 'The results were normal.'

Yes! I'm delighted and tell myself I knew it all along.

But a few days after that, Dr Tiny himself calls and leaves a message saying the results were *not* normal and I need to call. Which I do, leaving word for Dr Tiny to call back and thinking no more of it. It's almost Christmas and I'm buying presents to take to relatives in Australia as well as trying to rent out my house. A few days before I'm due to leave he finally calls back. I say I was told by his office that everything was normal and then that information was contradicted by his message. Suddenly angry, he hotly denies that I was ever told things were normal, says he will no longer deal with me and that I should get myself an oncologist. He hangs up. The arrogance, stupidity and simple lack of any human decency or manners is absolutely vile and to this day it makes my blood boil.

The warning bells are now sounding loudly—but I'm *still* convinced it must be a mistake and that I need to repeat the biopsy with someone who knows what they're doing. I'm just not the cancer type. A friend puts me in touch with a woman breast surgeon, Dr Peg, who did Sheryl Crow's breast cancer surgery (and who later did Angelina Jolie's) and I make an appointment for January, right after my Aussie trip.

In January I'm lucky enough to spend a little time with Hercules Bellville, my dear friend from London, who managed to fly to LA for a holiday—a farewell trip to see his pals, though he was far too stoic to say such a thing. With lung cancer that had spread to his brain and bones, it was shockingly clear his days were numbered. I remember sitting with him the last time I saw him, at dinner at the Chateau Marmont, and instead of having a joyous gossipy catch-up, it was hard not to break down crying during this precious time together as I could see the obvious agony he was in—even sitting—and I wondered how on earth such a witty, wonderfully vibrant lover of life could have succumbed to cancer. Like me, he wasn't the type.

A few days later I'm told I too have cancer. Having only returned from my four-year stint in Australia a year ago, I'm just now feeling like I'm back in the swing of things. Indeed, I've been longing for something great to happen. Some serendipitous bit of genius good fortune. *This is not it.*

The Oxford-educated Hercules Belville was independently wealthy and, to our Aussie ears, sounded very posh indeed. But he was in fact very democratic and not at all fond of the snobbish 'aristocratic' types he had grown up with. His passions were movies (he worked for Polanski and Antonioni, among others) and travel, and he and Michael were thrilled to take Gael and me for a weekend in Rome, checking out the sights and lunching with Bernardo Bertolucci.

CHAPTER 2

Aussie Sheila

S o how did an Aussie sheila, who didn't fly in a plane till she was seventeen, get to be at what seemed like the centre of the universe, having the time of her life with a job as the youngest reporter ever on British TV?

Well, it's not such a long story. I grew up in Melbourne in a pretty ordinary flat in the beachside suburb of Brighton, later moving to Black Rock, with extremely good, wonderfully kind parents who struggled to send me and my two brothers, David and Geoff, to good schools. Like my mother, grandmother, aunt and two cousins I went to Firbank, a Church of England girls grammar school where there were no fellas and a ridiculous curriculum in those days which meant that when I ludicrously mentioned that I wanted to be a doctor—just to please my hard-working parents—I was then allowed to focus solely on maths, science, French and Latin. No English literature needed. I was bright but an ill-read nitwit.

My father, Norman, or Nick as everyone called him, left school at fifteen when *his* father lost all his dough in the rag trade—my grand-father, Pop, pulled a few strings and got his son a job in the very same dicey rag-trade world, which he worked at till the Second World War broke out. He signed up and trained as a Spitfire pilot in Australia and Canada before being shipped off to Java in an ill-fated, ill-timed move. Their Spitfires were still in crates on the dock in Java when Singapore fell a day or two later! Their commanding officer handed them rifles and told them to hide in the jungle. Without even a day's training in combat, my dad and a band of six fellow pilots took off on foot, roaming the countryside for two months as they tried hopelessly to work out an escape route—at one point enlisting some locals to help build a raft out of palm trees and whatever else they could find. It didn't sink but lurked, submerged under about six inches of water, and realising this would not get them back to Oz, they wandered for a few more days before waking up one morning surrounded by Japanese soldiers.

My dear, darling gentleman of a dad: the handsome Norman Victor Hobbs. He joined the Royal Air Force and trained as a Spitfire pilot in Canada but, alas, never saw action as he was captured early and spent gruelling years as a Japanese prisoner of war in Changi, as well as on the infamous Burma Railway.

My good-looking dad and thousands of others remained prisoners of war, at first at the infamously brutal Changi prison before being sent off to work on the Burma railroad for the duration of the war, his friends dying like flies of dysentery and malnutrition. His family back home wrote letters, month after month for more than a year, to the War Department trying to find out if he was alive but to no avail. They also listened to the radio where weekly reports would list men who had been taken prisoner. After an agonisingly long eighteen months of silence, a local Melburnian listening to Radio Tokyo finally heard Dad's name read aloud one night—as one in a list of prisoners captured—and wrote a letter, which I still have. His family was over-joyed. But then another year passed without any more news until a postcard arrived one day—which I also still have—with my darling pa writing that no one should worry: 'lots of fresh air and tennis ... we're

An utterly life-changing note from a Mrs Carter in Port Melbourne to my grandmother, telling her that her missing son, Norman, feared dead after no news for over a year, was in fact alive! She had heard the news on Radio Tokyo, where prisoners' notes were read out. In a subsequent postcard, Dad lied hard and said he was 'quite well and had plenty of sports and games and was living in lots of sunshine'. I finally persuaded him to write a short memoir of his war years. Totally factual and without a drop of self-pity or emotion.

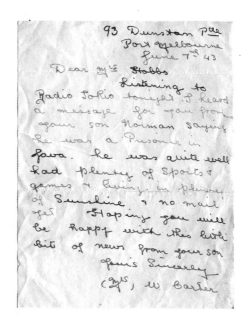

being treated very well'. A classic understatement by my cool dad who didn't want anyone to worry! The truth was they were almost starving to death, virtually dead on their feet as they worked on the railway in the heat, beaten regularly by their Japanese jailers. A third of Dad's fellow Aussie prisoners did not make it out of there.

The war ended and they finally staggered off to waiting ships and back to life in Melbourne—a massive anticlimax with no psychologists back then to work through the engulfing sense of shame and humiliation that men like my father felt at having never seen any action and being treated like dogs by the Japanese for three years. I'm not sure he ever got over it. I only truly realised the extent of his shame one day a few years ago, before he died, when I tried to convince him to come—even in a wheelchair—to the Anzac Day parade in Melbourne, which honours the men who fought for their country. At that point Dad, aged eighty-nine, was one of just a handful of surviving POWs from the Burma railway. He'd virtually always begged off going to the parade. (Alas, it pains me now to realise his war experience was a massively taboo subject, never discussed during my childhood. But I must have overheard a snippet once because I told my teacher in kindergarten that my dad had 'been in jail for years' and the head of the school promptly called my mother to coldly inquire if it was true. My mum quickly explained the real circumstances—and it was swept under the rug once more.)

In recent years these Anzac parades have become an ever more important ritual to Aussies—those who have realised the huge sacrifices made by so many. But Dad finally confessed that he 'didn't actually feel he deserved to be there'—not having ever even gotten to fly a Spitfire or see any action. They felt like losers, not heroes. It was such a sad, sad thing to hear him say it as we sat at a cafe at Rickett's Point right on the beachfront in Melbourne. I wheeled him back to the car once we'd finished our cappuccinos, glad he couldn't see my tears. It haunts me to this day. I was tongue-tied at the time and barely knew what to say to Dad, so I was pleased when, while rummaging through an old box recently, I found this letter I finally wrote to him:

March 15 2004

Dearest Pa

It occurs to me, very belatedly, that although I fully intended to, I never got around to responding to—or thanking you for taking the time to write down your memories of your time as a prisoner of war. It can't have been easy to do since it brings up so many emotions and a sense, for everyone, of so much that has never been discussed.

It's a difficult subject—and it's often been hard to know how or when or even IF to bring it up. In fact it brings up SO many emotions—even for the children and friends of survivors of the prison camps that it quite simply is a difficult topic!

And that's normal. It's difficult to discuss what was clearly the most harrowing experience of many men's lives, which is why it's easier to put in writing a response to your memoir and also a response to an extraordinary admission you made about 14 months ago ... We were having coffee down at Rickett's Point. Anzac Day was approaching and when I asked why, to my knowledge, you'd never marched in an Anzac Day parade, you said, with unusual candour, that as prisoners of war you didn't really feel, having seen no action, that, I think the word you used was 'deserved', to be in the march—that you hadn't somehow earned the right to be there.

Dad, I just want to say here and now—in response to that sentiment and in response to what you wrote, that I am unbelievably proud of you and what you went through during the war. You survived, a huge feat when so many friends and fellow soldiers around you were dying or already dead.

You managed, despite extraordinary hardship, horrifying conditions, sickness, fear, death, malnutrition and both physical and mental torture, to actually survive. It was an incredible achievement—a massive exertion of willpower, determination, courage and strength. It demonstrated a powerful will to live, a powerful desire to return to Australia and friends and family that were still waiting for you. You also exhibited another type of courage when you finally came back and had to try to rebuild a life.

And that, in many people's opinion, is where the need for courage and strength of character really kicked in. Because here you were back home—after years of being virtually left for dead and years of your family having almost given you up for dead.

But suddenly the war is over and the boys who went off to lay their lives on the line for Australia, are free.

A boat ride home, the remnants of a uniform handed to you for show and here you are, a mere week later, at Flinders Street Station, your mum and brothers overcome at this thin young man who left at 22 and is now 27 before them.

There's a reception at the MCG for the returned POWs and Uncle Alan, who's acquired a car since you last saw him, whisks you off straight there, not realizing that *you're all meant to walk a few blocks to the Melbourne Town Hall where, in a sadly inadequate show of public gratitude, crowds were waiting to cheer you on. Each returning POW was given 6 bottles of beer and some cigarettes!*

Meantime you and Alan and the others sat waiting at the empty MCG, an hour early, waiting for the Town Hall mob to make it there. Your mother, quite understandably, was furious. You had missed out on the one public moment of hometown glory after years of incarceration and deprivation.

A couple of weeks later, your parents had a small party to celebrate your safe return during which your father Gibson got up and made a speech which, according to you, was along the lines of 'We're glad to have you back after all these years, you've had a rest for a couple of weeks, now it's time to buck up and get on with your life!' Short, sharp and to the point but lacking in empathy and understanding for what you'd been through and what it would take to reassimilate.

Of course, unlike today, there was NO psychological counselling, therapy or support groups to help you POWs make sense of what happened and heal from the full-blown trauma of what you'd been through.

There was nothing—no help at all. Everyone was living their lives and you men were meant to snap out of it and start to fit back in. It's not surprising that you would occasionally be found lying back in your old darkened bedroom, in the middle of the day, staring into space.

The stamina and sheer guts to carry on once back on home turf is really just as, if not more, impressive than the guts it took to withstand an ordeal that the rest of us can simply not even imagine.

The fact is that POWs, all over the world, for many centuries, have all felt the guilt and shame of being captured. It's no one's fault. It goes with the territory.

But, as ever, it's completely unjustified guilt and shame.

You should be extremely proud of how you dealt with your war years—and how you dealt with the inevitable demons in post-war years. You were always a gentleman, to the core. A decent, utterly honest, utterly honourable, kind good man—never bitter or angry, never a word of complaint about what you'd been through.

Nothing—for decade after decade. You even went to Japan and did business with the Japanese and still not a mean, angry word—never a hint of what you'd had to suffer. Stoic, silent years where men would/could only suffer in silence—apart from very occasional reminiscing over a beer with a few fellow POWs or blokes who'd also gone off to war. Stoic years where you worked hard, making sacrifices to send us all to good schools.

Dad, you've been a good, kind, wonderful father and a good, kind, wonderful man. I, like everyone else in the family, could not be prouder and you should be very proud of yourself.

And we all would be honoured this year, even if it's just 100 yards, to walk in the Anzac Day march with you. Think about it and you'll decide.

I love you very much.

Lindy

Dad did not make it to the parade. His health was going downhill.

My mum, Pauline, was blonde and fun and gorgeous but with a streak of melancholy that seemed to reach massive proportions as she

My very pretty and witty mum, Pauline Broome, about the time she met the charming, urbane Peter Hales, her first husband and the father of my two wonderful brothers, David and Geoffrey. She was working in a munitions factory doing her bit for the war effort.

grew older. She left Firbank at sixteen and, after a stint as a hairdresser, she joined the war effort and went to work in a munitions factory, assembling parts for planes. Wartime romances blossomed with lightning speed. She upped and fell in love at nineteen, marrying a lovely man called Peter Hales at the Melbourne Town Hall. They had a son, David, and four years later another son, Geoffrey. When Geoff was just eight months old, Peter died after a drawn-out battle with cancer and my mother was left a widow with two small sons at twenty-four. I don't believe she ever really got over it and her loss was never discussed. Three years later she married Nick Hobbs, the still-dashing ex-POW, and the two wounded souls began a life together with my two brothers. A year later I came along.

They struggled and sacrificed like mad to keep it together and, quite apart from the total lack of any fripperies, holidays or restaurants ever, I remember the dread and panic caused by the rent man knocking on the never-used front door at our St Kilda Street block of flats on Saturday mornings

My earliest memories are of feeling lonely much of the time at the block of flats where we lived on St Kilda Street in Middle Brighton. My brothers were at school and there were no kids my age. I wandered around the concrete jungle and, although forbidden to go anywhere near the burning incinerator, I found it a lot of fun to hang around, getting my favourite red knitted moccasins burnt at one point. I still have that dolly!

every month. My mum worked as a pay mistress (an unqualified accountant who did the salaries for an architectural firm) and my dad kept trying to flog his fabric samples, trudging up and down Flinders Lane in the city of Melbourne—the heart of the rag trade then, but now filled with the hippest, most sophisticated cafes and coffee bars, boutique hotels and chic loft-style apartment conversions along narrow nineteenth-century alleyways. I'm so impressed now, as I occasionally resort to mentioning money and school fees to put guilty pressure on my poor son, that never once did my parents mention the sacrifices they made to send us to expensive private schools, which I realise now, despite some financial help from relatives, must have been a crushing burden.

For me, the whole neighbourhood still evokes the sad memories of the time. A few months after first getting my licence at eighteen, I was driving down Flinders Lane and spotted my dad coming towards me on the sidewalk, limping badly as he trudged along carrying his heavy briefcase full of samples. He looked tired, sad and defeated and tears sprung to my eyes. I tooted the horn and he immediately straightened up, trying to hide his limp and smiling proudly as he saw his girl. Poor old Dad. I think Mum made more money than he did, and that isn't saying much as back then women were paid so much less than men. Overhearing all the arguments about money each night as I lay in bed, I would rush home from school to make beds, dust, do the dishes and tidy the house for my mum, who would arrive home from work exhausted, before I hit the books to try and do well in school. And on the track. I was very darn quick out of the blocks and an extremely fast runner. I loved the annual combined schools sports days when I was put into many age groups above my own—to win all the hundred-yard sprints against students from a dozen other schools. I joined a running club and Dad would take me to all the meets. I trained at a St Kilda gym with Bill Lyons, an Olympic trainer who had very high hopes for me. Bill had me lifting weights—strength means speed in sprinting—and worked me incredibly hard. 'A natural with beautiful style,' Bill would tell me.

But during my last year at Firbank, my attention to my stellar sprinting career and academics flagged somewhat. My pot-smoking photographer brother Geoffrey and his wonderful fashion editor girl-friend, Honey, decided I should star in a photographic comic strip called 'The Adventures of Lindy' for *Go-Set*, a hip music magazine they worked for. I would play the part of a rock'n'roll reporter inter-viewing the local stars and any famous visitors we could get our hands on … it was madcap and utterly nonsensical but I would dutifully pose, notepad and pencil in hand, with folk like Roy Orbison, ride on the back of motorbikes, meet cute young musicians and generally have more fun than was to be had at my straight-laced all-girls school. In fact, about twenty minutes into our first photo session, my eyes were opened and my horizons widened when I smoked a joint and in a blinding flash it hit me—my schoolgirl world was claustrophobically tiny and certifiably dull! Furthermore, the weightlifting started to seem strange, and having my coach pour hot wax onto my bare thighs to repair pulled hamstrings after leg-lifting 300 pounds seemed really weird! So sprinting was over. And to be frank, the whole concept of becoming a doctor was utterly insane, given that I'm the most squeamish person I know. The doctor plans were over too.

When *Go-Set* offered me a job as a real pop reporter on the paper, I had to decide between that and university, but as I was young—just seventeen—I realised I could reserve my place at university for a year and take the gig. So I said yes in a heartbeat. I was never quite free from that day on, though, of the guilt that I'd disappointed my parents most horribly by not becoming Dr Hobbs.

Life sped up. I worked hard and, as the only 'straight' person on staff at *Go-Set* (everyone else was 'high' all day *every* day and found my ambitious earnestness hilarious), managed to get about six stories in every issue—more than the now infamous Aussie music guru Ian 'Molly' Meldrum, who teased me endlessly before finally finding me a tad annoying. We argued and once he chased me out onto a window ledge, though I don't recall why. I was still too young to drive and a long-suffering boyfriend, Ronnie Charles (who I only fancied when he was on stage as lead singer of a local band, The Groop, crooning a rather brilliant version of Robbie Robertson's 'The Weight'), would wait around till midnight to drive me home in his Mini Minor after I'd typed like a demon all day, revelling in my new role as a 'journo'. For all that hanging out he would get nothing more than a quick kiss before I rushed inside to hit the hay.

The hard work paid off and about six months later I was offered a job producing my own page—'Lindy's Page'—every day on a

Newsday Living — Monday, September 15, 1969

The day my brother Geoff buckled, too!

The Age newspaper took a crack at an evening paper to compete with the Sun, launching Newsday, where I was given my own page when I was seventeen. My contract stipulated I appear most days in photos, so I was obliged to act like a narcissistic nitwit. Here I wrangle my 'good sport' brother Geoff to help model belts.

brand-new evening newspaper in Melbourne called *Newsday*. The contract stipulated that I had to appear in at least one photo each day so, legally obliged to act like an obnoxious narcissist, I had to elbow my way into any number of situations and pose next to songwriters, fashion designers or pop groups to ensure I would be in the photo—or choose a few frocks and model 'em. As I was *still* too young to drive, dear Mum had to drive me to work at seven-thirty every morning and collect me at six each night. Sundays I slept till about 3 pm.

The newspaper folded after about seven months and I segued into a radio gig at 3AK where I compiled 'The Happening Report' every day. That meant I would simply get my hands on the six-week-old copies of English music magazines *Melody Maker* and *New Musical Express* that had just arrived Down Under and then announce the groovy goings-on in London and New York as if I'd just witnessed them firsthand and was fresh off the plane. 'The Happening Report' and its author were then invited onto a new TV show called *Turning On* (an Aussie version of *Bandstand*), hosted by a smarmy local DJ called Baby John Burgess. Unfortunately, as well as 'pop correspondent', they insisted I be one of the show's dancers as well. I was spectacularly bad with almost no natural rhythm, and I would screw up the dance routines constantly, turning the wrong way and sending some furious dancer flying into the wings. I can't remember if I got fired or if the show was axed first. But soon it was back to being heard and not seen—on radio.

Now, the radio station I worked for was tucked into a corner of the Melbourne headquarters for TV's Nine Network, and I soon found myself wandering up the stairs to the newsroom and lurking, uninvited, in the back of the news director's office during the morning conference.

One day they were a couple of stories 'light' and so from the back of the room I suddenly piped up that I had an idea.

'Who are you?' asked Mike Schildberger, the news director.

'I'm Lindy Hobbs,' I answered cheerily.

Women's Lib was all the go then and, fancying myself a bit of a feminist, I suggested that I invade the men-only dawn world of the 'Icebergers', a hearty bunch of blokes who swam every morning of the year in the icy dark-green water at the Middle Brighton Sea Baths. Women were *not* allowed.

'Give it a go,' said Mike, 'but you'll have to work out a way to swim with 'em!'

Sure enough, the chance for the Icebergers to show off their Aussie male bravado trumped the 'no sheilas' rule and, secretly thrilled at the attention, any initial shock at the sight of an actual female soon abated and they were tickled to be interviewed by me outside the changing rooms. I had even asked my brother David to show up—he was how I knew about the morning activities—and when I asked why he did it, he muttered, clearly hungover, 'It gives you a terrific start for the day and it's a great cure for hangovers!'

Then, under the guise of recording these brave specimens of manhood plunging into the icy depths in their budgie-smugglers, we headed out to the end of thc baths and set up the camera. But the real point, I told the gobsmacked crew, was for me to explain to the poor downtrodden women out there in viewing land, in a broad Aussie twang, 'Anything the boys can do, we can do better!' and with that I

3 you lin

(the girl who

● Photographs and story by Geoff Hales with the assistance of Honey and Terry Cleary

In what I assume was a pot-fuelled flash of brilliance, my brother Geoffrey and his girlfriend Honey Lea pitched the idea of me starring in a preposterous photographic comic strip for the music magazine Go Set. *It changed the perspective of a cloistered girls' school student and instead of going on to university to study medicine, I reserved my place and took a job at* Go Set *as a real music reporter, never looking back.*

peeled off my groovy moleskin pants suit, revealing a striped towelling bikini. Only because I now had to, I dived into the hideously cold, choppy water—signing off as I emerged, shivering, with the line, 'Well, come on down, girls, and join the men for a refreshing morning swim. But just be warned—and as a lady I will simply say—it's as cold as it looks! This is Lindy Hobbs for GTV Nine News.' The story went out that night, I invoiced them for twenty bucks, and hey presto, I was a TV reporter. And no, the irony of 'breaking down male barriers' while flaunting my bod in a bikini was not lost on me, but a girl's gotta do what a girl's gotta do.

And that's really what I said to camera. I know because when I was leaving the job I 'rescued' a can of film clips marked with my name. It sat in a trunk for thirty years until I took the footage to be transferred to DVD. When I played it, I thought someone had made a mistake because it was in black and white—but then I remembered that in 1970 colour TV had not yet come to Australia!

There's also rare vintage footage of a time when I persuaded Barry Humphries, fresh out of a home for recovering alcoholics, dolled up as Edna Everage (a shapeless dress and coat, no wig even—just lanky, greasy long locks), to take me on a bus tour of her birthplace, Moonee Ponds ... 'When I was a child, Lindy, you could eat off the streets in Moonee Ponds, you could. It's not like that any more, Lindy,' said Edna, stifling a sob. 'There's too many "New Australians" now.' (The latter being a put-down not in common usage any more for migrants, usually Italian or Greek, who had recently been naturalised.) I did about five or six pieces with Barry, and I'm proud to claim that I was the one who introduced Barry to Michael White—who would put Dame Edna on the London stage—convincing him that a straight man pretending to be a vile, snobbish Aussie housewife was very funny.

While my friends fretted over boyfriends and university marks, I'd forgotten about all plans for further learning and had no interest in boys at all. The work was the thing—and I was desperate to prove I wasn't the dopey chick who'd gotten the job solely based on my looks. (Especially once I'd made what I considered the mistake of agreeing to be the Channel 9 fill-in weather girl when the regular, Rosemary Margan, went on holiday. I'd forgotten to wear a bra and so the microphone was attached to my bare chest … thus broadcasting the sound of my beating heart. One had to write backwards on the clear perspex map—and actually write the darn weather report oneself. I tripped, I laughed, I flubbed—but folks seem amused. Though news pieces comparing me to a giggling Goldie Hawn on *Laugh In* were not quite what I was going for … even if it did get me publicity and Bert Newton invited me onto his show.) So I worked round the clock and pitched dozens of semi-serious stories. They weren't about to send me off to interview politicians, but I succeeded in being sent out on stories about education, expensive new hospitals and consumer watchdog reports on too many additives in washing detergents.

During my stint as fill-in weather girl on GTV while I was still working at Newsday, *Bert Newton invited me on* In Melbourne Tonight. *I think he teased me about my attempt to write backwards on the perspex weather map and so I teased him right back, suggesting he give it a go. He joked that I should be removed from the studio pronto.*

It was a constant trade-off, though. For every story that could have been done by a guy—that is, which had nothing to do with me being a female of the species—the quid pro quo meant I had to swallow my pride and succumb to prevailing sexist attitudes, such as putting on my pink velvet hotpants with white vinyl knee-high boots and heading off to some of Melbourne's classiest restaurants where they'd banned women in hotpants. With lights blazing, camera and sound rolling, I would enter, smiling broadly, and enquire of the maître d', 'Hi, I'm Lindy Hobbs and I'm wearing hotpants, but I don't believe I'm going to offend any of your diners. May I stay or are you going to kick me out?' Very politely but firmly, they refused me admittance!

I preferred a little more action, and when a boat full of Cambodian 'pirates' who'd taken control of a commercial vessel was seized and everyone ordered to stay on board while the captain was arrested and interviewed, I went down, somehow got a boat out to that bigger boat with some other journos, leapt aboard and was the only one slim enough to climb through a porthole to interview the occupants. Of course, they barely spoke English but I managed to cobble a piece together and sold it to the *Sunday Observer* anyway.

I once got more of an adrenaline rush than I'd bargained for when I was cruising in one of the camera cars on my own (having just got my licence) and I heard on the CB radio that a portion of the almost finished Westgate Bridge had collapsed. Well, I was fairly close so I took it upon myself to turn around and head right over there. I wasn't prepared for what I saw. Absolute chaos and destruction and the first of dozens of dead bodies (I'd never seen a dead body before) being brought up from the site by paramedics. I started doing live reports on the situation from the two-way car radio. They went to air in emergency bulletins right away and as I waited for a camera crew to arrive, I thought this might be my big shot at a breaking story. The crew arrived and as I stood there, incredibly excited, ready to do my first already-memorised piece-to-camera, a veteran reporter arrived, who didn't have the decency to tell me I'd been doing a good job, and without further explanation took over the prime spot I'd been saving, with an amazing view of the bridge, in front of the camera. I fumed that night as I watched my colleague's report on the news, convinced I could have done just as good a job.

In order to stay really busy, I also wrote regular pieces for the *Sunday Observer* and various magazines, profiling people like Germaine Greer or visiting celebrities. In one memorable piece that became a double page 'comic strip', I took Edna Everage on a marathon Christmas shopping trip that began at posh Georges and continued to Myer, Buckley & Nunn and finally Big M, where Edna almost came to blows with a fellow shopper, telling her, 'Christmas spirit, fiddlesticks! I saw it first, you grasping woman!'

Several months later, a legendary Australian newsman, Mike Willesee, announced that he was launching the first-ever national current affairs show but that he would not be hiring any women because he didn't think viewers 'identified' with them. I was livid.

A few days later I was on my way to the airport to interview Dudley Moore and Peter Cook who were in Australia doing their show *Beyond the Fringe*. I'd already interviewed Dudley for Channel Nine as he played, in a successful publicity stunt, on a grand piano plonked right in the middle of Melbourne's main square. He'd invited me to join him on his piano stool for the interview and, as the notorious lady lover he was, flirted with me like a madman. By the end of a funny and successful interview, he had my phone number. About six weeks later after the show had finished its run, he got on a plane to London, decided he had fallen head over heels for me and caught the *very* next plane back to Melbourne, holing up, to my horror, in a motel for weeks. Both Fleet Street and fellow Melbourne journos were obsessed with the idea of a romance between Dudley and me. Just before he left London to return to see me, he had announced his separation from Suzy Kendall, and newsmen were staked out across the road from the St Kilda motel where he was staying. The now-defunct tabloid *The Truth* was all over it and ran several stories, even successfully snapping me once leaving the motel—after innocently dropping off some food for poor old Dudley. Mum was thrilled he'd come back and I'd invite him over to our flat, where he and Mum would listen to records over a glass of wine or three as I worked all hours of the day. I tried to find time for Dud though, and I recall one sunny Sunday I dragged him down to Anglesea, where my pal Mandy was staying with some friends. She insisted we all hit the beach; Dud went along with it and eventually had to take shoes and socks off as we trudged through the sand. It was then that I discovered he had a clubfoot and I felt quite guilty, but he had not mentioned it to me, was determined to enjoy our outing and was such a bloody good sport about it.

Meantime, on this first trip Dudley persuaded me to do a longer 'in-depth' interview up in Canberra, and after quickly flogging the idea to a newspaper, I was on my way to catch a plane for the one-hour flight to the nation's capital when somehow I drove into a barrier on the side of the road in my first VW Bug. (I was a bad driver and still am. I failed my first two driving tests miserably and only nailed my third because Dad insisted on hopping in and chatting to the tester bloke about footy!)

So I got out of my immobilised car and was standing on the side of the road weeping, wondering how on earth I was going to make it to the airport in time for what would be my second trip ever on a plane. A car suddenly pulled up and, to help the damsel in distress, out hopped a man I recognised from all the publicity as Mike Willesee.

'Can I help?' he asked, with a grin.

'Yes, you can give me a job on your new current affairs show,' I shot back and promptly hopped in next to him in the back of his chauffeur-driven car. I explained that I was a local reporter at Channel Nine and that Melbourne's viewers didn't seem to have any problem whatsoever in 'identifying' with me. His quote about viewers 'not identifying with women' had stuck in my mind—as idiotic, grossly sexist and ridiculously old-fashioned. And so naturally I felt I had to bring it up immediately and argue that he was dead wrong. God knows how I had the gall to say such things but I did. The confidence of youth was on my side. He certainly didn't say yes by the time he dropped me

NEWS□ MOVIE PREVIEWS□ PROGRAMS□

Threats to life —TV man quits

NEWSMAN Tim Skinner has resigned from Happening 71 in Melbourne following threats to his life.

Skinner a panelist on the ATV-0 pop program, will remain off camera while a series of incidents are investigated by the police.

The trouble started a fortnight ago and last week Skinner received a threatening telephone call.

A station spokesman said the caller gave the message "We haven't finished with you yet." Then he hung up.

Police said they were taking the matter very seriously.

Last week Skinner's home in Ferny Creek, Victoria, was broken into and two valuable antique pistols stolen. A police spokesman said the front door of the house was smashed and goods valued at $400 to $500 were stolen.

"We are investigating this matter and taking it very seriously" he said. "If this is a vendetta against Mr Skinner, it is someone who knows him."

The spokesman said the phone wires of the house had been cut.

Skinner was not available for comment this week, but ATV-0 news director Mr Ian McFarland said: "This has happened over a period of several weeks. First Skinner's car wheels were loosened and then the car was burnt to the ground"

McFarling said the car did not explode but caught fire, he believed, in the early hours of the morning.

"Tim had many of his personal things in the car including a typewriter and they were all destroyed in the fire. The car was a Porsche valued at about $11,000." McFarling said the car was insured.

A police spokesman said this matter was also being investigated. "But we can't be sure, the car may have burnt as the result of an electrical fault," he said.

McFarling said Skinner had also received threatening phone calls. "I believe there was three in one day," he said.

McFarling said that Skinner, who also appeared on ATV-0's Breakfast A-Go-Go, just wished to remain off camera and take every precaution.

□ LINDY HOBBS may be Michael Willesee's "girl-in-a-million." Lindy is the only female reporter on Willesee's new current affairs program on TCN-9 starting this week. Lindy will join the team of Tony Ward, Geoffrey Luckock and Kevin Hamilton on the 30-minute program titled A Current Affair. Eighteen-year-old Lindy, a freelance journalist, was selected by Willesee despite an earlier statement that he couldn't find a female reporter suitable for his program. See page 17.

The white knight who came to the rescue after I crashed on my way to the airport was none other than Mike Willesee, who, a few weeks earlier, had announced he wouldn't hire any women for Australia's first-ever national current affairs show as 'viewers didn't identify with them'. I got the job.

off at the airport but I sensed that it was one of those lucky 'kismet' encounters that would lead to change and, sure enough, a few days later, before he'd even been in touch with me, a Melbourne newspaper announced that Mike had changed his mind, had talked to my boss and was *actually* hiring a female after all. I was described, in ludicrously hyperbolic terms, as a 'girl in a million'. But it was a big deal for me—and I moved to Sydney for it.

The first night *A Current Affair* hit the airwaves across the nation, I was wildly disappointed as I didn't manage to get a story on air. I knew my parents would be glued to the set down in Melbourne, and friends were sending telegrams saying they'd be watching. On day two there was a story about the sharks at the famous tourist attraction the Manly Aquarium biting the feeders. Well, Mike looked at me with a wicked twinkle in his eye—he was very attractive—and said, 'I think this might be something for you, Lindy. Oh and why don't you go get your bikini, in case you get wet?'

I remember bristling at that suggestion but the daredevil side of me often won out over anything resembling common sense. It truly didn't occur to me that I could actually say no to a story—and had I said no, I suspect my days would have been severely curtailed, so it was a no-win situation in many ways. I often felt very vulnerable and alone, especially without an agent or any other women to confide in, but I was desperate to please and keep my job and that was the end of it.

So off we went to Manly. The feeders were in the pool wearing wetsuits, throwing fish to the sharks—a popular highlight for the tourists. I was instructed by a hotshot cameraman that I should tread water and do the interview in the pool. I complied but *then* he announced he'd just pop down to the underwater window which allowed tourists to get an extra close-up look at these lethal mammals—and would I just dive down a couple of times so he could film me from there? Anyone with half a brain would have said, 'Bugger off, we've got enough,' but I willingly dove down a few times, eyes shut tight.

An hour or two later, changed and dry, I sat back to watch the footage. First the interview and then shots of me down *among the killer sharks*. The editor, a complete pothead, was puffing on a joint and went crazy cheering his approval and soon everyone was crowded into the editing room to watch. Even Miss 'Gung-Ho, I'm as Brave as a Bloke' Hobbs got the shock of her life. There I was, diving in the murky depths with my eyes closed, surrounded by hungry sharks. It was outrageously scary footage and Mike Willesee, clearly stunned by the danger factor, had me in the studio after the story went to air to commend me on my bravery and point out to the viewers that the diving was not his idea. A few minutes after the show my feisty mum was on the phone, demanding to speak to Mike and give him a piece of her mind. I was secretly quite pleased with myself.

After about eight months of *A Current Affair* it was time for me to up anchor and head to London. The decision was partly inspired by having become instant fast friends with my fellow Melburnian and best pal to this day Gael McKay (now Boglione, after meeting and marrying the wonderfully chic Italian Francesco Boglione—of Petersham Nurseries fame), who was heading back to London for the second time, having won a modelling competition at seventeen to work for Nina Ricci for twelve months in Paris.

It had also become crystal clear that despite hiring me, Mike Willesee was still no flag-waving feminist. Although some of the stories I was assigned were decent and even thrilling—such as riding in open helicopters with bold army dudes—many others were downright idiotic. In one I donned a flesh-coloured body stocking to pretend I was the 'Nullarbor Nymph', a mysterious female figure who'd been spotted running through the desert at twilight. One of the producers, John Cornell (who went on to produce *Crocodile Dundee*), thought it would be amusing to do a 'fake' piece as if we had captured rare footage of this outback version of Bigfoot. Ludicrously, I would play both parts—the reporter and the nymph. Perhaps they needed a ratings boost, but it was irritating since I was determined to prove I was capable of doing hard news. Alas, it was an uphill battle and all my ideas were squashed—or given to the male reporters. Any and all attempts to be taken seriously by my patronising boss led to tedious and pointless after-hours drinking sessions with him that I was too young and dopey to refuse in the first place. Eventually I learnt the drill. If you're a female, don't drink with the boss. If you're a guy, go right ahead.

Anyway, enough was enough. I was starting to feel uncomfortable about the workplace atmosphere—to put it mildly—and was lonely in Sydney despite the fact that promoter Harry M Miller had given a lavish party on a boat to welcome me to Sydney and was hot to trot (and had been for a number of years). He was hard to deter. Back in Melbourne I'd interviewed him in a sarcastic report I did on *Hair* finally making its way down to Melbourne with less production values than the original Sydney production and Harry could only complain bitterly to my mother as he watched it go to air in our living room, waiting while I got dressed for the big premiere that evening. He knew I was oblivious to his complaints and, used to getting his own way, he found me very intriguing.

Was it time to get the hell out of Dodge? Did I have the guts to leave Australia? It was almost unthinkably frightening, but I suddenly got a small payout from *Newsday*—the newspaper that had given me a twelve-month contract (but folded after seven months)—and Dudley Moore, still trying to seduce me, was trying his best to lure me over with letters that said things like:

England expects you to do your duty and get over here. Fast. I'll meet you at the airport and push food in you, carry your bags, show you my musical box/boomerang-shaped clothes brush and show you the London sights and sounds, the Queen, her parks and pigeons, the theatre etc., only COME QUICK—I'll be here for you and you'll like it here … hope to see you soon, sweet face, Love Dud.

Despite receiving nothing but discouraging advice about the chances of employment—slim to none—I bought my round-the-world ticket to London via Hong Kong and Athens, and although sad to be leaving my dear parents, I was firmly convinced it would be nothing more than a six-month jaunt. How wrong I would turn out to be!

CHAPTER 3

The Move to London

I ARRIVED IN LONDON in late summer 1972 at the age of twenty after a very weepy farewell to my darling parents. I knew some friends of friends when I stopped off in Hong Kong, but I knew no one in Athens, my second stop before London. I saw the sights, clocked the Acropolis, fended off Greeks at the Plaka and then cruised over to Mykonos for a week in those stunningly blue sparkling waters where Aussie tourists were no rarity—and I felt very brave, grown up and terribly sophisticated ordering moussaka and retsina like a local. Melbourne has the biggest Greek population outside Athens and so I knew a thing or two. I stayed in the most heavenly little whitewashed B&B with tiled floors, a pretty little white iron bed, a faded pink felt rug on the floor and not much else. I felt wildly cosmopolitan as I ordered Greek coffees in the cafe down the hill and smoked Marlboro Lights, while I feverishly wrote postcards and thought about how much my mum would love the hot pink and red geraniums blooming at so many windows and the old men leading donkeys up winding streets.

A couple of weeks later, suddenly very nervous, but thrilled with a newly acquired tan and the Greek peasant top that showed it off, I boarded the plane to the number-one destination for adventurous

Aussies—London, England. I tried to sleep but the flight was noisy thanks to a bunch of rowdy Aussie 'louts' who drank the entire way over, issuing repeated drunken invitations to 'little Lindy Hobbs' to join them for a beer. Being the rather shy prude I was, I ignored their raucous shouts but was secretly very tickled that they recognised me. I wished I'd been a little friendlier when I hit London and realised my luggage had disappeared. One of the plane boys then introduced himself. 'Hi Lindy, I'm Bryan Brown. Need some help, love?' My luggage turned out to be not far away on another carousel and Bryan gallantly carried my bags outside. We were not to meet again for another ten years, when he had just begun dating Rachel Ward, who was by then a very good friend of mine.

I had arrived in the mother country, and it was a stunning summer day that took my breath away.

My pal Gael wasn't due to arrive for two weeks but I luckily had one contact to look up—a Melbourne DJ whose rented house in Hammersmith resembled a grubby, messy boarding house, with endless Aussies in sleeping bags all over the place, dishes piled in the sink and the fridge filled with Foster's for nightly barbecues. Despite the bonhomie of these Aussie blokes, within a week I was staggeringly homesick and made one phone call to my folks where I did nothing but weep for about twenty minutes, threatening to get on the next plane home. It upset my parents terribly. My mum sent two telegrams and an express letter trying to cheer me up, begging me to call again right away using a phone card at the nearby phone box. I knew if I heard her voice I would just cry again, so I wrote back:

Thanks so much Mum, it was a really beautiful letter—one I shall treasure always. It makes me cry every time I read it. And thanks so much for telling me I'd be bonkers to come home already. I can't tell you how much that letter cheered me up. No I promise, there's nothing else troubling me as you put it. I don't know what came over me during that call. Well I do actually ... I just miss everyone like mad, especially you and Dad and I miss lunchtime cups of coffee with mothers and cauliflower cheese at night. But I can't be in two places at once so I guess I'll stay for a bit.

But precisely one week later I sounded decidedly more cheerful:

Please don't think I'm being too tragic. I did look up Clyde Packer's [the head of the Nine Network in Oz] 'man in London', Frank Coven and his wife Edwina. Such great people … They took me to the frightfully posh, exclusive Hurlingham Club on Saturday. The most superb vast area of lawn courts, croquet lawns, swimming pools, weeping willows, streams and bridges. It's like a secret fairy-tale world for the rich right in the middle of London. It was 'frightfully, frightfully'. Just listening to the 'Jolly good shot there, Charles' type comments was fascinating. Wish I'd taken a camera and a tape recorder. Mind you, they were all hopeless tennis players but insisted on praising each other to the hilt. A picnic lunch by the pool of Harrods pork pie and egg salad and very proper cucumber sandwiches. Such a treat but at one point I even wept thinking how I wished you were there with me!'

When my new best friend Gael arrived, the adventure really began. For a few wild, footloose months we lived like gypsies. A couple of weeks on a Chelsea houseboat that Gael knew from her previous trip (I wrote home, 'the tide's coming in and the boat's heaving mightily right now … oh dear, am so seasick, just threw up in a bucket—shit!'), a few weeks with friends of friends in Marble Arch and many nights on random sofas—and sometimes even floors—around London.

And then, as Mum kept asking if I'd seen Dudley Moore, whom she adored, I wrote:

Dudley got back to London a few days ago. Gael and I had been to see Marcel Marceau in the West End—Gael's thinking of going back to Paris to go to mime school! We could barely see him on stage though with our lousy seats till at intermission we noticed the binoculars in front of every seat for twenty pence. We even went backstage to meet him—but he was less than scintillating. Anyway, Dudley said he would meet me in the West End and take me on a tour of the sights. So Gael left to meet some Aussies and I waited in Leicester Square for Dud in his Maserati! Of course I was on the wrong corner and had to wait about an hour with endless blokes leering at me. But then we sped off to drive over Tower Bridge and past Buckingham Palace but by now it was about 1 am and all the lights were off. Nothing was lit up. Poor Dud was horrified: 'Didn't they bloody know I was bringing Lindy to show off the palace?' He carried on and was hilarious. So good to see him again but had to be firm that I didn't need to come and stay at his 'casa' in St John's Wood.

Yes, Dudley was crazy about me but, alas, I was not remotely attracted to him and we never 'did it'. I adored being with him and making him laugh and vice versa. Such a colossal drag when you find someone's company so riveting but just don't bloody fancy them.

Money was on my mind—though perhaps somewhat prematurely, I was fretting about finances and a job, just about six weeks after arriving. I wrote:

> The thought of failing to find anything with a future is omnipresent I'm afraid. I'm now considering a job at the new Hard Rock Cafe on Park Lane where my friend Belinda works, as a cashier (none of this waitress nonsense, I'm too clumsy) from 6 pm to 2 am for about thirty pounds a week.'

But then I found out there was a waiting list for such a coveted position. In the same letter I talked of my utter confusion about what to do:

> Sometimes I think perhaps I should head back to the Greek Islands for six months and have adventures—I mean, am I really here just to continue on my career trip? It is daunting having to sell myself.

Gael says I should get some photos done and join her in trying to get modelling work. I have been thinking about it. And I do have lots of alternative places to stay … But Gael and I agreed this morning that we would feel we 'belonged' and a mite more settled with a place of our own. We decided we should get up at the crack of dawn tomorrow and hit Fleet St by 9 am to get the first edition of the *Evening Standard* but now she can't go with me cos she's training it up to Norwich later today to visit Rick at the commune for a couple of days. She wants me to come but Frank and Edwina are having a dinner for me tonight so I can't join her. I must say I'm enjoying this gypsy life for a bit—sharing clothes and having friends around all the time. It's teaching me to be a better person, can't get up and be grumpy any more in the mornings. Oh dear, Gael's crying now—says she's homesick and she'd quite like to return to Melbourne. I agree but we must give each other strength!

Free feeds were very much appreciated by this budget-conscious Aussie but they came at a price. Again, I wrote home:

I looked up Johnny Nan's 'best friend in London' and arranged to meet him the next night at his 'fashion showroom'. Boy, what a creep. A condescending, pretentious Pommie twit though we didn't appreciate the full extent of his vileness till he took both Gael and I to dinner at Maunkberry's (an exclusive club) and blew about twenty-five pounds on a delicious dinner for us. Yes that was nice but honestly, he kept coming out with the most tiresome clichés about Australians—'I have the impression most Australians are terribly insular' or 'People don't really have a great cultural appreciation out there, do they?' Give me strength! Gael and I kept kicking each other under the table until we finally, politely, set him straight. And then after dinner we refused to leave with him and stayed on and at the club and danced till about 4 in the morning. Gael's friend who's a waitress there is dating the barman and so we got free drinks! We finally walked home across Hyde Park in the dawn light. It was so totally beautiful.

After looking at lots of flats, we finally ended up sharing a fabulous big three-storey, four-bedroom flat for thirty pounds a week with two other Aussies—including Frank Godby, whom I'd known since dancing class at thirteen, and who is a great friend to this day—and all sorts of ring-ins who stayed for a night or a month! It was right above the Nuthouse, a new vegetarian restaurant in Langton Street right off the King's Road at World's End. Thrilling! Our very own London address—and the stunning bonus of a wonky phone box about fifty yards away on the King's Road where you could make weepy international calls home for free. Another letter home:

Coming back from a schlep to the West End today to meet a producer of two ten-day Peter Stuyvesant commercials that would be shot in Kenya and Ethiopia (friend of a friend—a long story) when who should I meet at the bus stop home to Chelsea but my dear sweet best friend and flatmate Gael—laden, by gum, with eight letters that have been arriving at our old address in Marble Arch. It was quite overwhelming to get so many at once. And so insane reading the letter you sent to Mykonos, that was forwarded to London, out loud in our cosy, chatty, constantly people-filled kitchen where you wrote, 'Gael came to dinner last night,' and meantime Gael was right there in the flesh, giggling, next to me.

Gosh, I sometimes wonder how I'd be getting on without Gael and vice versa. It's not that loneliness creates any heavy demand for each other's company—anything but. But the fact of the matter is we simply have so much fun together and had a riotous weekend and it seems as if we were permanently doubled up with laughter as we went to see an old movie with Dud—Gael shrieking like a mad thing with her 27-pound velvet and feather extravaganza on her head that we bought at the Chelsea Antiques Market ... We spend hours making cups of tea and eating Vegemite on toast as we scour *Time Out* and plan events and outings for the coming week that would fill about two months back in dear old Melbourne … museums, galleries, the Serpentine … and in the last week we have seen both *South Pacific* and *Singing in the Rain* … and on Sunday night Gael and I were escorted to see *The Godfather* (with a pretty good-looking Al Pacino) by two creepy guys—one of whom hasn't stopped trying to woo me since we met at the bus stop at Barnes. Great movie—very violent though! Gael and I were constantly asked to 'stop screeching and shut our cakeholes'. Seriously, they are the exact words.

This was after a fabulous day walking right across Hampstead Heath—but in these dumb all-wooden shoes Gael and I both purchased! No give and we were in absolute agony by the time we stopped to stuff those cakeholes at the famous Hampstead Heath Tea Rooms with the most amazing selection of scones and cakes and pastries and fudges etc. Dudley's back in town after a weekend away in Sussex that I made excuses not to join him on—he has two letters for me—cannot wait!

There was a very frustrating delay in getting our home phone turned on—more important for me as Gael had already left town for a few days for a modelling job. As I wrote to Ma and Pa:

Finally, after ten days waiting for our phone to be switched on and frantic dashes across the King's Road to the phone box, I arrived home tonight and, automatically picking it up, was stunned to hear an actual London dial tone. My first call to Dud got no answer but then it rang—with an invite from the dreadfully enigmatic Robert Stigwood, producer of *Hair* and *Jesus Christ Superstar*, to a midnight soiree out at the Old Barn, his simply breathtaking fourteenth-century manor house out at Stanmore. (I had shown up for drinks at his office earlier this week and he'd clearly forgotten and wasn't there so I guess this was to make up for it.) Luckily I'd just picked up Gael's suitcase from a shipping friend of her parents and so I ended up wearing her fabulous Kenzo black velvet cape (with red lining) and skirt with my black beaded top.

After a sensible three-hour kip from eight till eleven, I sprung up, got dressed and was duly picked up by a big black limousine. It took ten minutes just to drive from the road to the most beautiful fairy-tale manor house you could imagine surrounded by sweeping lawns, tennis courts etc. and all lit up to perfection. The huge heavy oak door with iron reinforcements finally opened and the prettiest young butler you ever did see ushered me in.

It was a memorable night which lasted till 6 am with an exquisite supper, movies, ping-pong, long chats by roaring log fires, roaming through the house and a few laughs with Stiggy. I recall getting on very well with Paul Nicholas who was Christ in *Superstar*—feeling rather guilty, I might add, having been responsible for an innuendo-filled piece in *Private Eye* (where I had a two-week temp gig) the previous week that was based on my innocently telling a journo I'd met that Paul was living at the Old Barn with Stigwood! It could have been wrong—maybe he wasn't gay. But I was mortified that inadvertently I had anything at all to do with a piece about a leading man's possible gayness. Paul in fact called me about an hour after I left the party, at 7 am. And then two days later Stigwood called to ask if I had any interest. Confused, I said, 'Yes, he's great! I would love to see him any time.' But I never heard from the young man again.

I was living moment to moment during those days. It was good training though, and being as concerned as I was about money and employment, I was unable to see that only a short time after arriving in London I was standing at the edge of a major threshold. Things were about to take off for a homesick Aussie. I was in for some fun.

CHAPTER 4

Career Breaks ...

Career-wise, I'd had some lucky breaks in Australia, but I certainly didn't expect it to be as easy in the massive metropolis of London, in Fleet Street or in British TV news. Thinking I might have more luck with newspapers, I looked in the phone book, called up a couple, asked for the editor's office and proceeded to ask if I could have a meeting with the editor. Incredibly, I was not rebuffed everywhere. The *Sunday Express* editor agreed to see me, and after seeing some cuttings of pieces I'd written that I'd brought with me, said to call back in a week as he might have a casual Saturday-only job for eighteen pounds. I was delirious—mainly with seeing my very first Fleet Street newsroom in action. I wrote home:

> Wow, it was just like the movies. This huge room with what seemed like hundreds of short-haired blokes, sleeves all rolled up, typing away with hardly any elbow-room, making a huge noise, cigarettes dangling from their mouths. The place was filled with smoke and everyone was shouting 'Copy!' at which point young kids, maybe fifteen, would run and grab the copy from their outstretched hands and run it to the copy desk.

Of course, I had worked at a daily newspaper before, but *Newsday* in Melbourne now seemed a little like Hicksville compared to this. Before the month was up I actually managed to get a job at the *Daily Mail* working for the 'Diary'—the full page devoted to gossip.

> Am having a fabulous, hectic week at the *Daily Mail*. The smooth, good-looking acting editor Nigel Dempster says that he's most impressed with my consistent, daily supply of stories and it makes me hopeful of a permanent job … Looked at my CV and said he thought I 'must have started work at the age of five' … I must say I'm having a ball and think the newspaper scene is in my blood as I sit there working the phones and calling everyone I've met in just a few months … they have to drag me out to a Fleet Street bar—which they frequent every lunchtime—and most of the time I just say, 'No, gotta keep working boys … I'm a temp.' But of course, I've now got to impress the real editor who starts work again this coming Sunday. I'm a bit worried that I don't have too many leads right now—I'm about to call Robert Stigwood and see if he has anything to report, possibly without boasting about where I'm working …
>
> By the way I'm earning fifty pounds a week here at the *Mail* with expenses too and then extra for good stories. I got a tenner for the Michael Wilding Jnr piece …

Well, my networking—not that they called it that back then—leaves me gobsmacked. What happened to this go-getter of a gal? Where did she go? Another letter home tells of the kind of meeting I'd give my eye teeth for right now!

> Had an appointment yesterday with Rupert Murdoch's deputy, Mr McKay. Remember the case of the missing Muriel McKay— who was kidnapped by mistake when they thought she was Rupert Murdoch's wife and could blackmail him for millions? I wrote a letter and, on the strength of it, got a meeting. I was

ushered into the ballroom-sized, ultra trendy office and with my usual aplomb immediately tripped on the very thick carpet and fell on my face before seating myself on the wrong side of the desk! Well, these new-fangled, open plan offices, a girl can't tell where she is. He laughed a lot and then proceeded to spend an hour with me, fobbing off his other appointments. Not that this privileged appointment actually meant a job. He said there were no jobs going on any of their newspapers right now but he rang the people at Thames Television on the spot and got me a meeting for next Tuesday. And no, I didn't risk asking, as Mr Dudley Moore suggested, about 'old Muriel' ...

So sure enough, I headed up to Thames TV on Tuesday for my interview, dressing very conservatively, well for me anyway, and there were a few tricky moments, especially when he asked for my opinions of British television and what I thought of the news reporting, and I had to admit that I hadn't had time to watch much TV due to my incredibly busy schedule—which was utterly lame—and then I quickly added that of course I thought it was all of a very high standard, but the fact that I couldn't name shows I admired was quite pathetic and I felt like a moron! But he seemed fairly impressed with the amount of experience I'd already had and asked if I was interested in the light entertainment side of telly, and rather too hastily I replied that that would screw up my dignified hard news reporter image and he agreed. But I'm now kicking myself that I didn't ask what he had I mind! Oh well ... then it was off to Fortnum and Mason's for tea with Dudley and he ordered a bottle of champagne!'

I cringe now reading of my insanely casual approach—but there you have it. That particular letter ended with this:

Last Sunday—a momentous moment at approximately 2.22 pm ... the smell of fairly well-done roast lamb and slightly burnt vegies wafted to my nostrils as, 'Just a moment dear—I'll just turn up the oven,' was heard and seconds later, the long-imagined vision of Ada Moore appeared at the door of her tiny council house in Dagenham. Yes, I finally met Dud's mum—so unintentionally funny and preposterous that twice I nearly choked on the brussel sprouts and Dudley did in fact collapse in an hysterical heap on the floor. All the gossip and anecdotes from downtown Dagenham— no wonder Dud's never short of a sketch as has been the case for the last twenty years according to him. The lunch is followed up by dessert of licorice all-sorts and green grapes 'in a glass bowl— not on a plate, Dud, as we have a new visitor today,' insisted the adorable Ada. She must be lonely since her hubby died but has no self-pity. Just full of life and energy. People never cease to amaze me with their resilience … And by the way, your last letter was so lovely, Mother. Better than four new outfits—or five! No bawling this time—just in hysterics for half an hour. And when I read out the bit about Lizzie and her Black Rock drama with the plants and the dog and the kids and the architect, Dudley offered me payment on the spot for inclusion in a sketch. He very nearly careered off the road in mirth.

Only a month or two later, a newly divorced 36-year-old Michael White found himself without a date one evening for a Who concert and so invited his lively new friend Richard Neville (of *Oz* magazine fame). Richard, whom I'd just met a month or two earlier when I was staying in my favourite digs—a flat in Leicester Square with Aussie artist Martin Sharp and production designer Brian Thompson— couldn't make it but suggested that his new gal pal could perhaps fill his place. Richard called me and enthusiastically vouched for Michael and in fact was the go-between for this blind date—even making the arrangements with Michael so that we didn't speak before the date. Michael duly arrived to collect me on a Saturday evening in his sleek navy-blue Jensen convertible. I popped my head out the third-storey window of the flat above the Nuthouse and said I'd be right down. So the suave producer popped into a gallery next door, bought a painting and put it in the back seat in the four minutes it took for me to get down to the car.

I sunk into the lovely soft leather of Michael's brand-new sports car. Ahhh, now this was a new species of man I hitherto had not been hanging with ... a 'date', quite a bit older to be sure (he was thirty-six to my twenty), in a different league to the fellas who'd come calling back home. A trilingual sophisticate with impeccable taste in theatre, a well-travelled graduate of the Sorbonne for whom the word 'cosmopolitan' might have been invented. I had a feeling Mum would approve and off we sped.

He called intermittently over the next few weeks—always very cool and unruffled, as was his way, and such a relief from the over-eager Melbourne 'schoolboy' types (Dudley Moore even fits this category) who'd been whipped into a lather as I ignored them in my ambitious flurry of activity. But the relationship just seemed to happen, effortlessly. Without ever discussing it at all we were, within a couple of months, a couple.

Park Walk, San Lorenzo and Mr Chows were our top three restaurants where we could kick up our heels and have a ball ... they knew us, enjoyed our patronage and found us tables at the last minute—and I don't recall ever having a bad time. Hey, we were young and happy in the best city in the world. Here we're dining at Park Walk (I do believe Mr White is smoking a joint).

45

And I was impressed. He'd already produced dozens of plays, brought foreign theatre and ballet companies to Blighty and introduced the likes of Yoko Ono, John Cage, Merce Cunningham and Pina Bausch (the latter two both modern dance choreographers) to London audiences. He'd challenged censorship with both the erotic revue *Oh! Calcutta!* and a very avant-garde druggy play called *The Connection*—and basically his incredible cool and lack of boasting was just as impressive. Culturally speaking, he was leagues ahead of me, but I was a quick learner and soon 'au fait' with his accomplishments.

Now, there was a little bit of a crossover period. Just before meeting Michael I had met the very divine Earl of Pembroke. The late Henry Pembroke, tall, slim and very good-looking, was also on the outs with his pretty wife. I went to stay at his stately home, Wilton, with its famous 'Double Cube' room by Inigo Jones and its beautiful Palladian bridge, rose gardens and stunning grounds. It was featured in the film *Barry Lyndon*. It was my first very grand house and I was wildly impressed! It was summer and though there are bigger houses, like Blenheim Palace, it is definitely one of the most beautiful and its state rooms are top notch. On massive impeccable lawns I tried croquet for the first time (wearing high-heeled Chelsea Cobbler boots), played tennis with Henry, went on beautiful walks through the rose gardens and grounds that went on for days and swam in his glorious pool, always with a houseful of guests and all very proper for quite some time.

But Henry developed a huge crush on me, would have special vegetarian food ordered for me (during my brief six-month stint as a vego), bring plants from Wilton for my flat and even lent me his Mini Minor to drive round London. (Big mistake as I crashed it into a lamp-post soon thereafter.) He was utterly charming, not remotely stuffy and never wanted to be introduced to anyone by his title. He was a film director and found a lot of the duties connected with being lord of the manor quite tiresome, though he took them seriously. I recently found a very touching letter he sent to my mother that I had no idea he'd written. I guess he was trying to ingratiate himself and spoke of how incredibly 'fond of me he'd become in such a short time' and how much he admired my 'joyful, curious indomitable spirit'. It certainly impressed my mother and I now know why she often asked about him, hoping, I imagine, that I might even become the Countess one day— since his marriage was definitely on the rocks and did indeed end. We flew to Ireland together and a few weeks later, after I had just started seeing Michael, we went on an already planned trip to Marrakech. But by the end of the short five-day trip, I knew I was keener on Michael and encouraged Henry to try to make it work out with his wife.

Just one problem. Michael, whom I'd told I was on a trip with Gael, threw me for a loop the day I got back with what he thought was a fantastic treat—a trip to Marrakech, and we were to leave that evening! What to do? I couldn't tell him I'd lied and had just returned that very morning. I was stunned, exhausted and had a suitcase full of dirty clothes. Gael shrieked and found it hilarious but I was in a complete panic, wondering if I should come clean. Though I hated to be dishonest, there was no way of explaining this or hoping Michael would understand. I was convinced it would be the end. Gael lent me clean clothes and helped me quickly repack!

And yes, Michael had booked us into the very same glamorous old Mamounia Hotel I had left less than twenty-four hours earlier! The man at the desk gave me a very hard look and then, clearly recognising me, greeted me warmly, 'Ah you're back already!' I had to laugh, pretend he had me confused with someone else and hope he was discreet enough to keep his trap shut. But I felt hideously guilty and found it all very unnerving. The room service waiter nearly dropped the coffee when he saw me and one of the maids winked and nudged me. It was exhausting. And I had to feign surprise, shock and awe as we hit the markets of Marrakech and took photos of the same snake charmers I'd seen a couple of days ago! I got through it, was thrilled to finally arrive back to London and Michael was none the wiser. I vowed to never lie to a man again.

In retrospect, I think Michael was very taken by the girl he nicknamed 'Scoop' Hobbs and he also needed a partner-in-crime—a jolly, upbeat and attractive co-host. I fit the bill. He was definitely intrigued by my energy and early success, and he loved my Aussie cheekiness. Once soon after we met, Michael, a very keen racegoer who owned either all or parts of several racehorses, took me to the Derby. He hadn't told me the Queen would be there! I slipped off, slyly saying I just wanted to take some pictures, and somehow elbowed my way past the pros into the royal enclosure to get some close-ups of the Queen and the Queen Mum. I needed to get a few snaps of our lovely monarch for my mother. Michael apparently looked down from the grandstand and spotted me a few feet from Her Royal Highness, snapping away while the press photographers were all stuck outside the enclosure. He was astonished and boasted of my nerve for years.

He also loved the time I jumped into the basket of a hot-air balloon at the last minute at a wonderful, old-fashioned fete organised by the brilliant, inimitable Candida Lycett Green in Wiltshire. Why not? It was a divinely long, hot summer evening, the dashing Rupert Lycett Green was urging me to jump in, and though I didn't know where it was going or for how long, it was a hard invite to resist. In fact, we were up above the exquisite English countryside for hours when it went completely off course and ended up at least two counties away. Thrilling!

And for my part, what was not to like about Michael? He was charming, generous, witty and clever. He was cutting edge, taking risks with such an amazing array of avant-garde plays, ballets and 'happenings' … he was exciting and had the energy to match mine. More, actually. He knew everyone and we got on like a house on fire. I was happy. It felt very right. The adventures, which included Michael's three fabulous young children, Sasha, Liberty and Joshua, began. About three or four months after meeting, in February of '73, I moved in with Michael. We started off in a rented basement apartment just off Sloane Street, then we moved to a Mount Street, Mayfair, apartment and then to a stunning five-storey house in Egerton Crescent, Knightsbridge, where we stayed.

Michael was a keen race-goer and although I had no interest in most of the meets, I certainly agreed to go to Ascot the first time I was invited. When I spotted HRH The Queen in the Royal Enclosure I popped on down for a look-see, slipping past security, as you do when you're on a mission to get a snap of the Queen for your mum.

Joining forces with Michael at twenty also meant an instant family. He had three gorgeous and sweet children: Joshua, Liberty and Sasha. I adored them and loved every minute of our time together, especially holidays where we would all learn to ski or play tennis together.

But meantime, back in early October of '72, I wangled a meeting with a BBC radio gent whose name I'd been given back home. I gabbed for a while before he stopped me. He regretted, he said—and I'm paraphrasing here—that the BBC was not in the habit of hiring antipodean upstarts who hadn't bothered to attend a place of higher learning (even if they did already have experience), and that I must have had convict blood to have even made it into the building. He ushered me out the door offering a polite, 'Do let me know if there's anything I can do to help,' and to his surprise I thought he was being serious.

'Well yes, I really want to meet Nigel Ryan. Do you know him?' Nigel was the head of ITN and, having heard they weren't as stuffy as the BBC, I thought it might be my only chance of making it onto TV. Well, blow me down! Somehow, the BBC gent managed to get me a meeting several weeks hence.

Oct '72

Dearest Ma and Pa

So you won't be too impressed by this bit of news ...

I finally nabbed an interview with Nigel Ryan the head of ITN—which is the big TV news place other than the BBC—and since I have nada in the way of a college degree I was hoping they'd simply be impressed with the amount of experience I've had and *not* dwell on the educational deficits. Studied the newspapers for days and made notes about everything going on in the world but still felt incredibly ill-prepared when the day came. Unfortunately there was quite a drama beforehand—I lost my front door key somewhere between the laundromat on the King's Road and our flat round the corner above the Nuthouse—only 300 yards away! You can't imagine the ensuing chaos. There I was locked out of Number 5, swearing and kicking the pavement—with my big ITN interview in thirty minutes! I was devoid of makeup! Anyway, I thought I had no money and just as I was about to jump into the nearby Thames, I discovered I'd cleverly put my purse into the laundry bag. So I gave my laundry to the man in the gallery next door and just had to cab it to the interview, pretend I went in for the 'au natural' look in my jeans and a coat I never took off— and then get a cab back to my posh landlord's art gallery and beg him for a key.

Well I think the no-makeup look worked. Nigel Ryan seemed to really like me though I almost think he thought I was lying about the jobs I'd already had—I was very upbeat and when I went back two days later, I did a mock interview in the studio and read some autocue—and got a job! It's on the lunchtime news called *First Report* hosted by a wonderful man called Robert Kee.

PS. Nigel says I may have to work on some of my 'broader Aussie vowels'.

(And indeed, the day came about three months later when they sent me off to Paris to cover the haute-couture fashion collections and in my voice-over, thinking my six years of French at school had finally paid off handily, I pronounced names like Yves St Laurent, firmly emphasising the final T in Laurent. The day the piece was going to air, I was called into Nigel's office and I walked in, terrified that I was about to get the sack. But with a supercilious smirk, he simply raked me over the coals for my atrocious pronunciation. 'No hard T at the end of St Laurent, my dear girl' … and he went through a list of frog names I'd gotten wrong. I had to rush into the booth and rerecord my voice-over. The piece went out that day on all the news shows—not just the lunchtime report.)

Having a firm job starting in a month meant there was time for a fabulous jaunt to Milan with Gael, who was meant to be pursuing her modelling with a round of daily 'go sees'—making appointments to see photographers and ad agencies to show them her folio of photos. We did a few 'go sees' but we mainly took diet pills, drank cappuccinos all day and sat in cafes smoking and talking nonstop before heading back to our lovely old *pensione*—filled with beautiful huge pieces of mahogany furniture—late at night for boiled eggs, a slice of gorgonzola cheese and a few prunes. We lost some weight and were very pleased with ourselves. Michael had offered to meet us at Milan Airport, hire a car and drive us up to St Moritz for a weekend—an offer we took about ten seconds to accept. We had a cassette recorder with us, and as Michael walked out into the airport, Gael and I planted the cassette player on the floor next to the arrivals door, turned it on to loudly play Carly Simon's 'You're So Vain' and then hid.

Michael was mildly amused. We thought it utterly hilarious and reached new heights of hysteria as we ascended the Alps, had a couple of puffs of a joint Michael lit up, and by the time we got to the famous St Moritz cake shop, Hanselmann's, were so stoned that we collapsed onto the floor of the restaurant, barely able to breathe we were laughing so much, utterly wasted and light-headed in the new altitude, not to mention half-starved from our diet. Michael was certainly thrilled to be swanning around a chic ski resort with two gorgeous young things—but slightly appalled by our Aussie joie de vivre. We couldn't help it. We were so happy to be 'in the snow' and not used to such luxury, high-falutin living.

The very swanky Palace Hotel where we stayed was like Disneyland to the girls from Black Rock. We marvelled at the softest, whitest sheets we'd ever slept in and our eyes bulged as the room service trolley was wheeled in each morning with its array of chocolate croissants, eggs and fresh fruit, pancakes, hot chocolate and coffee. And though we loved to tease him, Michael, who'd been sent off to school in Switzerland at the age of seven for his asthma, impressed us no end as he switched from French to German to Italian and back to French in the course of a walk through the hotel. Heads turned as Michael strolled through the lobby with Gael and I on each arm, and if anyone thought a groovy ménage a trois was going down, Michael did nothing to change their minds. So Gael and I were thrilled by the fabulous wood-panelled Swiss restaurants, strobe-light nightclubs and—as in some corny romance novel—flowing champagne, women in furs and jewels and handsome tanned ski instructors. Once we hit the nightclubs there was no stopping us. We danced together like whirling dervishes, and made something of a spectacle of ourselves, albeit 'an attractive one' according to Michael, as he reported that international playboy Gunter Sachs thought we must be professional dancers. I was not very good but Gael was, and is, a fantastic, incredibly sexy dancer.

A few days later it was back to London, and my first serious job at *First Report*. Any pieces I did would go out that lunchtime—and if decent, would even make it onto the nightly news. One had to work at absolutely lightning speed. I rarely had time to finish editing any story properly, leading, most of the time, to live voice-overs for stories—a high-wire act that might have terrified someone without my Aussie experience. It was truly an adrenaline-pumping time and, happily, I was treated for the most part like one of the guys and sent off to cover 'serious' stories like the divorce referendum in Rome or foot-and-mouth disease scares for farmers in the wilds of Wales.

It didn't mean the guys at work actually liked me (let's be frank—who *would* warm to an annoying upstart twenty-year-old with no degree who's nabbed a great job?) and they were desperate to whip up some gossip, but luckily, I was attached and thus there were no office romances for me. In retrospect I was a staggeringly dull goody-goody prude who absolutely had no idea how to flirt and who barely knew when someone was coming on to me. I'm pretty convinced I could have gone further if I'd had a few more feminine wiles. It's amazing the number of men who mistook my lack of finesse in 'chatting them up' for rudeness. Men who said they took a dislike to me because I apparently gave them the cold shoulder. I blame the all-girls school upbringing which led to a general fear of men, but really I suspect it was innate shyness. You're either born to flirt or you're not.

Anyway, I had a great job, a great guy. Life was pretty amazing and I knew it.

CHAPTER 5

Trouble with Oncologists

IN STARK CONTRAST to reminiscing about the good ol' days, this next stage of my cancer story makes me crazy and freshly guilt-ridden beyond belief just thinking about it. Such colossal stupidity on my part. But I will say that I am simply scared stiff and in a blinding panic, which, when coupled with my innate impulsiveness and urge to get the show on the road, makes it somehow comprehensible that I have my lumpectomy and then I only see one oncologist and stick with her.

I simply do not do my homework. And this is where I want to warn readers—*please* do it. I do not seek the guidance of three or four oncologists before making a decision. I go with the first one I meet—a female oncologist I'll call Dr C—who has perfect grooming, power suits and a calm, composed demeanour. Many people have recommended her and a new friend who was diagnosed a couple of months ahead of me adores her. Plus my good friend Diantha's son-in-law has also just been her patient and likes her.

I've already spent several days schlepping on my own into Cedars-Sinai, to the code blue nuclear section where they pump your veins with radioactive material so that the machines—yes, the ones where you're slid into the nightmarish tunnel thingo for what seems like lonely hours on end—will detect any spread of the cancer.

Spread? When the technician spells it out, I'm in shock again. If you can fathom such stupidity, I'd actually forgotten about this possibility. And as it's finally sinking in to my thick head, they put me in a foul, cold isolation room for hours to wait, incommunicado, between tests. I'm not allowed to go to the regular waiting room—where cell phone reception is much better—because I'm contaminated! We even have special toilets—so that our toxic bodily fluids are kept isolated from the general public.

When it's time for the big meeting with the oncologist, I weaken and ask Lola to come with me. Dr C tells me I have cancer (stage one invasive ductal carcinoma, ER positive) and that despite the tumour being small, and no cancer having been detected in the lymph nodes, chemotherapy would boost my chances of survival by about 40 per cent. According to many specialists and the leading UCLA oncologist I find three months later, the real number is much lower. Some say it is just 2 per cent and that the 40 per cent figure refers to tests showing a shrinkage of tumours for a period of just twenty-eight days, but Dr C pretty much makes sure of our business by adding that if the 'cancer is not contained in the breast and metastasises and spreads, there's nothing more we can do for you. We have no cure. We can only prolong your life.'

That's all she says, but it's pretty potent and somewhat overly dramatic stuff. I can think of nothing to say as I look over to see my darling daughter in tears. Lola, who said she would take notes and who's normally hard-headed, cool and exceptionally smart and curious, is looking down, weeping quietly. Guilt at having dragged her there courses through my veins. Obviously, I simply do not know where to begin with follow-up questions. But I do ask, 'Do you have any suggestions for diet or supplements I could take to boost my immune system while I'm on chemo?' I guess I'm trying to prove to myself and Lola that I still have my wits about me.

'Oh well, I guess you could take a multivitamin,' she replies, adding, 'if you like.'

That one response alone should have been enough to send me running for the hills. But at that point it simply seemed like confirmation that doctors are still in the Stone Age and know nothing about nutrition, supplements and complementary ways to boost one's immune system and stay well. In my experience, most doctors are not taught about nutrition or preventative medicine. It's not about wellness. It's about drugs. That's how they are taught—in medical schools often largely funded by pharmaceutical companies.

Ten days later, I begin the chemo. A week beforehand my dear friend Buck Henry, the 82-year-old writer of *The Graduate*, sends me an email—'Welcome! You're in the cancer club now whether you like it or not—with all us old codgers!' And when I tell him I'm off to the Beverly Hills oncology centre, he actually utters the words, 'I'm jealous.'

'You're going to love it there,' he insists. 'I used to look forward to it. They're sooo nice. They bring you warmed blankets, ladies come round with snacks (or hand-knitted beanies if you're going bald) and you can even order meals from about a dozen restaurants.' All true, I discovered—and they bring it straight to your numbered recliner chair.

The toxic combo of drugs I am given, Cytoxan and Taxotere, are administered in the chemo lounge, a massive 3000-square-foot area consisting of several nurse stations and about forty widely spaced recliner chairs—all with their own TVs and uncomfortable side chairs for the poor old friends or spouses who sit grim-faced and uncomfortable for the four hours that most chemo treatments take … though in my case, the chair is empty for most of my first session as Lola finds the proximity to Barneys a tad irresistible, especially as there is a sale, and I selflessly encourage her to sprint down there and come back to give her tethered old mum a show and tell.

Having read about all the possible side effects in a cheery pamphlet, I am here to state that I get every last one, quite severely. But I get one that is not even in the books, and one late-night call to my oncologist has her insisting that the wildly painful itching that makes me want to jump out of my skin, has me pacing up and down all night and scratching so hard that my skin is left red-raw and bleeding is *not* a side effect of the chemo. I'm sent to a dermatologist, and when it only gets worse after the second session of chemo, my oncologist concedes that it must be connected and the chemo drug cocktail is altered.

Another testament to my idiotically sensitive system is that my hair starts falling out about ten minutes after the first chemo infusion. Instead of two or three weeks later, it falls out in huge handfuls within a week. That first present on my pillow clearly freaks Nick out—as he walks past my bed to find the school novel I had been reading to him the night before, he sees the clump of hair and shouts out like he's seen a ghost.

'Mum! What the hell?' he yelps.

I start to laugh, a bit manically, it's true. He looks at me like I'm insane as I simply run to my closet and pull on a new cashmere beanie that I bought online for this very moment … and it's off to school.

Now, I'm the first to admit that having soft, silky hair-free legs— and since I'm a prude I won't mention other places—is a boon, but the transition to hairlessness on my head is swift and cruel. I become fascinated and a smidge OCD about the fact that just the gentlest tug, which produces *no* feeling at all, results in a handful of hair in my hand.

Three days later, I'm sitting on a chair on top of a towel in the living room in my apartment, surrounded by Lola and two brave friends, Brooke Adams and Richard Baskin, for the shave-off ceremony. It's time. Nick has sensibly skateboarded off to visit a friend in the hood and I've asked Mario, an old friend and a hairdresser, to come and do the honours. Champagne is drunk as we wait and chat, but Mario's not answering calls or texts. With my receding hairline and huge patchy bald spots, I look like a crazy old bag lady. An hour later we give up waiting for Mario and I find an old plastic razor in my shower that hasn't been used for weeks. Lola gaily gets to work and I put on a brave face as the rusty blade drags over my scalp. I see snaps Lola has taken of the back of my head and collapse in hysterical laughter. It's all patchy—I look like a leopard. Everyone starts to laugh and someone chuckles about how lucky I am to have a sense of humour. That's for sure.

As weeks wear on, my inner journalist kicks in, and although it's too late for me to be brave and call a halt to the chemo, I finally start to try and find out more ... I read books, search the internet and find out some disturbing news about chemotherapy and the fact that oncologists in America get the chemo drugs wholesale and then charge patients the retail price—thus making a very large portion of their income from prescribing chemotherapy.

No more bad hair days for sure—but not much else to recommend the out-dated practice of giving anyone and everyone chemotherapy, even when it is not needed. Three doctors would go on to confirm that my chemo was not appropriate ...

Right after I finish chemo, Buck Henry suggests I visit his friend and fellow breast-cancer gal, the *Spiderman* producer Laura Ziskin, who with Sherry Lansing founded Stand Up to Cancer, which has held two telethons raising almost $200 million for cancer research. Laura, who will sadly die in 2011, is surprised to hear I'm having chemo given my early-stage cancer and strongly recommends I see her oncologist at UCLA, Dr John Glaspy. I make the call, use her name and I'm in within two weeks.

I am blown away at first sight. This man has the kindest, wisest, loveliest eyes I've ever seen—and a charismatic, magical smile. I adore him on the spot. He's a researching, groundbreaking oncologist. All my records have been sent over. I quickly summarise them. 'One point two centimetres, nothing in the lymph nodes, a lumpectomy, twelve weeks of chemo, I now feel appalling and I don't know what to do next ...'

He immediately responds with, 'Well, if you'd come to see me sooner and told me you did *not* want chemo, you wouldn't have got an argument from me!'

What kind of heretical talk is this? I practically hug him on the spot—simultaneously devastated that I finished the chemo just two weeks earlier. And so I ask him if he agrees with the statistic that chemo would have only improved my survival rate by this alarming 1 to 2 per cent and he says *yes*.

Dr Glaspy even discusses the advantages of complementary treatments like vitamin C therapies and acupuncture. The guy is a veritable Renaissance Man. But I am finding it hard to focus. I've allowed three months of vile, toxic chemo drugs to ravage my body, when this oncologist says it may not even have helped! Since my now-tripled dose of the antidepressant Cymbalta is failing miserably in its long-cherished role of keeping my ever-ready tears at bay, I simply can't stop blubbering and we decide it's best for me to come back later to discuss the next move.

Well, the next move—the next conventional step—is radiation. But I'm now questioning everything that has been recommended and it seems that the side effects of radiation are very much played down. I go to see one of the top guys in Beverly Hills with Ilana, a friend from Australia. Now, I admit that by this time I'm a little short on respect for the by-the-book conventional wisdom, so when this guy starts saying that in his experience there are rarely any side effects whatsoever, my hackles rise and I start to pose lots of questions, especially about the likelihood of skin rippling, lumpiness and/or shrinkage due to my breast implants. These are well-documented problems and even Dr C mentioned them. But as I've now observed on many occasions, questioning these medical honchos does not go down well. He becomes—not unlike the radiologist who didn't spot the cancerous lump at my mammogram—hostile, arrogant and just plain rude.

This doctor simply denies that my having implants will increase the chances of side effects. Well, I ask, what about potential heart damage because it is my left breast that will be radiated and thus the radiation will be closer to the heart?

'Not any more. Our techniques are very sophisticated,' he claims, both pompously and condescendingly. I am flabbergasted and foolishly try to quote some of the research I've done. It's pointless. He's digging in his heels and refusing to even acknowledge the remote possibility of any side effects.

My feisty Aussie pal takes over and her voice quickly rises as she shrieks, 'We're adults here, doc. Could you just tell us the truth and not talk bullshit?'

He stands to rise. The consultation is clearly over. And we huffily take off, cursing him to ourselves like only a couple of irreverent Aussie sheilas can do. Well, that's one decision quickly made. For me radiation is out!

My next option? In retrospect, I believe I would have been well advised to do nothing more than concentrate on wellness. Eating the best, freshest, organic food I could find, supplements, acupuncture—you know the drill—but instead, it pains me to write that I've been told that the newest version of a mastectomy, the skin-sparing, nipple-saving double mastectomy, would be the way to go. Although I am racked by indecision and confusion, I move headlong into a tiring, expensive round of appointments with three different breast surgeons and six different reconstructive surgeons.

Two surgeons are needed for this extraordinary surgery that will supposedly reduce my chances of recurrence even more. The breast surgeon is responsible for making the ridiculously delicate cut around the nipple (keyhole surgery) before removing the breast tissue, and then the reconstructive surgeon puts in expanders—temporary implants which, as their name suggests, can be expanded at intervals through a port to slowly stretch the now delicate covering of skin. A six-hour surgery. And then the reconstructive surgeon will of course be the one who monitors you, pumps up the expanders and then operates again several months later to remove the expanders and put in permanent implants.

My goal is to find two surgeons who take my insurance, but I make sure I get to see all the top guys whether they take insurance or not— which means exorbitant consultation fees for some. But, late in the day it's true, I'm determined to do my homework and I want to hear all my options. Some surgeons who've been highly recommended turn out to be dinosaurs who only do the old-fashioned method of lopping off the tits and doing things like a TRAM flap reconstruction, where skin, fat and muscle are moved from your stomach (leaving a ten-inch scar) up to your chest to create a breast mound. This results in scars, a flabby tummy devoid of muscles and a huge risk of hernias.

Other grim scenarios include taking a flap from your back or even the top of the thigh around the groin. Bizarrely, they proudly show me photos of their handiwork with livid red post-op scars on sad, hollow-faced women. Oddly, at least four of them ask me if I took fertility drugs at some point. I did and they all tell me that a striking majority of their patients have done so too. That's great—the agony of unsuccessfully trying to conceive with AI and enduring years of shots and procedures, and then breast cancer to boot! But how odd that I've never heard the connection before.

Trying to really do my homework for this decision, I go to see Dr Glaspy again and take along a dear friend, Richard Baskin, to listen to what he has to say.

But what a day—we arrived at UCLA about two hours after Michael Jackson's body has been taken there. It's bedlam. Richard is phoned by a music-industry lawyer pal as we sit waiting for the doctor. He says he's heard Michael Jackson overdosed and died. It is hard to take in as I feverishly study my questions for Dr Glaspy, the final sounding board for my double-mastectomy decision. He agrees with me that the side effects of radiation are very much played down and that using the new skin- and nipple-sparing techniques for mastectomies are definitely a good option. Dr Glaspy tells me my chances of recurrence are down to 1–2 per cent after a double mastectomy, and yes, he'd recommend it.

It's easy to make the decision to stay with Dr Peg as my breast surgeon—she did the biopsy and the subsequent lumpectomy—but harder to work out which of these others should have the honours with my mastectomy. However, after dozens of phone calls to friends and friends of friends who've been through cancer to get recommendations, the name of a Santa Monica surgeon, whom I'll call Dr Bob, is mentioned and I Google him. Unlike others, he has a slick website—and the photos of his work are spectacular. He does it all—stunning facelifts, lipo, eyes, noses … and beautiful breasts. He takes my insurance. And when Lola and I go to see him he couldn't be nicer or spend more time explaining the surgery, making drawings and answering any and all questions. We like him. He's never worked with my breast surgeon before but is happy to do so. The decision is made. Off with the tits!

CHAPTER 6

The Swinging '70s

Now, WHEN MY daughter, Lola, sometimes looks at my albums, she cannot fathom the glamorous, action-packed life her mother led and occasionally feels a tad dispirited because her life—backpacking on rickety buses through Argentina as I write—bears no resemblance to mine. The times, I tell her, are simply different. Quite apart from the trips to Gstaad, St Tropez, Aspen, Rome, New York, Marrakech, Jamaica and LA, and all the weekends spent in stately homes in England, most people simply don't entertain the way they used to—and certainly not the way Michael and I did. Barely a week went by when we weren't hosting cocktails or a dinner party or a massive 'bash'. And for some reason, I felt compelled to start taking pictures of it all—now pasted into (at last count) about 110 photo albums.

The aristo-heavy country weekends at big old piles were fascinating and I was the full-on Aussie rube who loved meeting po-faced butlers and discovering that housemaids unpacked for you and that, come morning, cooked grub would be waiting in chafing dishes in the 'breakfast room'. But not as thrilled to find that old customs had survived and women were still expected to leave the gentlemen at the dinner table and quietly retire elsewhere when coffee and port were served. The first time it happened, coffee was brought in and the women, without a word being said, all rose as one and slithered out of the room. I thought they were just all off to the loo at the same time until Michael nudged me.

'What?' I asked.

He finally had to explain that this was time for the menfolk to chat alone. 'It's tradition.'

'Bugger that! It's ridiculous. What is this? The Middle Ages?' I sputtered and refused to budge. Fortunately, this lot were amused, and with Michael quickly explaining in his customary teasing fashion that I was 'fresh off the boat', I got away with it. But frankly, it was less-than-scintillating man talk and, having made my point, I didn't bother to stage another sit-in. I would soon tire of the country. As much as I enjoyed the evening charades, games of croquet and joining the shoot for elevenses, I'm such a city girl and by Sunday evenings I would be thrilled to make a getaway. It was London that made my pulse race. Give me a big grimy capital any day.

Just a few months after I moved in with Michael, a thunderbolt struck and things would never quite be the same. Sensing something new, original and utterly entertaining, he took one of his famous gambles and put on a full-blown, brand-new musical whose title was changed at the last minute from *It Came from Denton High* to *The Rocky Horror Show*. Michael had visited the author Richard O'Brien, Australian director Jim Sharman and composer Richard Hartley in a little flat nearby and they played him a few songs and he agreed to put it on. Just like that. No mucking around for Michael. Split-second decisions that, more often than not, paid off. After just two previews it opened at the tiny 63-seat experimental space upstairs at the Royal Court Theatre in Sloane Square. I remember going to a rehearsal and watching from the back with Michael and Jim Sharman, who I knew from Sydney where he'd directed *Jesus Christ Superstar*. It was utterly thrilling. I couldn't stop moving as the music played. It really made you want to dance—one of the reasons it turned into such a massive cult hit. Such rollicking good fun and totally accessible to everyone since author Richard O'Brien had come up with the winning concept of combining fantastic music with the unintentional humour of B movies and the preposterous dialogue and ideas of bad schlocky horror films. It was a hoot and by opening night (I still have the original programme), I was singing along to the tunes.

The rest is history. A critical and commercial hit, it soon transferred to the Classic Cinema on the King's Road, and then in one of his genius unconventional moves, Michael transferred *Rocky* to the bohemian King's Road Theatre—which he saved from demolition by putting *it* on there, and it ran for seven years! The set designer was another Aussie pal, the very talented Brian Thompson. Nell Campbell, who played Columbia and is now one of my dearest friends, was from Sydney, though I hadn't known her there, and the star of the show— the utterly divine and delicious Tim Curry—remains one of my best friends to this day. It was pretty thrilling stuff and in my mind signalled the start of the 'good times'. Michael and I were very much united in that we were both intent on sharing these good times.

And it was possible because Michael's generosity was virtually unlimited. (Michael produced 101 stage productions and twenty-seven films—from *A Chorus Line* and *Annie* to *Hound of the Baskervilles* with Dudley Moore and Peter Cook to *Monty Python and The Holy Grail*, from a 'happening' with Yoko Ono to an edgy film about new wave music called *Urgh! A Music War*, which I produced with him.) His reach was wide. Quite apart from the countless number of people whose careers Michael jump-started he somehow felt it was his duty to entertain London away from the theatre as well. We hosted endless big dinners at San Lorenzo or Park Walk or Mr Chow and Michael would always insist on paying the bill—even with seriously rich people in tow or should I say *especially* with millionaires around since they were often investors in his shows. In fact, the evenings with potential investors were definitely in the 'hard work' category and I must say I dreaded them—not least because they were always such late nights and the effort to appear at work in sparkling form at 8 am was monumental. I wrote home:

> After the fiasco with the Arabs deciding not to invest in *Chorus Line* at the eleventh hour, it looks as if many long drawn-out evenings with some Persians will pay off. They've promised to invest and after soirees when it seemed the caviar and champagne would come out our ears and after one occasion when Hassan (the shah of Iran's cousin) lost 100,000 pounds in an hour at the gambling tables and couldn't care less, it seems they're for real. Phew! I don't know how Michael stays cool. Even when he's incredibly short of money for productions he doesn't seem to fret. But when I hear of some of his money problems, I feel faint on the spot.

Depending on the season we would host dinner parties either in the gorgeous ground-floor dining room at Egerton Crescent, which featured groovy walls of copper, in the big eat-in kitchen (painted, in my first decorating effort, fantastic shades of chartreuse, acid yellow and a darker green with a red fridge) or in the pretty back garden. They were often catered affairs and once, after Michael went to Tokyo, we had a novel dinner, long before it was popular, of Japanese sushi with our very own sushi chef. But most of the guests, shocked and appalled by the idea of raw fish, went home hungry. Chris Reeve later told me he headed straight for the nearest Indian take-away.

But that was a rare dud of an evening. When evenings weren't catered, Michael's a great cook and, in a slightly dizzy Auntie Mame kind of way, would effortlessly whip up, with help from our surly Spanish housekeeper, things like pasta or roast lamb or a fabulous fish pie. He'd come to terms with the fact that I was useless in the kitchen and had once jokingly telegrammed (yes, telegrams—my kids don't know what they are!) my mother to ask, 'Dear Pauline, why didn't you teach Lindy to poach an egg?' and so I'd generally be ordered to stay out of the kitchen, thank God—and would spend time feverishly scouring the papers for story ideas for the next morning's meeting.

I would simply set the table or do a big shop at my 'local' market—the ridiculously overpriced Harrods Food Halls.

I confess that 'economical housekeeping' and I were not remotely acquainted, and indeed I felt positively saintly during the week when I managed to find five minutes at work to phone in a delivery order to the Piccadilly tourist trap Fortnum and Mason's for a lot of outrageously pricey out-of-season fruit or to Harrods for a few staples like coffee, wholemeal bread, big jars of Vegemite, Bendicks Bittermints or a dozen brown eggs. I could in fact soft-boil the latter— just! I know, I know, I sound spoilt and lazy but, seriously, you try keeping your head above water with a demanding cut-throat job at Thames TV, where I'd joined the staff as a reporter on the evening *Today* show after two years at ITN, and a demanding showbiz legend of a boyfriend whose idea of lolling around was to stay in one night a month. In fairly obnoxious fashion, I wrote home:

Dearest Ma and Pa

Well it's been a whirlwind of activity just for a change. I'm sorry to sound like a pill but I'm just so tired!

I've just done an interview with a British Rail Supervisor who was put on leave for making witty early morning jokes and wisecracks when announcing the arrival of trains over the station amplifier … But they reinstated him and there was clapping and cheers when he began again today … Tomorrow I'm doing a tour of Soho with the newly appointed vicar and then, it seems, an interview with Princess Anne—about what I know not yet—and Friday a story about a dog who plays football. Two nights ago I did an extraordinary interview with a woman who became a rich old Etonian's mistress at the age of seventeen (having been put under licence to him at fifteen after running away from home) and stayed for eighteen years. He was killed last year and after a big court case she's been thrown out of the house he bought for her and her daughter.

As for night life—non-bloody-stop! I organised a very nice small dinner party for Barry Humphries so that Michael could get to know him … It was just six of us—me nearly choking as Barry, in excellent form, sat next to me, elbowing me every thirty seconds as he made a crack, quite sure of a patriotic, faithful, always good for a chortle audience in yours truly … Anyway after much encouragement from me, Michael's meeting him tonight to talk about trying to put on a Dame Edna show in the West End very soon … I'm sure it will work …

(It did and Michael to this day credits me with insisting that he encourage Barry back to London and 'talking him into' putting him on in the West End, followed by a very costly disaster when he then took Barry to Broadway. It was a flop and cost Michael a lot of his own money, and Barry repaid him by then deciding to produce the next show himself back in London so Michael could not recoup any of his losses.)

Then last night I took Gael and some other Aussies to a party for the cast of *Chorus Line* at the Hard Rock Cafe. The Aussie gang was thrilled to slip through the waiting crowds with us, nod to the bouncer and waft inside. Tomorrow night it's dinner either at Germaine Greer's or the new head of EMI (probably the latter going on to the former's), Wednesday it's dinner with the Greeks (bound to be late as the Niarchos boys like to indulge!) followed by a dinner party here on Thursday night for Tim Curry and Russell Harty the talk-show host. But do not feel bad for me, Mother … I don't actually arise at dawn to market and peel potatoes … More like get home at seven or seven-thirty after a ten-hour day at the studio, then a bath, get dressed, return a few calls from folk asking to get invited in after dinner and then a little check on the drinks situation to see if there's enough ice.

Yep, it's the life of Riley for me, though no doubt I'll be in for a nasty shock one day! But thank goodness we're off to the

Lycett Greens' for a lovely weekend in the countryside and the kids are coming out from boarding school to join us. Rupert is organising a croquet tournament for Sunday afternoon (and boasts that I'm a gung-ho Aussie ever since I jumped into the hot-air balloon at the last minute, with him ending up in a field in the middle of nowhere with cars trying to follow us and make sure we survived!)

And then Monday I'm off to Rome to do a report on the divorce referendum with an Italian crew who will barely speak English. Hopefully I'll get some decent digs in against those hypocritical prigs from the Catholic Church and I've got them to agree to let me stay an extra day to go to a feminists rally where they will be loudly insisting that women need the right to divorce.

So we didn't swap recipes or cook together and, yes, 'Chalky' White definitely could be a nag and a bit 'fussy' and unsexy in the way he often treated me like one of his kids, but fortunately he and I did share a love of hanging out with people, often. As a child, I don't recall my parents ever having a single soul to dinner in our drab flat and perhaps because of that, I was swiftly a dab hand at rounding pals up for our London soirees. My parents were outgoing and both had wonderful senses of humour but no money to entertain, so this was a novelty and I loved the idea of creating fun by putting so many different, random folk together. Small talk and approaching strangers has always terrified me, but as a hostess, I found it liberating and a way to hone my conversational skills.

Some of my party rules? Always over-invite and make sure they're folks from different walks of life, keep the lights low and flattering, always serve champagne when they walk in the door, say yes to friends of friends, make tons of introductions and try to give that time-honoured but wildly effective tiny capsule description of each person as you make the intro.

'Barry, this is Jack. Jack, Barry has just starred in a one-man show in the West End as a bigoted Australian housewife, Edna Everage. Barry, Jack's here in London going to a lot of parties but during the day he's starring in *The Shining* for Stanley Kubrick.' Or 'Chris, I'd like you to meet Salman Rushdie. Salman, Chris Reeve is starring as Superman in a film right now and Chris, Salman is a writer ...' Or, 'Susan, this is Boy George, the singer ...' before being interrupted with shrieks of glee from Boy George, who's already kneeling at the feet of a flattered Susan Sarandon. That sort of thing.

It's been gratifying over the years to hear, often long after the fact, from so many people that they met their future best pal, boyfriend, wife, director, agent, leading lady—all through me and Michael at an Egerton Crescent soiree. We insisted on fixed table placements. Except on Casual Sundays.

So this gorgeous five-storey house (with the live-in housekeeper installed in the basement) was perpetually stuffed to the gills with all manner of folk, from earls (Henry Pembroke remained a great friend) and poets to antipodean upstarts, but the witty showbiz crowd dominated. Writers, actors, musicians, set designers, directors and media folk of the day, from Tina Brown to Harold Evans, David Frost to David Dimbleby. And then there was my fabulous high-energy and especially witty Aussie coterie of pals, which included my best friend, the beautiful, fun-loving and charismatic Gael McKay (now Boglione), the late Bennie Gannon (*The Boy from Oz* producer), Brian Thompson (*Rocky Horror* production designer), Stephen Mclean (author of the Peter Allen biography) and Little Nell (Columbia in the original production and movie of *Rocky Horror*) as well as people like Norma Moriceau (designer of *Mad Max*), Geoffrey Robertson, who went on to become a famous QC and human rights lawyer, and of course Barry Humphries, a fellow Melburnian!

I shan't dwell on it and I'm loathe to sound nationalistic but I do feel we Aussies brought a certain sense of gay abandon and hilarity to the party. We were so thrilled to be there in the most exciting city on earth, not afraid to show it and I think our exuberance definitely helped create a joyous atmosphere. We were also just plain silly. One night Barry came to dinner and somehow we starting reminiscing about childhood 'cossy sucking', which is to say, sucking the straps

Boy George was beside himself with excitement when he spotted Susan Sarandon. As I was about to introduce them, Susan shrieked at the sight of him and rushed up for a big hug. Mutual admiration society. My dear pal Johnny Rosza rests his head on Michael.

Dining rooms may be considered a waste of space these days but ours at Egerton Crescent was a lively, much used and much loved room. Its copper walls made it oddly cosy and Michael constantly swapped out the art we bought. I introduced him to Martin Sharp and this one above the fireplace (barely seen, alas) was a gem. Barry Humphries was a frequent visitor, as was Little Nell Campbell, who played Columbia in both the stage and the screen version of The Rocky Horror Show.

or some portion of your swimsuit after an ocean swim to taste the salt from the seawater. Barry didn't drink and I barely ever drank, so inebriation is not our excuse for such inanely childish behaviour but … we did find it hilarious and I have photos to prove it—of a maniacally grinning Barry sucking on a swimsuit. Yes, very silly.

One of my favourite guests was the utterly divine and truly beautiful son of a preacher, Tim Curry, who reigned supreme on the King's Road as the lead in *Rocky Horror* for so long and who was so extraordinary reprising his role in the film. Now, Tim knew how to flirt and since he was so ridiculously good-looking and charismatic, he was a great dinner-party guest and could easily hold a table of guests spellbound as he revealed some juicy bit of backstage gossip, doing

The opening night of Dame Edna in the West End, produced by Michael White—thanks to, as Barry acknowledged, my insistence that Michael meet Barry and give him an opportunity to showcase the wonderfully witty Edna Everage at the Apollo in 1976. Housewife Superstar *was a huge hit and Michael naturally threw a big party afterwards. I always insisted on inviting my best friends, including Tim Curry, who'd recently starred in the original stage production of* Rocky Horror *and its now legendary film adaptation.*

everyone's voices because he's a brilliant mimic. It was always a tiny bit troubling to me, though, that despite being the life of the party he would always come alone, go home alone and to my knowledge never once had a boyfriend. Tim, who now lives in LA, is as witty and wicked as it gets, with a steel-trap mind that remembers every showbiz tale from the minute he got his break on stage in *Hair*. If ever there was a brilliant raconteur who should write a memoir, it's him.

And it was always a treat to see model Penelope Tree and her sexy boyfriend David Bailey, who I instantly liked, as he reminded me of an Aussie with his cheeky irreverence. We met just a few months after I started dating Michael when we all happened to be staying at L'Hotel in Paris. It was my first trip to Paris and I was wildly excited—even if Michael's reason for going was less romantic than it might have been. He was very curious to see *Deep Throat*, which had been banned in the UK. Michael was a big defender of freedom of speech in the 'arts' and as it was the first porn film to have decent production values and a story—as well as humour—Michael wanted to see what the fuss was about. I was shocked by it, as it was the first porn I'd ever seen—though of course I acted very blasé. Michael was quite cranky when halfway through I got something in my eye and we had to leave! After going to three French pharmacies we ended up at the eye hospital where they numbed it, removed some dust and gave me a big eye patch. (I'd had very sensitive eyes since doing a piece way back in Melbourne on tan-through bikinis. Like a nitwit I had done repeated takes of my piece-to-camera in the tanning booth with no goggles on and had burnt my eyes, ending up unable to see for several days!) Back to Penelope. I thought she was incredibly glamorous and chic with her mysterious, unusual looks—but just the other day, still a great friend, she told me that when she met me in the hotel corridor in Paris, she thought I was the mysterious one in my eye patch and Kenzo cape!

We saw a lot of Chris Reeve, who was in London for a month, barely able to believe his own luck as he had the title role in the *Superman* film. Such a sweetheart, truly humble and endlessly grateful for his good fortune as an actor.

After an interview with the very sweet Chris Reeve, who had just starred in Superman,
*I offered to drive him to the airport—not realising that he packed 'like a very rich girl' and had
huge suitcases that were hard to fit into my yellow 'Jeans' VW Bug (with true denim seats)!*

And of course people loved to call up at the last possible moment, begging to bring an extra guest, knowing they were never refused. We were endlessly squeezing extras in at the round table for twelve—in the round being a 'must' for lively exchange. Or when we couldn't fit even a very thin model at the table, we'd simply say, 'Do come in after dinner.' So suddenly Prince Andrew would be sitting on the sofa, having been brought by girlfriend Koo Stark, Eric Idle would slip in with a Python or two in tow, Robert and Celestia Fox would appear with their new best friend, the actor Rupert Everett, or the very, very chic Tina Chow would appear with or without Michael Chow. From the corner of my eye I might suddenly spy the impossibly beautiful, clever and glamorous Edna O'Brien, who could flirt like nobody's business all night long and still come off as serious and literary.

Out of nowhere it seemed, the angelic, ridiculously stylish Jasper Conran would be sitting next to Sabrina Guinness or Tom Stoppard (now together and wed!)—or Manolo Blahnik and Michael Roberts would arrive after dinner, giggling and raving about some extraordinary fashion show or party they'd just attended, and with all barriers down, Lady Diana Cooper would be seen chatting to Goldie Hawn, Karl Lagerfeld, Dustin Hoffman, Warren Beatty, Lauren Hutton or Diane von Furstenberg, since so many Hollywood stars and New York jetsetters would somehow find their way to Egerton Crescent. It was a startling change for me. I felt like I'd won the lottery. It seemed very indulgent and more than a little bit decadent to entertain on the scale we did … week after week. I remember feeling guilty occasionally as it would occur to me how much it was all costing, but when once or twice I mentioned it, Michael looked at me like I was mad and insisted it was good for business and that it looked very much like I was having fun. And I was.

The clever, wise and always deeply amusing Robert Fox, looking debonair at the opening night for Dracula. *Robert was Michael's long-time assistant before going into business on his own, and is now one of London's most successful theatre producers. Fantastic taste, razor-sharp wit. One of my good friends to this day. I'm a lucky girl.*

Even Lady Diana Cooper, a witty writer and a legendary beauty in her time, was captivated by the charismatic Jack Nicholson at an Egerton Crescent dinner party, sending a note the next day to apologise for having never turned to her left as was polite at a change of courses. She explained that she could not take her eyes off him—even though she couldn't always follow his drift.

Although reluctant to smile in photos, top decorator Nicholas Ponsonby Haslam was (and is) one of the best party guests ever. Witty, fun, a total stayer, an outrageous gossip and a fantastic snob, who would be sure to flatter any visiting stars. Here he is with the gorgeous singer Marianne Faithfull, who had the prettiest soft blonde hair—totally natural—and very sexy bedroom eyes.

I truly was … but the minute the last guest was gone and the last candle blown out, I remember feeling lonely quite often as Michael drifted back into introvert mode. It was virtually impossible to get him to have a good old rehash of the evening. No chitchat or gossip. He'd crack open some weighty biography and ask me how far I'd come with Proust's *À la Recherche du Temps Perdu*!

'You are such a snob. I will read it when I'm good and ready … so far it's bored me rigid,' I'd say as I stomped off up the stairs, and Michael would tell me not to stomp and wake the children. Almost like an actor, Michael was someone who needed an audience to perform for, and I had no idea how to break through or even attempt to broach the subject. Truly, I was usually too intent on getting some much-needed sleep after jotting down a note for the housekeeper— 'Please make carrot/apple juice, porridge and coffee at seven o'clock … Thank you'—and finding clothes for the next day if it was a weekday, to really mind. Or to know exactly what was missing from the relationship. I was so grateful for the gorgeous roof over my head that I absolutely felt I had no right to complain about a thing.

Anyway, Michael did enough complaining for the two of us. He would complain about my clothes. They weren't 'grown up' or sophisticated enough for him. They might be too 'hippy' and baggy as I went through a long stage where I favoured flowing, voluminous Kenzo clothes. Or they would be outrageously silly and madcap when I would wear white painters' overalls dyed pink or waiters' blue-checked pants … or khaki army shorts with black tights and Margaret Howell Fair Isle cardigans … All a bit unorthodox and in retrospect slightly ridiculous. But my outfits were fun and original and I never tired of walking out the door at Egerton Crescent, jumping into the bright yellow VW Bug Michael had bought me with *denim* interior (it was called a 'Jeans') and in minutes reaching Knightsbridge or the King's Road and the shops! I was earning decent money and could actually purchase what I wanted. I didn't have extravagant tastes at all and never bought jewellery or designer bags, but I did appreciate and splurge on some lovely Bruce Oldfield cocktail outfits, some great vintage dresses and I absolutely—like many women—adored shoes and boots. There was a time when I simply did *not* possess a single pair of flat shoes. I had my own walk-in closet and a little office off the bathroom at Egerton Crescent and I got quite a kick out of seeing the two dozen or so pairs of high-heeled boots and stilettos lined up. Country weekends? I would tramp muddy fields, much to Michael's annoyance, in high-heeled Chelsea Cobbler black boots. No flats, no sneakers and proud of it! (When he joined the Queen's Club eventually I had to give in and buy sneakers to play tennis.)

He complained about many other things ... that I was always late (true), that I took too long to get ready to go out (not true), that I told everyone what I thought way too candidly (true), and that I was too speedy and scattered (very true) ... I was so scattered that once, just a few days after we'd finished some renovations and added very pretty pale blue and fluffy white cloud wallpaper to the ceiling of our huge double-sized living room with its eclectic mix of Clarice Cliff pottery, modern art and pale pink sofas, I began to fill the tub in our bathroom upstairs and then zipped back down several flights to make Vegemite on toast. I believe I then called my mum in Black Rock, completely blanking on the rapidly filling bathtub directly above the living room. Michael was abroad, and the ceiling collapse happened about an hour into the call ... I heard a roaring noise and suddenly huge chunks of the ceiling were on the living room floor as I had very successfully flooded the bathroom above.

I rushed back down to the kitchen to Mum—who was waiting on the phone to find out what disaster had befallen me—and I was simultaneously hysterical with laughter at the sight of the freshly 'clouded' ceiling in huge soggy lumps on the new rush-matting floor and appalled and guilt-ridden, dreading Michael's nagging for the next few weeks and noting Maria the housekeeper's annoyingly smug expression as she passed me on the way down to her basement lair. She loved it when I got into trouble. Seriously, she lurked in the doorway with a grin when Michael came back from his trip two days later and stood surveying the damage, whining that we wouldn't be able to entertain for weeks!

CHAPTER 7

The '70s Swing On

I N THOSE HEADY days of socialising, we met all sorts of fabulously interesting and diverse characters. A truly mad mix of people. Once in a while, a very pretty, fragile-looking wisp of a girl appeared in something chiffony. Anna Wintour. She looked like a strong gust would send her flying but appearances can be deceptive. Apparently Michael had been having a flirtation with the future *Vogue* dynamo just prior to me. Before he'd moved out of his family home, he would take his three kids to Holland Park and introduce Ms Wintour as a nanny he was vetting. Apparently, although sparks flew, there was no ignition. Once Michael and I got together, I recall seeing her at a dinner with Richard Neville in New York and thinking how utterly gorgeous, skinny and chic she was. Later that same night we went to the opening party for the infamous '70s club Studio 54 with Allan Carr, the tubby *Grease* producer, along with fashion designer Jasper Conran who, swathed in soft pastel shades of silk, resembled a woodland elf. It was an electrifying place. Many nights were spent there, never starting before midnight, and I always felt I was an oddly kindred spirit to Andy Warhol who would sit, like me, sometimes next to me, observing all night —barely uttering a word but seemingly mesmerised as folk like Bianca Jagger, Diane von Furstenberg, Fred Hughes and Calvin Klein all swarmed around in hyper-manic mode.

The legendary Anna Wintour back in the '70s. She was incredibly memorable even then, pretty as a picture and all girly and feminine in lovely floaty garb. Softly spoken, sweet, bright as a button—and now a global fashion force.

Thrilling trips to New York were fairly frequent as Michael wanted to know exactly what was going down on Broadway in the way of plays and musicals he could transfer to London—shows like *Annie*, *A Chorus Line* and *Ain't Misbehavin'*. I couldn't always go but when I did we invariably hung out with a couple of main 'sets'. One was the Lorne Michaels crowd, going to the always exciting tapings of *Saturday Night Live*, where we watched on the studio floor with Lorne as performers rushed past. The epic 'after parties' at different venues each week didn't start till 2 am, went on till dawn and left me shattered— parties where I met Griffin Dunne and Art Garfunkel, Danny Ackroyd and John Belushi … parties where one was offered many drugs but, thank God, I did not partake. (I was wildly sensitive to drugs and the few times I tried coke I was up for about twenty-four hours—with a blocked nose for at least three days to boot. I didn't see the point, though coke absolutely eliminated shyness in a fabulously liberating way for a spell. One could go up to anyone and chat—not something

I did easily unless it was a good pal. Even a strong joint would leave me so unpleasantly out of it and paranoid that I very rarely held onto anything passed my way.)

We also started heading out to the Hamptons, where the men are really separated from the boys when it comes to dough and the size of your spread. Lorne Michaels' second wedding to Susan Forristal was a huge and fabulous party at his amazing place on a couple of acres in Amagansett one Saturday afternoon and evening, and remains vivid to this day. Jack and Anjelica, John Belushi, Paul Simon, Bill Murray, Gilda Radner, Buck Henry and many, many *Saturday Night Live* alums were there and, unlike most weddings, there was no sense of formality or speeches, just a whacky 'we are rich, funny and young at heart' vibe—and I have to say, it was pretty enjoyable.

The other crowd was the one that gathered at The Factory around Andy Warhol, and for sheer unadulterated social-climbing fun, it

Dodi Fayed was always a very cool customer. In other words, he was laid-back, good-looking, travelled and rich, and the sophisticated world he moved in gave him access to many beautiful women. He was actually a sweet, gentle man and he and Gael flirted up a storm at many Egerton Crescent dinners.

was hard to beat the likes of Andy's best pal, business partner and 'social secretary' Fred Hughes, who set the tone of shallow fabulousness in this Studio 54 era, obsessed with gathering the rich and famous around him and Andy. If you had a trust fund or a hot album, or were amusing and glamorous, you were invited into their circle. And if you had a title or at least very aristocratic connections, you were fawned over by the dapper, Anglophile Fred, who wore tailored English suits and hand-made shoes, and was a complete and utter snob but after several drinks was proud to admit it! I did love going to The Factory. It was just that—a factory with dozens of fresh paintings lined up every day ready to be wrapped and shipped out. Fred was everywhere, shamelessly flogging the art to all and sundry and begging me to get

A trip to the Factory to pick up Andy for lunch always left me speechless. It really was like a factory, with a bevy of cute, young, male minions touching up the fresh work and then bubble wrapping each one beautifully. Andy liked to see them stacked, he said. Made him feel productive!

him invited to any swanky bash we were heading to that night. He came with us to one party at Calvin Klein's apartment, and at one point he and Gael and I found ourselves in the bedroom and thence the massive closet where we marvelled at Calvin's hundreds of pairs of shoes, shirts, t-shirts, cashmeres, overcoats and suits—all colour-coded and beyond immaculate!

Once in Manhattan, Michael oft made an excuse to head on out 'to the coast' to foster movie contacts, schmooze his new movie-star pals and generally soak up the sun. As is the case for many Londoners, palm trees, sunshine and hot weather were massively appealing to him. My first trip to Hollywood was with Michael and Aussie director Jim Sharman, trying to seal a movie deal for Jim's hit musical *The Rocky Horror Show*. Hercules Belville told Michael about his LA friend Lou Adler, an insanely laid-back, good-looking hipster record producer who also owned (and still owns to this day) the Roxy, a club on the Sunset Strip that could be the perfect offbeat spot to launch *The Rocky Horror Show*. It only had about four hundred seats, but a lot of big bands had made their debuts there and it was a very cool spot in a brilliant location. Lou expressed interest and so off we flew—only to be made to wait for about five days before Lou finally felt ready to receive us at his spectacular place right on the beach at Malibu, where he did business on an outdoor phone in the sun, smoking non-stop joints in a pair of board shorts. Frustrating to have to wait, but actually Jim and I were thrilled to explore LA and dragged Michael to all the tourist traps such as Disneyland, Mann's Chinese Theatre and Malibu Beach. But our favourite spots were the Chateau Marmont, where we stayed in the top-floor penthouse suite with its fabulous balcony overlooking Sunset Strip, and the divine Schwab's coffee shop on Sunset Boulevard, where we'd go every morning without fail for coffee, bagels and poached eggs as we read *The Hollywood Reporter*. What a crime that it was sold and torn down. A few trips later we upgraded to the Beverly Hills Hotel and when we weren't at On the Rox, the exclusive, very hip tiny nightclub above the Roxy on Sunset also owned by Lou Adler, we were hanging up at Jack Nicholson's house on Mulholland Drive—the very same house he's still in, where some serious drug-taking went down in his cosy living room, which was stuffed to the gills with his amazing $100 million art collection, including works by Matisse, de Lempicka and Andy Warhol—or at parties at Swifty Lazar's *or* some of the famous evenings at the late Sue Mengers' Bel Air house. The scene was very, very social in LA if you knew the right people.

One evening in 1979 at Sue's was a gem. She gave a dinner for sixty (preceded by a small intimate lunch—we attended both) for Princess Margaret. I have no idea how or why but it was a fabulous mix of folks—everyone from Gore Vidal to Jack Nicholson, Roddy McDowall, Ryan O'Neal, Californian governor Jerry Brown, Elliott Gould and Barbra Streisand. 'Every time [Princess Margaret] looked my way I curtsied,' a mortified Sue later recalled. 'I was curtsying all night! She thought I was an idiot.'

Two of my favourite men, and two true rarities—both sweet, kind and good men. Film buff Hercules Belville and famous environmentalist Ed Begley Jr, who for thirty years has been biking almost everywhere in LA—including to our fave LA hangout, On the Rox—to reduce his footprint.

Another night at our favourite club with Jack and Debra Winger. On the Rox was like being in your own cosy, cave-like living room: lots of 'deco' velvet sofas and mirrors, low lighting, a bar in one corner and a teeny membership list! Sometimes it would just be half a dozen of us. Twenty people was a big crowd.

Sue Mengers was persuaded to give a dinner for sixty to introduce Princess Margaret to Hollywood—and especially Jack Nicholson, who, it was rumored, she was dying to meet! He paid her a lot of attention and it was a colossally successful party, with the likes of Barbra Streisand, Ryan O'Neal, Gore Vidal, Jerry Brown, Ken and Kathleen Tynan and Michael White.

But I think that was just Sue spinning a yarn. She was the least stuffy and pompous royal host one can imagine, and I remember it being a raucous, jolly evening with Sue and Jack barely slipping out of view to giggle and smoke joints the entire night. Princess Margaret downed many drinks and rarely had her cigarette holder far from her lips. Not very smiley unless the likes of Jack were paying her rapt attention—which he did. A few weeks later I interviewed Sue for the *Sunday Times* and she told me, 'Princess Margaret put the wrong address on her thank-you note, the dumb broad! So it never arrived. Otherwise it could have been sold for a couple of pounds in my old age.'

Sue was at the height of her powers as an agent when I interviewed her, with a roster of stunning clients or 'sparklies' as she called them— including Ryan O'Neal, Woody Allen, Gene Hackman, Ali MacGraw, Michael Caine and Barbra Streisand. But as Sherry Lansing had just been appointed the first woman president of a studio at 20th Century Fox, I felt I should risk pointing out that perhaps Sue had been eclipsed by Sherry in terms of power, but she was having none of it.

'Oh, agents are more powerful than studio heads. There's no doubt about that,' she said with the cool calm conviction that had mesmerised producers for a decade. 'I feel utterly able to run a studio. But I'm not running one because I make more money than any studio executive. I make a lot of money. There's no woman today who can make a film go without checking with a man and I say it with all due respect to Sherry. On the whole women have subordinate jobs. It's hard for us but right now the agency business is very lucrative for me because million-dollar fees for actors are the norm. I was responsible for that but I blame the studios. They wanted my client Gene Hackman, who didn't want to do *Lucky Lady*. Finally they offered a million bucks. That started it because then Nicholson said, "Well if Hackman's getting a million, I should get two," and then Warren Beatty said, "If Jack's getting … " But with Burt Reynolds it's gone berserk. Five million dollars is a lot of bread.'

It's funny to think of Burt Reynolds being the biggest star in Hollywood at one time.

Michael also made an annual pilgrimage to the Cannes Film Festival—once he had followed producing *The Rocky Horror Picture Show* with several more films including *My Dinner with Andre*, Monty Python's *Jabberwocky* and John Waters' cult favourite *Polyester*. Occasionally I joined him and one memorable year we hung with our now very good pal Jack Nicholson, who loved the south of France and felt very at home there. Even the hordes of fans and paparazzi didn't seem to bother him there and we had lots of fun. Anjelica Huston didn't make it that year and Jack was in hyped-up gregarious mode, which meant some serious full-time flirting went on, but it was fun and infectious to behold—and directed at men, women and children alike. He was there with his friend and director Bob Rafelson and co-star Jessica Lange for the premiere of *The Postman Always Rings Twice*, and he was definitely pleased with both it and himself. He confided to me that he really enjoyed being sexy in the film. 'I got to be hot and heavy in this one,' he told me. 'I'm pretty good at it and I think it's time my sex appeal was fully appreciated by the world, don't cha reckon?' and at that he would roar with laughter and 'whoop' a little as heads turned and people grinned like fools at this rather loud Hollywood movie star.

And indeed, Jack was someone who enjoyed being a movie star, perhaps more than anyone in the movie-star ranks. Seriously, he got such an obvious thrill out of the fame, the glamour and the opening nights, and it was very infectious and quite thrilling to witness. None of that shy, tortured lurking in corners or behind closed doors for Jack. Michael and I joined Jack and director Bob Rafelson in the limo one night to face the hordes of paparazzi at the foot of those famous stairs at the opening of *Postman* at the Cannes Film Festival. A roar went up from the crowd as the limo door was opened and Jack was spotted. He turned to me, his face lit up with that megawatt smile and said, 'Are you ready Tine? The fun begins now,' and he meant it. He had a ball, simply thrived on all the attention, and was never happier than when surrounded by adoring fans as one was nearly blinded by the popping flashes. He loved to dress like a movie star, too, and after *Chinatown* he took a massive liking to the beautifully tailored suits that

Jack in playful mood, enjoying his fame, poolside at the Carlton Hotel in Cannes at the annual film festival. He loved France and any opportunity to hit Cannes.

costume designer Anthea Sylbert so expertly made for him. Jack had a huge wardrobe of stunning clothes, including a lot of fabulous vintage suits (with pleated trousers that suited his athletic 'chunky' thighs), waistcoats and jackets, some of which he still wears to this day. He once confessed that he had not had huge luck with women before becoming a movie star—'Not tall enough, thighs too short,' he explained—but once he made it, sex appeal seemed to ooze from every pore. He took to fame like a duck to water and never looked back.

After a while I was bold enough to entertain back in London even when Michael was out of town. I wrote:

Dear Ma and Pa

Actually I've become quite the hostess for a week now. Michael's been away in Marbella with Liberty and Joshua so one night I had a dinner for Ian Meldrum—eight for dinner and lots in afterwards and the very next night I gave a dinner for Jack Nicholson—eight again and about fourteen in afterwards. Jack's such a charmer and loves being the centre of attention (no, of course I didn't cook—we have a new Italian housekeeper, an absolute gem who cooks wonderfully, and when she saw Jack, she didn't mind about two dinners in a row). Went to two more dinners the following two nights—one for Michael Roberts who did the *Sunday Times* piece on me and another at Joan Buck's, the new features editor at *Vogue*, and by the time MW was back I was exhausted. Before long everyone had exaggerated my entertaining to 'a week of rave-up parties'.

A bit of weed-smoking went down, but mainly it was champagne to start, decent wine, plenty of vodka and very snappy, lively conversation. But the real tricks to successful entertaining in my book? First, work on the 'atmos'! Odd to realise it now but scented candles had just appeared so I always made sure a couple of pine-scented Rigaud candles were burning. I would keep the lights way down low, put on some music, but not too loud, and make sure the house was warm enough. And then? Invite funny, jolly people to encourage tons of laughter. I can hear it now under the cloud-covered ceiling in our big upstairs living room, with rush matting instead of carpet, the pink linen sofas, huge plants, some deco lamps and vases and Michael's cool art collection—and often a pyjama-clad child peeking in from the corridor. Don't get me wrong. Evenings were not devoid of lively debate and it was just as important to invite some clever, argumentative types like the famous theatre critic and writer Ken Tynan, playwright and QC John Mortimer or Lord Hesketh, who was given to controversial right-wing views on religion, politics or sex. And Nicholas Ponsonby Haslam could always be relied upon to give hilarious pronouncements—often about what he considered 'common'. It was a long list and included everything from serving fish at dinner parties (too stinky) to being ill and eating tomatoes. Once, when Nicky was just back from a trip to Tangiers, someone asked if he had jet lag. Nicky gave the poor questioner a withering look and haughtily replied, 'Don't be ridiculous! Jet lag's frightfully common. I wouldn't dream of it.'

Nicky, now arguably one of London's most famous interior decorators, was worth his weight in gold as a guest—chatty, quick, anxious to charm but not afraid to offend. As funny as anyone I've known. A real stayer, entertaining till the very end of the evening. Not unlike Jack Nicholson, whose attendance was an iron-clad guarantee of a hit evening—but also a very late one since he seemed determined to be the last to leave and folks rarely like to leave before the star. It's been said before but it has to be said again: Jack seriously oozed charisma and was always, hands down, the sexiest man in the room. Jack could say, 'Pass the salt,' and make it sound like a come-on. We put him next to the once legendary beauty Lady Diana Cooper at one dinner party and she called the next day to apologise for her rudeness. 'I completely forgot my manners and didn't turn to speak to my left all night—but I'm afraid I just couldn't take my eyes off Jack. Didn't always follow his drift but goodness, what a gorgeous man.'

She couldn't follow his drift? Who *could*? Jack was always so stoned that as the night progressed, it became harder and harder to follow what he was saying. I remember often talking to him at dinner or parties and wondering if I had gotten a contact high. It was virtually impossible to keep track of the conversational zigzags. But no—he would just be on a drug-fuelled roll that, after many circuitous detours, would sometimes (but not often) make sense.

But he just had to give you the 'eye' or a wink or one of his wicked grins and you instantly felt attractive—as if a real guy had just checked you out and approved. He made men feel special too and that's quite a gift. At the huge opening-night parties for both *Annie* and *Dracula*, Jack worked the room without discrimination. At one point I sat gazing at him (as a *Daily Mail* photo captured) as he raved incoherently—and somewhat disloyally to Michael—about how magical I looked, and I found myself under his spell for a good five minutes. It was one of the rare occasions when I knew I looked good after actually applying eye makeup and wearing my strapless black velvet dress with matching bolero that Bruce Oldfield had whipped up for me. I knew I should be doing 'my duty' and greeting guests but I was rooted to the spot, rendered immobile under Jack's steady gaze! I finally came to my senses as he rambled on, and being the loyal prude, I thought he was being a tad inappropriate and thus quickly went back to my job of working the room as Michael's consort, chatting up guests and actors such as Terry Stamp and Chris Reeve, Bianca Jagger and Nicholas Soames. But waiters and toffs alike would be equally charmed by the gregarious Mr Nicholson, who had a penchant for nicknames. He called me 'Tine'—which is short for the full nickname he bestowed of 'Little Tiny Little'. Anjelica was 'Toots', Carol Kane 'Whitey', Warren Beatty 'the Pro', Sabrina Guinness 'Beans' and Michael White 'the Chalkster'—to name just a few.

During the long shoot for *The Shining* in London with Stanley Kubrick, Jack—joined by Anjelica at various intervals—holed up at the Dorchester and so when he was not ordering a *lot* of room service in the suite, we took him to the theatre, to country weekends at the Lycett Greens, to dinners and opening nights—and the tennis club where he and Michael would spend most of the time teasingly accusing each other of cheating, and we could barely play for laughing. (We also skied with Jack in both Gstaad and Aspen. A very laid-back skier!) Once Jack came straight from the set of *The Shining* to join us at Mr Chow's. They'd been shooting the ending and Jack still had blood in his hair and a wild look in his eyes. In fact, he was acting utterly insane, making mad utterances as his eyes literally rolled around in his head and he winked at any cute girl whose eye he could catch. Michael Roberts and I found it hilariously over the top. 'The cameras have stopped rolling, Jack. You can calm down,' hissed Michael, whose wicked sense of humour has served him well in his many roles dealing with stars from being fashion director of *Vanity Fair*, *The New Yorker* and *Tatler* to his endless sessions both writing and photographing for *Vogue* and *The Sunday Times*.

The huge after-party for Michael's West End production of Dracula *(with Terence Stamp in the starring role) was definitely a hit thanks to the presence of Jack Nicholson, who was in town shooting* The Shining. *I was finding it hard to tear myself away from his bloody gorgeous gaze!*

Anjelica, of course, was no slouch in the charm department and we all adored her from the minute we laid eyes on her. Tall and lean and incredibly beautiful, she simply dazzled and was—and remains—one of the best raconteurs I've ever met, holding an entire dinner party spellbound as she reminisced, for instance, of her dad at their home, St Clerans in Ireland—doing fantastic imitations of all the characters concerned. Like the rest of us, even Jack would seem almost mute as Anjelica brilliantly spun her yarn—clearly enjoying the attention and preparing for the time when she too would finally shine on celluloid. There were others with the gift of the gab. Like both Jack and Anjelica, Lorne Michaels is an Anglophile—never missing a summer trip to catch both the theatre and Wimbledon—and definitely someone who could talk up a storm but never fail to fascinate as he explained, always seriously, why a film or an actor or a sketch was funny.

And then there was the most enchanting and divine Diana Vreeland, the legendary fashion editor at both *Harper's Bazaar* and *Vogue*, who was a total dream—witty, smart, incredibly energetic at seventy-six, with a deep husky voice but no discernible accent at all. We met her through Jack, and one night she and I and Michael and Jack all went to a long Bob Dylan concert, her first, which she was ridiculously enthusiastic about—as she sat grinning and swaying, hour after gruelling hour, in a black cashmere turtleneck, knitted green trousers, lots of gold jewellery and her trademark overly rouged cheeks and pinky-orange lipstick.

We became great pals and age didn't seem to matter to her a whit. I would visit her in her suite at the Dorchester, marvelling as a secretary worked the phones, kept on till eight every evening to cope with the flood of calls. I was there with the arch-priestess of American fashion one afternoon as she confirmed the evening's activities. First there was to be a little dinner downstairs in the Orchid Room with Bianca Jagger and Andy Warhol. Then Jack, late from the set, would be joining them for coffee before escorting her to an art auction at Sotheby's and then on to a party for four hundred being given for Andy in Eaton Square.

What is there to say? They made a glamorous couple, but in the early days one was infinitely more famous than the other. It made for a power imbalance that Anjelica always felt. That and Jack's innate need for attention and other women meant that Anjelica finally got her act together and began to act too—and how!

Former Vogue *editor and fashion world legend Diana Vreeland had never seen Bob Dylan perform and was very excited to join Jack, Michael and I at the Albert Hall to watch him sing. She was the most terrific gung-ho sport ever!*

A true original, Diana was in town to research her eighth major costume exhibit for New York's Metropolitan Museum of Art but found time to attend the theatre, the opera, the Dylan concert, seven restaurants and six parties—all given in her honour—in just ten days.

During an interview I did with her for a magazine once I arrived in New York—where she welcomed me with open arms, the woman who discovered, among others, Lauren Bacall and Halston, and made cult stars out of Penelope Tree, Veruschka and Swinging London in the '60s—she told me:

I owe it all to England. I learnt everything and my whole life was formed there. I arrived in London in 1929 with my husband Reed and stayed eight years. I love it.

At first we knew nobody. I spent long days just sitting and reading. But during our first six months in London, Reed and I went to the theatre every single night—which was very easy because there were almost sixty plays running. And every night my husband wore a white tie and tails. I was dressed to the teeth too—long dresses, oh my word yes. Beautifully dressed. It was very festive.

Usually in the spring I went to Paris and Rome. Travelling was easy then. We had trunks and a maid. You didn't even have to go to your hotel on arrival. Have lunch with a pal, go home, in the evening there it all was. It sure did save a hell of a lot of time.

Well, yes—I imagine it did!

And if it all sounds so glamorous, it was. I was utterly aware of how lucky I was at every moment and thus the gushing letters back to my poor parents. But because of this acute awareness of my privilege, I found it almost impossible to say no to Michael when he wanted to both go out and entertain so relentlessly. How could I turn down any of the amusing evenings or openings or dinners with fascinating folks who my contemporaries, struggling to make ends meet in tiny flats in Earls Court, would be thrilled to meet? But I truly paid for it by being permanently exhausted. To my continued disgust I'm someone who needs eight to nine hours' sleep but rarely if ever got that much and would drag myself into work some days completely shattered.

I often wanted to stay in and prepare for the next day's interview—but, remembering the old adage, 'It's the things you don't do that you regret,' I'd usually pull on a frock and join in the fun. Michael's tastes and friends covered the waterfront. Suddenly Graham Greene would be knocking on the door for tea, or Harvey Keitel would appear on the doorstep, having been invited over for cocktails, or our next-door neighbour, the TV interviewer David Frost, would show up because Michael had told him to come and join us at San Lorenzo that night. He forgot to warn me about half the visitors he issued invites to—but I learnt to adapt and *never* show surprise, no matter who appeared. And of course it did mean more contacts for me and access to people in the news. I was the one who got the Sex Pistols into the studio for their first-ever TV interview, and when the infamous Sloane Rangers story by Peter York first appeared in *Harper's*, I was the one who'd met enough legitimately posh, aristocratic Sloane Rangers on enough weekends—when we'd stayed with them in their wonderful stately homes—to whip together a half-hour documentary special, in which I interviewed many of them, at hunts, on horseback, at play, during posh dinners and shopping for their Hermès scarves. It was quite a coup and I only wish a copy of the tape existed today.

CHAPTER 8

We Get Around

WELL, UNLIKE THE divine Diana Vreeland, we had no trunks or maids, but we did travel. A lot. Though there was never a trip where a huge screaming match didn't first take place over the amount I packed for my good self and Michael's kids. Michael packed well and light—in minutes—but I'm convinced it's an art you're either born with or you're not. I was born with the 'pack as if your ocean liner will sink and you might have to stay for six months' gene. Plus, I'd never 'travelled' anywhere till I met Michael, having only taken three local plane trips to Sydney before I left for the UK. Well that's my excuse.

In my first two years with Michael we went on two extraordinary boat 'cruises' hosted by the wonderfully witty, larger-than-life spendaholic Lord Hesketh. The first boat was called the *Southern Breeze*, and when Michael invited me I refused at first, terrified of seasickness and the idea of being cooped up at sea for God knows how long. Who knew that the captain made all manner of daily stops in glamorous ports and beaches from Capri to Portofino? Who knew there'd be a swimming pool on board and nonstop fun with some hand-chosen guests like Lady Anne Lambton, Christopher Sykes, Betty di Robilant, Tom Benson and someone called Chunky? Exquisite food. Private planes to get to the boat. Laundry on board. I was such a novice but

Lord Alexander Hesketh, who went through a good deal of his fortune by singlehandedly financing James Hunt and his Formula One racing team, also spent lavishly on holidays and generously hired a private plane to take us to Genoa to meet the Southern Breeze, *a boat he had rented to take us on a memorable summer sea cruise prior to the Monte Carlo Grand Prix.* (Photo by Christopher Sykes)

it's funny how quickly one can get used to the ol' high life, ordering breakfast or witty cocktails on the high seas.

But generally for summer fun, we upped stakes and invited a few of the gang—like Gael, Candida and Rupert Lycett Green, Robert and Celestia Fox, Nicky Haslam, Hercules Bellville, Nell Campbell, Peter Eyre, the Australian producer Ben Gannon and Katherine Tennant (the *Telegraph* astrologer)—to join us in a stunning tiny old village which had been turned into a holiday compound called Le Nid du Duc, which we rented from director Tony Richardson in La Garde-Freinet near St Tropez. Now owned by Tony's daughter Joely Richardson, it's listed on the chic Petersham Properties rental website:

This idyllic hamlet is tucked away in a quiet valley in the hills above St Tropez. Tony Richardson found the abandoned little village in the 1960s and turned it into a magical compound of houses and guesthouses. Featured in many books, the house is a secret hideaway to countless actors and writers. The pool has even been painted by

David Hockney. Beautiful, rustic and private, this is the perfect place to escape, yet unique in that it has easy access to the beaches, shops and nightlife of St Tropez, which is thirty minutes away.

Looking back, it's almost *too* idyllic for words. I've yet to go anywhere that comes close to matching up. Michael, an early riser, loved to drive off alone at about 7 am to the nearby village market on cobblestone medieval streets to buy the day's produce. As the rest of us were just staggering out of our little stone houses, strolling past the peacocks that wandered the property and sitting down at a huge outdoor table right in front of the main house for coffee, the wildly domesticated impresario would arrive back, with straw baskets laden with fruit, vegetables, fish, fresh bread and croissants for everyone. What can I say? He loved to do it.

Then for the rest of the day the routine would alternate. We'd either lounge by the pool all morning and after a delicious lunch under the olive trees we might take a siesta, play Scrabble or read.

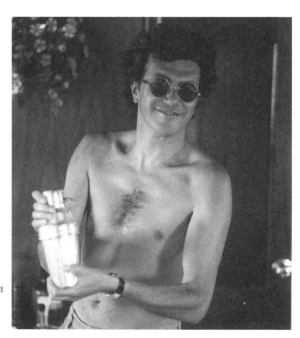

Michael 'Chalky' White in jolly holiday mood, whipping up a mean martini on board the Southern Breeze *– a boat big enough to have its own swimming pool.* (Photo by Christopher Sykes)

After getting dolled up, we'd then hit St Tropez and the clubs by night. (These sorties usually ended with a late-night feast of French fries from the famous place loved by Brigitte Bardot, Le Gorille cafe, wolfed down as we strolled along the port to our car.)

Or we would go to the famously glamorous, topless beaches of St Tropez like the Aqua Club or the Cinquante Cinq, which are still stunning but were *really* fantastically divine and not overcrowded then. They had severely overpriced outdoor restaurants that served delicious, irresistible things like grilled white fish and fries and raspberry tarts and chilled wine. First we would park ourselves in front of our favourite restaurant and nab the thin mattress-like loungers covered in striped cotton ticking to lie on. They didn't come free, of course, and generally the kids would be allotted just one between them, so a fight often ensued as they jostled each other to get to a mattress. Gael and I, sporting groovy Cutler and Gross sunglasses, would remove cute Kenzo miniskirts—or in Gael's case a fabulous frock or pair of pedal pushers from a stupendously stylish, now-defunct Sydney shop called Flamingo Park—so that, once down to bikinis, we could oil ourselves and the kids up with something utterly devoid of SPF.

If we tired of our books we could wander on down to the cute little shacks right on the beach, which sold *pareos* and tops and hats and espadrilles, and slyly check out all the topless and sometimes stark-naked folk that we prudish girls from Melbourne thought a little vulgar and coarse. Michael and Hercules would tease us both endlessly about our reluctance to bare our breasts—but the more they did it the more we insisted on retaining our already-miniscule tops. And besides, I was a stepmother of sorts to Michael's adorable three young children and felt very protective of them when the poor darlings, all sent off to boarding school at a young age, were with us. And I was a journalist for God's sake! The truth is I really was a bit 'square' and, by today's standards, totally clueless when it came to sex. The extent of any sex talk from my parents was the moment when my mother said to me, as I was heading off one night with a date at the age of about fifteen, 'Never let a boy touch your breast.' That was it. I truly had barely

heard of an orgasm till I got to London and was embarrassed by sex
for a good few years.

As you might expect, there were no simple picnics on the sand
for us. Michael lived large and it was a proper three-course, sit-down
lunch for us every day. Hang the expense. Michael did not believe in
any sort of economy when it came to dining and restaurants and I was
very happy to go along with it—though in retrospect, it's insane how
extravagant he was. But Michael thought of eating and entertaining
as part of his role as the convivial, generous producer, and more often
than not, he would spot someone on the beach or in St Tropez—from
John Mortimer to Roman Polanski to our favourite designer, Kenzo—
and invite them to lunch. Who knew when John would write a play or
Roman need a producer for a film. Michael was networking!

Then after a nap or a late-afternoon stroll of the St Tropez shops
and perhaps a sorbet or a cocktail at a bar, we would drive the forty-
five minutes back to our compound, stay in that night for a delicious
dinner cooked by houseman Jean-Pierre and then play charades or
scrabble. Nicky Haslam and Michael were wildly competitive and
for some reason had the most outrageous argument one evening over

*My favourite country weekend:
staying in Wiltshire with the Lycett
Greens! We took pity on the visiting
movie star and allowed him to join
in with tennis, croquet and Scrabble!
He and Michael, both stoned usually,
bickered about whose ball was over
the line, endlessly accusing the other
of cheating, as Rachel and I laughed
and laughed until we told them to just
bloody well get on with it!*

whether 'oil line' was two words (Michael's view) or, as Nicky contended, could count as one coveted seven-letter word. Neither would give in and so, on empty stomachs, hilarious long-distance calls were made and bets taken as Gael and I whipped up yet more rounds of Camparis for everyone, searched for the missing dictionary and forgot about the burning chickens in the oven. The debate lasted the entire holiday—and it still rates as one of the best vacations ever.

Another favourite summer getaway was in fact going to stay with our dear friends the Lycett Greens in Wiltshire because a) I adored Rupert and Candida and their five kids and b) it's hard to beat long, late twilights in the English countryside with a Pimms cup after an afternoon of croquet or tennis, or a picnic on the downs that we rode to in old pony carts. Simple, old-fashioned picnics somewhere exquisitely beautiful were one of Candida's specialties, and Jack, Anjelica and Rachel Ward were utterly charmed by one weekend there, which seemed heavenly then and more so now. We went to grander stately homes but it was never as much fun.

And then there were trips to Morocco, Jamaica or, on several occasions, the constantly buzzing Ibiza, which I wrote home about:

Aug '74

Hi folks … Just thought I'd pop off a very quick note to say g'day as the proper letter-writing seems to be taking forever.

Gael, Michael, Liberty and I are lying aboard John Bishop's yacht off Ibiza—the others having swum ashore to get a table for lunch … If I was strong I'd stay here and miss lunch but I expect I'll dive in and head ashore for the best fish and chips I've ever tasted. We got a lift out here from some friends of John's with a big bright yellow cruiser (very kitsch with lots of zebra skin and inlaid mother-of-pearl cabinets). The sky is mauve on the horizon, the sea pale green and the strip of peninsula beach almost white … but Ibiza, which is really fun, is getting more popular every year—it'll soon be another St Tropez, I guess, so we're lucky to be here now.

We're staying in a fantastic villa and all guests who came for a week, like Gael and Bennie and Michael Roberts, have decided to stay on another week! Too tired to pack and leave I think—lunch is at 7.30 pm and dinner is never till midnight. Then it's outdoor clubs to dance till 4 am.

Then last night, just as we all decided we needed a quiet night, Michael decided we had to return some hospitality and whip up a dinner party for thirty-five! Just finding a spot near the market in town was a major undertaking. Then once home, the Aussie nanny insisted on writing out the most elaborate, pretentious cordon bleu menus of about ten dishes which annoyed Michael no end ... orange and lettuce salad, prawn curry, oeufs en cocotte and so it went on. The kids ran wild as we all pitched in. Gael and I did the fruit salad and arranged the flowers. Fabulous hibiscus and pink vines and lots of shrubbery and we put candles along the balcony and round the pool. We all felt like going to bed by 11 pm—with not a guest in sight! It got going around 1 am when the owners of the best nightclub in town arrived ... Between you and me, despite the view, the food, the friends, the beaches and the great Scrabble games, I long for the structure of work again in chilly London.

But one summer night in Ibiza stands out as close to perfection. A Bob Marley concert at an open-air bull ring on a hot balmy evening under the stars with icy-cold French champagne and, for some, a teeny hit of acid too. The best reggae on the planet, the best friends (Gael, Rachel Ward, Bryan Ferry, and David and Jose Olivestone—big-time partiers, and Jose ran the agency Models 1) and youthful exuberance that led to running down cobblestone streets at dawn ... it doesn't get much better.

Michael was also good friends with Chris Blackwell, the very charismatic record producer and Island Records founder who introduced Bob Marley and reggae music to the world and once gave me a joint during our time in Jamaica—the likes of which I've never known.

I couldn't speak for about six hours and just watched Chris doing deals on the phone, chatting to visitors, playing backgammon with Michael and being his cheerful, very cool, sexy self for hours on end—smoking joint after joint all the while. I truly realised then that for some people there are no boundaries between work and pleasure and they enjoy every minute of the day as they work. He was a fascinating figure— very good looking, with a beautiful slightly upper-class British accent that would then break into Jamaican patois, having grown up there with his rich 'white Jamaican' mother Blanche who was Ian Fleming's long-time lover. Chris then bought Goldeneye, Fleming's famous villa where he wrote all of the James Bond novels, and was already an extraordinary entrepreneur by the time I met him. He was one of the few men during my ten years with Michael whom I found sexy and utterly irresistible, but I would no more have thought of flirting with him than flying to the moon. I never developed that flirting muscle and more's the pity is all I can say.

A hot summer night in Ibiza. An open-air bullring. Bob Marley playing. A teeny bit of acid. Simply one of the best nights of my life. We partied until dawn and ran down cobblestone streets in fits of laughter. I was a lucky girl.

14 April '75

Dearest Ma and Pa

Just had six days in Jamaica … impossible to describe the mixed feelings we experienced there—on the one hand, pleasure in the heat, beautiful surroundings and Planter's punches. On the other, amazement and pity at the exploitation of the locals, their ludicrous wages and shocking living conditions. Several of them are very excited when they learn we're from London, telling us that their dream is to come and move in with relatives in Brixton …

Had a fun time with Chris Blackwell, who discovered Bob Marley, practically invented reggae and is like the king of Jamaica … Learnt how to suck sugarcane and swam under this fabulous waterfall …

Then, in wild contrast, we stopped off in New York and stayed in the most beautiful genuine '30s Art Deco furnished apartment belonging to Francis Ford Coppola which is in the Sherry Netherland Hotel. When he's not around he rents it out. It has so many gadgets cleverly concealed—there's a button next to the bed which you press and suddenly a husky female voice says, 'It's 8.30 am.' Neat. Oh and we met Uri Geller at Stigwood's penthouse in New York. He bent me a fork!

My mother was completely intrigued by the famous psychic who claimed some of his powers were from extra-terrestrials, which she found a fascinating concept, and she'd gone to see him when he was visiting Melbourne. I knew she'd be thrilled with a souvenir and so I popped into Robert Stigwood's grand dining room in his penthouse on Central Park West, commandeered a heavy silver fork that was laid out on the table for supper, and asked Uri to do his thing. Quite impressively, he bent me a fork right before my eyes as I held it and he gently stroked it, and sure enough, when I produced it months later at Christmas, Mum was impressed and very tickled.

Now, thanks to my monied boyfriend, this was clearly a hedonistic, deeply shallow and frivolous life I was leading. No ifs, ands or buts. No mention of charity work. No poor folk were being fed by yours truly. But from where I sit right now, scrupulously hoarding the few frequent-flyer miles I still have (without a credit card, no more are being racked up) and virtually grounded when it comes to travel, it sure sounds swell. But it's not just the trips to far-flung places I miss. It's also the idea of a partner. Just having a kind soul (yes, preferably smart, funny and sexy) to help plan outings, someone to go out *with*. I'm definitely a girl's girl but there should be a strict limit to how many times one dines with fellow female singletons each month. I'd love a partner in crime. A poor but lovable movie-going partner would do the trick. An informed lefty Democrat to help schlep groceries from the car. I miss those days for that reason alone.

Simple picnics or sandwiches on the sand were out of the question for Michael. Hey, it was St Tropez, and fancy three-course meals at the restaurants right on the beach were de rigueur—and incredibly tasty, too! No complaints from the Aussie sheilas. From left to right: me, Michael, Gael, Hercules, a friend of the kids, Joshua, Liberty, Sasha and the fabulous late Ben Gannon.

CHAPTER 9

Never a Dull Moment

EuROPEAN WINTERS MEANT summers Down Under, of course, and most years I made it back to Melbourne for Christmas, thrilled to bits to spend time with family and friends. Gael was often on the epic 24-hour plane ride with me, and our newly acquired sophistication slipped away as we neared our home turf, excitedly practising our Aussie accents (we didn't want folk to think we'd become stuck up!), reading any Aussie newspapers or magazines they had on board to catch up with the local scene, and always hoping it would be a good summer and we could get a tan in record time. We usually went overboard with gifts for everyone. In my case I spent months shopping before the trip—lots of clothes from Harrods for Mum and always cashmere sweaters for Dad. To this day my kids and I share the cache of cashmeres my darling dad left behind.

And to prove I was doing well and that my family could be proud of me (because it wasn't as if they could view my TV exploits on YouTube in those ancient days), my cases were full of yet more clothes for brothers, cousins, nephews, nieces, aunts and uncles. One year we cut it fine and arrived on Christmas Day itself and the bored immigration guys decided to pick on us, opening every last one of our multitude of suitcases, unwrapping gifts and generally going through our belongings with a fine-tooth comb. It was terribly mean. We fumed and started 'giving lip'—but it didn't help and probably made it go on even longer. We changed tack and tried to joke our way out of it and eventually we headed through the doors to find two sets of worried parents waiting for us.

Traditional Christmas lunches would follow—and barbecues and visits to the beaches of our youth. But as heavenly, relaxing and heartwarming as it always was to be back in the bosom of our family, I think we both felt the inevitable pull of our fast-paced lives, and in what seemed like a flash, it was time for those gut-wrenchingly sad farewells and we were off, usually to visit Sydney pals before winging back to Blighty. In my case it was often to join Michael on the ski vacations he adored in Aspen or Gstaad. There was a memorable

*Some summers we Aussie expats would all find ourselves back home for Christmas! I was always torn—family and a few wonderful pals were in Melbourne, but other good friends waited up in Sydney, so I would invariably tear myself away from Melboure and head up to Sydney. Top row: costume designer Norma Moriceau (*The Road Warrior, *Crocodile Dundee*)*, Nell Campbell, Gael, me. Bottom row: Fran Moore, Jo Shorrock, Jenny Kee, Sally Campbell.*

New Year's Eve with Roman Polanski, Jack, Anjelica and Peter Sellers where Roman wore a pig mask and hogged the Fortnum's caviar. I wrote home:

Dec 1976

Dearest Ma and Pa

Well after a week here in Gstaad, this is the first night we've been back in time to hear the ye olde Swiss clock chime midnight. We're in a big Swiss chalet which Roman Polanski and Andy Braunsberg (the guy who produces a lot of his movies) rent out every year. There are six bedrooms and ten of us here ... Roman and two French birds who refuse to speak English most of the time but aren't too bad for Frogs, ze typical German ski champion Hans and his girlfriend—a former Miss Sweden called Va Va who's a cute blonde bundle of fun—plus Andy and his pregnant girl-friend, a sweet Southern girl called Daisy. As well as a pal from London, David Olivestone—a total raver, mad lunatic and all-round party boy—who appears at breakfast each morning looking like the wrath of God. But he's tons of fun and very sweet—if a complete alcoholic.

Well it's been a ball. One long party and lots of late nights—Michael in his element skiing by day, which he adores, and partying by night. My skiing is tragic and it's very discouraging that I'm so lousy and quite terrified of some of the incredibly steep runs ... Roman kept insisting that because I'm an Aussie I must be great. But when he finally saw my atrocious skiing, which ended with me on my bum as I skied up one day to join the guys after a lesson, he was stunned and laughed for a good two minutes.

So we had the number one New Year's Eve Party at our chalet—a big success! It was catered for by the Palace Hotel (it's the flashiest here) and we had forty people for a buffet supper and about two hundred after dinner. Roman took great delight in directing the preparations beforehand so that the more responsible, like me, were allowed to blow up balloons and decorate the living room with streamers hanging from ceilings, walls, windows and every spare corner and cranny available. That's not to say we were given an entirely free hand. Roman would inspect the work every so often and complain that I'd put 'far too many streamers' (in that thick Polish accent everyone can and does imitate) in some obscure corner and they were being wasted. Yes, like many directors, he paid attention to detail. Then all the party paraphernalia and things to throw at midnight were placed at select points for we in the 'know' to hand out. Every so often Roman would insist that I record him posing by the food, under the balloons, in a mask ... with my trusty Instamatic.

Things sure went off with a bang—especially the fireworks display that Roman organised on the front lawn. There was lots of dancing—started off by Michael, who turns out to be a brilliant jiver, and myself wearing my rock'n'roll skirt with two stiffened petticoats underneath. The French girls loved it. At least the stilettos and '50s look made a witty change from all the 'sumptuous' evening gowns and jewels (my God, the jewels—you shoulda copped them ... my eyes nearly popped out of my head several times) worn by most of the guests ... a very flash lot of rich Italian, German and French folk like Gunter Sachs and his brand of playboy along with lots of actresses and models.

Also here is Peter Sellers who's shy and sweet and puts on a very bad Aussie accent every time he talks to me. 'How ya goin', sheilah? Are you all bloody right?' He's very funny, if a tad needy, and insisted I sit next to him at dinner two nights after New Year's Eve. At one point a glam femme fatale came up and began talking in French to Roman and some others, and Peter suddenly said, 'Watch this.' He stood up and, as he held out a bottle of wine, he began talking in nonsense French—but really good nonsense French you understand, with a serious expression and arched eyebrows, so that for a moment even I was fooled till he turned and winked at me—People started giving each other quizzical looks, frowning and saying *'Qu'est que tu dis?'* and *'Pardon?'* Finally, people started to twig. Frankly, I think he just needed to be in the spotlight, and like most comedians, he probably feels he's disappeared unless he's the centre of attention. This dinner is a tradition, given by friends in a chalet up the road and part of the tradition is a 'food fight', which got rather out of hand this year with Roman going crazy and hurling cream wildly at everyone in sight.

(Yes, Roman's done some very regrettable things since those days but he was nothing but charming to me back then.)

Now I know these letters make it sound as if I had a ball on these holidays, but truly, I was just as happy working. I felt compelled for some reason to always make my parents think I was having a heavenly time. But I was so happy to get back to my job which meant the odd tiff with Michael when I refused to ever extend a holiday and sometimes actually did insist on leaving early to get back to work. Thus, the letter above continues with a new burst of enthusiasm as I talk about my newest project:

Sorry, it's two days later now and I'm back at work finishing my half-hour special on the Sloane Rangers for tonight's program. There was a big, controversial article about them in *Harper's* last month. 'Sloane Rangers' refers to that smart upper-class breed of gel who wears blazers and skirts, Gucci shoes, an Hermès scarf knotted under the chin and spends her life in Harrods and Peter Jones thinking of her weekend hunting and shooting. It's been such a blast—and surprisingly all the toffs have been thrilled to talk to me. So today was spent putting on the music, mixing the sound, doing promos and generally getting quite nervous as it's had lots of publicity!

And Michael is now convinced no one will talk to him after tonight—since he's assuming I take just a slight dig at the upper classes. I do! Last night at dinner Henry (Earl of) Pembroke had me laughing as he insisted my show would bring another million votes to Harold Wilson (Labour Party prime minister), and he and Michael teased me throughout dinner, generally getting carried away. We're having a little soiree tonight for some of the stars of the special at Egerton Crescent. Michael keeps reminding me that five million people will be watching and that he hopes it's good. It *is* funny, I think, and that's the main thing. Meantime, it's Michael and my third anniversary tonight! I bought him a giant koala bear. And another anniversary Michael is dreading far more is his fortieth birthday next week. I think I'm going to give him a surprise party—he's always said he'd hate that but do people really mean it?

Michael was turning forty and I decided that London's number-one party thrower should himself be feted and so I planned, meticulously, a surprise party to be held at his assistant Robert Fox's apartment in Wapping. The surprise actually worked and I know Michael was secretly thrilled at the massive turnout.

Well, too bad if Michael did mean it, because I did in fact go ahead and pull off the fortieth surprise party for him. It was the only party anyone ever organised for him. And it was a huge success, though not without a lot of stressful moments. I devised a plan to go to the theatre and then to Robert and Celestia Fox's for dinner. Michael decided he wanted to eat at a restaurant in the West End rather than schlep to Wapping (to what was the beginning of the radically chic concept of loft living down by the Thames). He was used to getting his way and I had to insist that their babysitter had cancelled and we *had* to go to them for dinner. Then the theatre ended earlier than I anticipated and I had to call Robert on Michael's car phone (yes, he had one of the earliest car phones ever, long before mobile phones—it was huge and cost a small fortune), tell him in a pointed tone that we were on our way and insist to my beau that we stop for wine—at which point the canny Michael started to smell a rat. But I persisted and when I finally dragged him in the door, it was indeed a wild scene of hilarity and joy as so many London pals excitedly screamed, 'Surprise!'

I know he was secretly thrilled with being the guest of honour for once in his life and the party was a fantastically memorable one, though I did go home a little worse for wear after my net dress caught fire thanks to some low-lying candles. The net exploded in flames in a split second, and shrieking guests started throwing glasses of champagne and wine at me and the dress to put it out as I hopped around, half screaming and half laughing. Apart from the smell, the damage was mainly to the outer frou-frou layers of net. No big deal and the party was a big success.

Michael vowed to surprise me back—especially as my twenty-first birthday had been insanely low-key. We'd only been dating a couple of months then, and without any family around, there was no one to organise a party. My dear parents had airmailed a small package a week earlier, begging me not to open it till my birthday. The night before, Michael took me to the theatre and then we drove over to Glebe Place, just off the King's Road, to visit his best pal Hercules Bellville in his fabulous house filled with his teeny tin toys and a wildly eclectic art collection. Well, the boys smoked a big joint and I sat waiting for midnight to open my present, which I'd stuffed into my bag before leaving home that evening. Midnight came, Herc cracked open a bottle of champagne, and I swiftly opened the box to discover the most beautiful long strand of pearls with an opal clasp. Naturally I wept immediately and felt incredibly sad and homesick, but Hercules, quite stoned and more of a tease than Michael even, cheered me up no end by telling me that my parents were clearly thrilled to have gotten rid of me and I should abandon any thoughts of returning home, since they'd finally found some peace without me. Darling Herc could always make me laugh.

Four years later, Michael decided he would not let my twenty-fifth birthday pass without a party. I too was secretly thrilled. I'd never had a birthday party—not even as a kid—so this was a great novelty.

Another night at Egerton Crescent … but this time it's my 25th birthday, and Michael repaid my surprise bash for him with a surprise party for me. Here, frequent Egerton Crescent visitor Manolo Blahnik is manhandled by two Aussie broads: fashionista Jenny Kee and my bestie Gael. Who can blame them? Manolo is witty, sweet and fashion royalty.

I remember Gael and I sitting in the kitchen at Egerton Crescent on a Sunday night, almost on the eve of my quarter-century birthday, commiserating about how old we were getting. Michael's attitude to age was always so healthy that he'd get furious if I mentioned my boring, conventional fears about the passing years. Likewise, he was utterly unsentimental about birthdays and could not understand the ingrained Aussie penchant for birthday hoedowns—but he kindly made an exception this time and about 150 people were sent invitations, but only with a week's notice. Michael decided to make it 'high-powered', as he put it, and so as well as the usual gang of Aussies, he invited some important businessmen and showbiz people. In other words it was 'a party for him as well as me' as I wrote to my folks at the time. For events like this Michael would hire party planners to cater and they would provide a maid, a barman and a butler. Michael would do the flowers, his bustling three-storey office, presided over by the fabulous Audrey at the posh address of Duke Street, St James's (right off Piccadilly, almost opposite the Ritz), would do the invites and I just had to try and get home by the time it began on the day. I wrote home three weeks after the party:

> Sorry not to have written with news of the quarter-century birthday party before this, but it took about a week to recover and have just spent the last two weeks finishing off my run of 'Hobbs's Choice' for Thames TV before coming to New York with Michael, where I'm now ensconced on a wet, windy Sunday afternoon—admittedly in a vast, lovely suite at the very deluxe Pierre Hotel opposite Central Park. It's bliss but I've had a shocking cold and felt lousy and it does make one realise the importance of one's health.
>
> We're here because of Michael's film *Jabberwocky*, which opened a couple of weeks ago, and much to his distress, is not doing well here. The guy distributing it hasn't sold or marketed it right but has wasted enormous amounts of money on things like a full page *New York Times* ad, which appeared the day we arrived, to impress Michael. Foolishly, Michael signed a personal guarantee of 200,000 pounds and if the film doesn't do well in America

there's little hope of recouping in England ... the gambles of a life in showbiz.

But back to my birthday night. Spent the morning filming Princess Margaret for my Jubilee edition of 'Hobbs's Choice', then had to cut it down to three minutes, submit my commentary to the lawyer (a weekly procedure but this time more hazardous as the lawyer is female, sixty, uptight and *loves* the royals) and then for the first time ever at Thames, due to technical reasons, do the commentary live in the studio at 6 pm ... with guests arriving back at Egerton Crescent at 7 pm! And then the director informed me there was surprise champagne for me in the bar after the program so I couldn't belt off home. I did the commentary, no fluffs, slugged back champers, made some excuses and rushed home, arriving, late night shopping and traffic jams notwithstanding, at 7.15 pm, rushing past some guests to head upstairs and into the bath. Luckily there were two maids and two waiters plus the housekeeper to open the door, not to mention Chalky who'd left work at 4 to come home and get everything ready. He really is fabulous. Anyway, sprinted up the stairs, into the bath, total panic and in he comes with a 'little pressie', having already bought me this gorgeous hot-pink taffeta skirt and top from Kenzo. I have a funny feeling that cos it's so little it must be some sort of jewellery.

I was right. It was a totally stunning star-shaped diamond ring. He certainly wasn't down on one knee but mumbled something about it being an 'engagement ring if I play my cards right ...' Typical Michael. As with anything potentially serious or important, it was said half mockingly. Eventually, with Joshua, Liberty and Sasha hovering about and excitedly handing me shoes and frocks, I rushed downstairs to an amazing room full of wonderful friends, a pianist at the piano, gifts being handed to me and champagne everywhere. About two hundred people came—and it must have been fun as the last guests left at 5 am! As I finished up my letter: 'A memorable night and I'm a bloody lucky girl.'

I truly was lucky. But the word 'engagement' was never discussed again. Frankly, I was relieved. My life was such a whirlwind, and avoiding any introspection, I deliberately did not ask myself if I was in love. And I do remember the feelings of guilt if I ever questioned why our relationship didn't feel more romantic. I was acutely aware of how lovely my life was and it did feel right in so many ways. And since I also adored Michael and his three children, I had no intention of rocking the boat.

In retrospect, perhaps the concept of marriage was too much for Michael to even consider. He was *so* busy. At one point in the mid-seventies, Michael had six shows playing simultaneously in the West End, and within twelve years he had put on more than ninety of them! I think he must have been more stressed than he let on about the vicissitudes of making money as a producer in the West End, having to continually raise money and deal with creative but difficult folk. He wasn't one to share the burden or perhaps to even worry about the financial side of things enough, and indeed I do wish he'd employed someone sensible whose sole job was to guide and advise him and make sure he made better deals. Michael was a notorious 'gambler' on shows, and some paid off—but many didn't. He made up his mind about a play over a breakfast sometimes, and agreed to back a movie and write a personal cheque for something like *My Dinner with Andre* after one cocktail and a brief description of the project. He was basically crazy, which is what was also so lovable about him, but he truly was his own worst enemy in the sense that he was not the sharp businessman he needed to be. And since I didn't ever mention marriage, it simply did not crop up. People never ceased to be amazed by my casual attitude and it was hard to put into words the sense that it was not something that was meant to be.

So, we worked on and we partied on. Our only rivals for giving great parties in London were art dealer Martin Summers and his very lively and witty wife Nona. They had some great and wild parties at their gorgeous house in Glebe Place—one memorable one featured the entire visiting Aussie cricket team—Dennis Lillee included, of course—and ended with an actual rendition of 'Knees up Mother Brown' as cricket lovers Mick Jagger and Mark Shand acted like fawning groupies. We spent a lot of time at clubs after dinners out: Maunkberry's and the Embassy Club among them, but mainly the ritzy Annabel's in Berkeley Square. I dreaded clubs more than almost anything, always have. Noisy, can't hear oneself speak—but Michael just hated to call it a night.

We also went to a heap of balls—when I think back to the '70s, I think *balls*—many, many balls—the Pied Piper Ball, the Bedford Ball, the Red Ball in Paris with Mick Jagger and Jerry Hall, Bianca Jagger, Yves St Laurent, Andy Warhol, Paloma Picasso and Roman Polanski, plus all the fanciest Frenchies alive. The Red Ball was a doozy. Every woman in attendance was required to wear red and it was quite a thrill to see what an effort everyone had made. We admired each other in

The Aussie cricket team, led by Dennis Lillee, was in town to play the Poms and my good pal Nona Summers was inspired by Mick Jagger's love of cricket to quickly invite them over to her house in Glebe Place. Sitting next to Dennis are the late Virginia White, and Laraine Ashton, a modelling agency owner.

the glow of spectacular fireworks that went on for hours on the edge of the Bois de Boulogne, and I have a great photo from the moment when Roman grabbed my camera saying, 'Ah you look stunning, but who is photographing you?'

And with that he gave the camera to a passer-by and grabbed me in a pose as fireworks exploded behind us. I'd had a red lace two-piece outfit made—a long full skirt and a bustier top worn with red satin gloves, deep red lipstick and red Manolos … The only man who wore red was Mick Jagger, who sported a shiny red damask suit and knew very well just how fetching he looked. I rather judgementally recall a massive amount of pre-ball cocaine being consumed in Lou Adler's suite at the Ritz by all but me, and what would today be called an impromptu after party at La Coupole.

Another gem? London's premier socialite Nicky Haslam's summer Hunting Ball at his exquisite Hampshire Hunting Lodge (leased from the National Trust)—with the snobby dress code 'tenue de chasse' ('hunting outfit')—that ended at dawn and was perhaps his most successful party ever. I translated it to a 'hunting love' theme and went as some ludicrous version of Cupid, wearing a long slit-up-the-thigh black velvet skirt lined in pink taffeta, a heart-shaped bustier in pink taffeta and a matching pink taffeta arrow through my top-knot. It was a baking hot summer night with tons of people crowded into a fabulous but very, very hot white tent. The good news? Sweaty, jostled folk always think they're having a good time. Indeed, the party was going strong at 4 am! One of my favourite photos is of a lithe young blonde thing wearing little but a loincloth and a leopard skin flung over her shoulders, the leopard tail swinging between her legs as she as she walked away from the big tent in the stunning dawn light … Rupert Everett held a spear aloft, indicating he was some kind of native with much war paint on his lovely face, others went as *Clockwork Orange* thug 'hunters' on the prowl, Joan Collins wore glam safari, Bryan Ferry went as a Big White Hunter—or perhaps himself … and Nicky was a black-faced turbaned Indian Raj (which would not go down well at all these days, but it was still the politically incorrect '70s).

One of the best balls ever was the Red Ball in Paris, given by the late Brazilian playboy Nelson Seabre. Women were asked to wear red. And we all obeyed—Bianca Jagger, Jerry Hall and Paloma Picasso included! Yves St Laurent was there, along with Andy Warhol, Fred Hughes, Valentino … As Roman Polanski spotted me taking snaps, he demanded, 'But who is photographing you?' With that, he grabbed my camera, gave it to someone and here is the result.

Nicky Haslam's hectic but hugely fun hunt-themed ball at his exquisite Jacobean hunting lodge in Hampshire was utterly memorable. A fabulous turnout in a sweaty, hot tent—and they stayed till dawn. Here Bruce Oldfield, a charming dress designer to the stars, charms Joan Collins and the late writer Pat Booth.

121

Two very jolly additions to any party: the witty and chatty actor and writer Rupert Everett, along with one of the most sociable and outgoing actresses I ever came across, Susan Sarandon.

There was Davina Phillips's fancy dress ball where art dealer Earl McGrath wore a witty jacket with about twelve knives 'stabbing him in the back', and since everyone else was in Edwardian dress, I'm not quite sure why I thought a mauve see-through Liz Emanuel dress was appropriate ... The Berkeley Square Ball with Princess Margaret was an absolute bun fight ... There was Dafer Dakhil's very twee fancy-schmancy ball at the famous Art Deco Savoy Hotel with Tina Chow looking exquisite in an impossibly chic cream satin gown ... simply balls galore and I never quite got over feeling like a common country bumpkin at the very fancy formal ones, where posh women wore gigantic real diamond tiaras and a great dancing partner like Rupert Lycett Green would desert you as soon as he smelt the steaming hot kippers being brought in about 1 am.

Never a week went by when I didn't dutifully write home, describing these quaint customs I'd never heard of—like breakfast being served about half an hour after dinner at English balls—and including snaps of the parties, people and places I'd witnessed to amuse my parents. Thus, much to Michael's annoyance, I *always* carried a camera wherever I went! And I got away with it because (a) we were very often the hosts and (b) everyone got so used to it. And I was trusted—it's not as if I was flogging the photos to *News of the World* or the *Daily Express*.

CHAPTER 10

Moving On

IT'S FUNNY, REALLY. We had no texting or iPhones, no computers, Facebook or email but we sure managed to 'hook up' pretty successfully and have a bloody good time.

Our miraculous ability to communicate and plan to see each other with only—barring the occasional cryptic postcards and telegrams— that near-extinct instrument known as the home telephone continued smoothly into the '80s. We partied on. But I had left TV—foolishly, I believe with hindsight—to direct. It was silly because I was doing well and in the summer got to live host a series of summer-only shows that Thames produced. I think I could have had a long satisfying and exciting career in TV but I also knew I had more in me and liked the control and creativity in directing. I decided to turn 'Hobbs's Choice'—a very ahead-of-its-time melange of music, fashion and fads, originally a show within a show on Thames TV's *Today* show—into a half-hour film for the cinema, covering among other things the fashion shows in Paris. Gael and I starred in most of the big staged scenes, dressing in pirate-look clothes by Kenzo to gallivant on a fabulous old barge on the Seine, gorgeous evening wear in stately homes across England and glamorous 'punk' clothes by Karl Lagerfeld and Vivienne Westwood as we hand-jived at the Ritz in Paris till we got thrown out. I got a kick out of guerilla filming and didn't like to take no for an answer.

I followed that with another short on the new era of 'new wave' nightlife, music and clubs in London in the early '80s, called *Steppin' Out*. It featured roller-skating parties, the craze of Vespa-driving mods and their favourite mod bands along with events like 'Come as Your Favourite Blonde' night and other special nights at some of London's hippest, most stylish and often quite gay clubs. It's become something of a cult film and thanks to Google, my design website now gets enquiries about *Steppin' Out* as well as requests for my design skills!

It was followed in quick succession by my first foray into a scripted film—another half-hour short for the cinema called *Dead on Time*, written by Richard Curtis (of *Notting Hill* and *Four Weddings and a Funeral* fame) and starring Rowan Atkinson, about a man who goes to the doctor and is told he has thirty minutes to live. I gave Greta Scacchi one of her very first jobs (that enabled her to get her Actors Equity card) and Rupert Everett, still a gorgeous unknown (pre–*Another Country*), appeared out of nowhere all the time, begging for a part—*any* part! I finally relented and had to make up a role, casting him as a blind, cane-tapping extra. He ate up the screen like a mad fool and had to be restrained from trying to steal every scene. I was incredibly nervous as I drove up that first day of shooting but by 'It's a wrap' a week later, I had the bug. It was such fun and I felt like I'd finally found my niche. It went out in the cinema before *The Turning Point*, the ballet-themed feature starring Mikhail Baryshnikov, Shirley Maclaine and Ann Bancroft.

Dead on Time won awards and became my new calling card. I was now a director and felt I must head to America to 'follow my dream'. Besides, my romance with Michael had finally cooled. But it was just so upsetting to imagine leaving London, a place I now considered 'home'. I couldn't face the trauma of it for the longest time.

TODAY 17h30-18h15 PALAIS DES FESTIVALS, SALLE A

93 GIRLS IN 27 MINUTES?
"HOBBS'S CHOICE"...
First-of-it's-kind
"Fashion Extravaganza"
- a choreographed musical revue
from Paris and London...
"A winner"-Ritz
"Amazingly erotic"-Evening Standard
"A refreshing breakaway from short films of the past"-Sunday Times

**First-ever screening since
London Premiere with Turning Point.**

FOR SALES CONTACT: **DAVID RAPHEL**
Suite 100 CARLTON HOTEL Tel: 68 9168
or at ICM 66 Champs Elysees, Paris 75008 Tel: 7233553
All Territories Available

Michael had a movie at the Cannes Film Festival and after selling my 'fashion musical' short to Twentieth Century Fox to go out with The Alien *in UK cinemas, we decided to have a couple of showings at the festival in the hopes of selling it overseas. I was incredibly nervous but it went over very well and we sold it to several countries—including France.*

I took 'Hobbs's Choice', my bi-weekly musical fashion spot from Thames TV's Today show, and made it into a half-hour cinema short based on the Paris Collections. Kenzo came out with some 'pirate-look' clothes and so there we were, shooting on the Seine in Paris ... like a bunch of fools!

125

To shoot the half-hour cinema version of Hobbs's Choice, *I enlisted my beautiful best pal Gael to come to Paris and take part in the filming. We shot at the Ritz in Paris and took tea under the chandeliers with some cute punk dudes. Great makeup by our friend, the talented makeup artist Yvonne Gold.*

And since I was crazy about Joshua, Liberty and Sasha, I would lie awake silently weeping at night as I guiltily tried to imagine leaving the fold—or 'deserting them' as I described it to friends. I truly was like their mother for quite some time, their own mother having disappeared for a few years due to some substance abuse problems that she eventually overcame. I bought them clothes and read them bedtime stories and agonised over Christmas and birthday presents. We took skiing lessons together and shopped at Harrods—which they loved—and I cried when we dropped them back at boarding school after holidays together. I took them to dentists and occasionally with me on a job when it was appropriate. Joshua, the oldest, was thrilled when I took him with me to interview John Aspinall for the opening of his wildlife collection to the public. In somewhat unusual fashion

Margaret Howell is a British designer who has always made beautiful Enid Blyton–type duds: shirts, Fair Isles and lovely houndstooth jackets. At one point, if you brought in a portrait photo, her band of little old lady knitters would knit a jumper with the face on it. Michael insisted he wear one of me and, in a rare romantic gesture, secretly had it made.

Dead on Time

<u>Running time:</u> 33 mins.

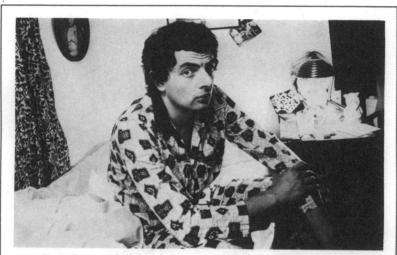

Forty-five years of life expectancy are crammed into half-an-hour for a young man who is told he will be dead within 30 minutes in "DEAD ON TIME", a black comedy starring Rowan Atkinson, who has written the film in collaboration with Richard Curtis. He describes it as a tragic comedy. Filmed entirely on location, it tells how a young man named Bernard Fripp hits the streets in a fervent panic when told of his impending fate. He is determined to live, in the short time remaining for him, the potential of the 45 years he had hoped to enjoy.

Every minute counts as he sprints through the environs of New Covent Garden and the valley of the shadow of death. He falls in love twice, comes to grips with great art, great literature, great music, religion and other things he had never really had time for, culminating in saving a child's life. The ending provides an ironic twist.

The off-beat film has been produced and directed by Lyndall Hobbs. Executive producer: Michael White. Associate producer: Simon Milne.

The first scripted short I directed was Dead on Time, *starring Rowan Atkinson and written by his good friend Richard Curtis, who would go on to become famous for writing* Notting Hill *and* Four Weddings and a Funeral. *On day one, I drove up to the location in an old disused bank, utterly terrified. By the end of the day, I realised that directing was a huge rush.*

129

they encouraged close personal relationships between the keepers and the animals, and Joshua was tickled pink when I went into the lion enclosure to interview John. The kids loved the dinners and parties and would always sneak downstairs to peek at the fun.

Although it was all a tad unorthodox, I truly loved them and their dad. Hard to say why Michael and I couldn't figure out a way to work on our relationship but I suspect largely because we simply didn't pay it enough attention. And Michael was tough, very withdrawn and closed down when it came to communication. His childhood—being sent to boarding school in Switzerland at six because of his asthma and then rarely visited by his parents, who let him spend certain holidays as the lone child left at school—clearly had something to do with it. I was not much better. Our romance was the 'B' story in our lives when it should of course have been front and centre, the main plot, the 'A' story. Should we have sat down and tried to express our feelings, wants and desires? Of course. But this was not about to happen with a man who said he loved me perhaps once in ten years. Feelings and deep intimate discussions were not on the menu. And he was becoming *more* obsessed with his social life as he got older—not less. So, with an incredibly heavy heart and almost a year of soul-searching, I took off on a trip to New York and left Michael, his three kids and my life—and did not return. Between us, I also had a giant crush on a movie star by this time!

CHAPTER 11

Plastic Surgery—but Not the Good Kind

A FEW DAYS AFTER the double mastectomy, some kind folk are emailing me to ask, 'How's it going?' Part of me wants to shriek, 'It's a miracle that I'm alive!' I mean, *was* the combo of a jet-lagged plastic surgeon and a sleep-deprived breast surgeon really ideal for my bilateral skin-sparing, nipple-saving mastectomy with right lymph-node removal and then reconstruction?

The morning before the operation, the glam young reconstructive surgeon Dr Bob is boasting of two weeks of wild nights in Ibiza till 5 am—which had ended just one day earlier—as he asked me, 'Are we', (yawn, yawn), 'saving the nipples or not?' He scans his notes, clearly trying to remember who the hell I am, so I helpfully offer to call the breast surgeon, Dr Peg, to ask her. Alas, I can't hear her answer because her baby is screaming in the background and she sounds croaky and shattered. Should I run for the hills now? I ask myself, but I falter as Dr Bob reappears, smiling but still trying to stifle a yawn.

I go home feeling quite disturbed. As I write this, I wish to God I had cancelled the whole thing, but I didn't.

In fact, I decide to pop out and buy a *lot* of goodies (Chinese food, vodka, chocolate, cigarettes) to stuff into my face before the midnight deadline. At 2 am (okay, I cheat a lot)—after one last mouthful of cheese on toast—I stagger into bed, guilt-ridden about the nicotine. But now I just wish I had taken a photo of my rather stunning pre-op bosoms.

I do survive the massive seven-hour surgery saga (they cruelly intubated me to make sure I would), despite the South African anaesthetist being a mean buzzkill and only giving me about one and a half seconds of fun before I am out cold. I had begged for a few minutes of stoned euphoria and the 'good Michael Jackson stuff' but he was not amused.

My three days in hospital are all a blur. I know Dr Bob is not around. He has taken another vacation! I remember little else but the giant white labrador some bossy lady brings in for 'healing purposes', who is trained to get up on the chair next to my bed but not trained to show a whit of interest in me as I pat him. He won't even look me in the eye—bastard!

Once home, I spend drug-addled days lurking in bed and stumbling round the apartment. My sweet Lola Nightingale takes me to see Dr Bob, just back from his holiday, and he announces that the drains must stay in another week, drains that tend to leak onto the 800-thread-count sheets you've been saving for that fab hot date— or, in my case, the day you return from tit surgery. I have so many questions but try to keep them to a minimum, especially when my opening salvo, 'Do you think my breasts will ever look less horrifying?' is met with a chuckle and, 'You're such a character!'

A couple of days after my drains are taken out, my breast swells like a balloon and the doc has to get out the horse needle and drain my breast since fluid is collecting right around the underside. Now, this is a day or two after another horse needle has injected *more* fluid into the expander ... I'm like a human pin cushion and keep asking why my breast gets redder by the day. But Dr Bob says it 'all looks fine' and who am I to argue?

But I'm feeling *bad*—really bad, like, 'Can I actually stay awake and alert enough to keep driving home?' I suspect that I may be ill when I don't even have the energy to nag my son about his homework every ten minutes. I can't even get up and make the breadcrumbed chicken breasts I had promised to cook after three nights of takeaway, so I'm deeply grateful when Nick offers to microwave some mac 'n' cheese (organic, natch).

At about 8 pm Nick goes down to the underground car park to search for his special 'composition' book in the car, and I wonder whether a quick nicotine hit will give me the energy to help him with the mission statement for a fictitious charity he's just told me he has to write for English. I swiftly turn on the stove's gas burner to simultaneously light a stick of incense and my cig, and then in a flash of brilliance decide to get a protein hit with a quick spoonful of peanut butter.

Uh oh. I hear Nick putting his key in the front door lock and so, grabbing a paper towel to wipe peanut butter from the counter, I make a lightning dash to my bathroom where I shut the door, take a last drag and spray the non-aerosol air freshener. I slip out a few moments later, feeling positively light-headed, and dash to Nick's room to see if there is any way humanly possible to help him with the essay— other than by actually writing the whole thing myself. I lie on his bed waiting for him to find his agenda and the essay directions (that'll be twenty minutes).

But right about then I smell something burning and then there's a *deafening* alarm going off. Is it our smoke alarm or the building alarm—or both? Okay, I don't actually recall turning off the gas burner and I *may* have flung the paper towels in the general proximity of the stove but, in any event, the roll of paper towels is now very much alight on top of the stove!

I shriek like a banshee as my brave son comes to the rescue, grabbing the frying pan and hurling the flaming missile into the sink before turning off the stove and turning to give me an accusing look. 'What did you do?' he shouts.

'Nothing!' I shout back as I grab a towel and start waving it under the alarm. But as Nick opens the front door we see residents fleeing to the stairs carrying small dogs, cats and crying babies. 'Oh, I bet it's a false alarm,' I mutter guiltily—though it does seem like a weird coincidence. Any thoughts of sticking it out soon leave my pounding brain. The alarm is insanely loud and so I reluctantly don Uggs, grab keys and follow my son, who's thrilled to ditch homework and join the throng of residents hurrying down the stairs.

And there they are—the entire population of this enormous Hancock Park apartment complex gathered outside at the back of the building. But look, it's a lovely hot evening, a brilliant red sun is setting, little kids in their PJs are running round like wild things, overexcited teens are texting their pals, and people are laughing and cracking jokes as they pet each other's pooches. Okay, so a few cats in their carry boxes hiss a little and one new mother with a screaming infant seems stressed but generally there is a sense of bonhomie, especially when about ten burly firemen arrive and everyone cheers. And there is no proof it's my fault.

People are back in their apartments twenty-five minutes later, I haven't been charged with arson and I still have to write the bloody mission statement as Nick is way too frenzied now to focus. I practically hallucinate as I write the last sentence at 11.35, Nick now snoozing happily in bed.

Next morning my chest feels like it's on fire. I try to be a good mother and make school lunch but—can I be really frank?—making lunches bores me rigid and Nick never likes them and so I hurl a few snacks together, give him the six bucks for school lunch, hand him his morning drugs (Adderall for the ADD and Accutane for skin plus some multi-vites!) plus his bowl of Cheerios and milk that is eaten in the car with a towel on his lap, and off we head to school, late as usual. Johnny Depp's children's bodyguards—two gigantic black gentlemen who hang out at school next to their equally humongous black Escalade all day—snap their heads round to look as I loudly roar to a halt. I smile insincerely and wave as Nick cringes, swearing under his breath. They stare back stone-faced and off I zoom to Starbucks for my morning Venti. Too tired to even wait for my order in a standing position, I have to sit, the sweat pouring off me.

I call Dr Bob. No response. So I call Dr Peg who, shockingly, is available in one hour. (She is not the doctor in charge—it's Dr Bob— but what's a mid-reconstruction sheila to do? Be your own advocate and call the next surgeon on one's list, the one who made the first cut and scooped out all the breast tissue. I like her and wish she did reconstruction as well.) Dr Peg takes one look at my luminous red breasts and declares, 'Jesus, you've got an infection!'

Just as she's expressing diplomatic surprise that Dr Bob didn't notice this infection, my mobile phone rings and when I see it's Dr Bob calling I ask Dr Peg, somewhat panicked, what I should say. I'm actually feeling guilty that, out of fear and frustration, I've gone behind his back to get a second opinion on my heat-radiating boobs. Dr Peg just grabs my phone and tells him very matter-of-factly that I have an infection and she is prescribing antibiotics. Okay, great. But I keep wondering whether Dr Bob's going to be upset with me. After all, he's the one who swears he will deliver beautiful breasts again and I am feeling somewhat captive and inclined to keep things jolly and pleasant. And so, when he calls me an hour later insisting I come to see him tomorrow, I don't ask why the *hell* he did not even diagnose this infection.

Once the two weeks of the Augmentin antibiotic are up, it's back to Dr Bob. My breasts are still the same bright red. I nervously suggest that perhaps I should go to see an infectious-disease (ID) doctor. His response? 'I know an ID doctor and I think I'll call him.' He comes back and informs me the ID has suggested I switch to Clindamycin. Now, while I am *not* the shy and retiring type, I just do not have the energy to ask why the hell he is not sending me to *see* an expert in infected breasts.

These new antibiotics make me feel like everything else I've been through is kindergarten. I'm almost comatose. And my left breast is still a very angry red after five weeks of swallowing enough antibiotics to stop an angry rhino in its tracks. At my check-up, Dr Bob enters and like some robotic hooker, I open my robe as I greet him. He pokes. It hurts.

'Still red,' I say.

'Yes, but a little better,' he counters.

'What about seeing an ID guy?' I venture again.

Silence. He takes notes.

'Maybe IV antibiotics *are* the answer at this point?'

'No, I think another five days of Clindamycin is the way to go.'

I feel beaten but using every last drop of energy I have left I manage to ask, 'And you don't think it makes sense to check with the ID doctor you spoke to last week to see what he says?'

'No, try these again,' he says, handing me the prescription.

'Okay,' I say meekly and start to dress. But as I speed back to Hollywood I boldly dial Dr Peg and leave a message asking if she thinks a sixth week of antibiotics is the best way to go at this point. Eureka! She calls me back and, after angrily asking if she's heard correctly and I *still* have the infection, makes an appointment for me with an ID doc for the very next day.

So, with an infection that's been raging for five weeks without being diagnosed by my esteemed reconstructive surgeon, I'm now back at Cedars to see Dr Sam. Apparently, a crimson-coloured breast is all an experienced ID doc needs to see before demanding the name of my oncologist. Before I can say, 'Will I live?' he's called my oncologist, Dr C, on her mobile and is saying, 'Lyndall's had a staph infection for five weeks and has only taken oral antibiotics so far. Can she come down right now to start on an IV?'

Fifteen minutes later I'm back at the oncology centre, a place I hoped never to set foot in again. I'm hooked up in the chemo lounge in record time. Just a burst of pre-closing time efficiency I tell myself, till Dr C comes rushing up, aggressively pulling the hospital-like curtains. My usual waiting time to see her is usually about ninety minutes. She gives me no verbal greeting, just a big hug and an uncharacteristically pointed, 'I cannot believe your surgeon! Why did he let it go this long?' She motions for me to lift up my tank top and her eyes widen a little, but before I can ask if she thinks my breast will fall off she chides me for not having come to see her earlier. I am tempted to point out that her scheduling assistant never responded to my email but fear it would sound ungracious.

Dr C then proceeds to inform me that an ongoing infection should be treated with oral antibiotics for no more than five to six days before getting aggressive with IV antibiotics. 'At least three weeks too long,' she says and then justifies her claim by painting a very grim potential scenario. 'If the infection is allowed to take hold and then really won't budge, at some point you will have to be opened up, and both the expanders and the Alloderm have to be removed. The problem then is the breast skin tends to stick to the chest wall like superglue and when you try to pry it all apart, the resulting cosmetic effects could be—well, *less than ideal.*' The ID doc has already warned me of this. Funny how Dr Bob never mentioned it.

'Aggressive treatment as soon as possible is the only way to go. I want you to do IV for two weeks, seven days a week. The IV antibiotics bypass your stomach. I can't imagine how you feel after five weeks of them. Very bad for your system, you know.'

'Well yes,' I say, suddenly very close to tears as I notice a good-looking man holding his wife's hand tightly as the nurse inserts an IV. To think I might have avoided three or even four weeks of the bloating, diarrhoea, toxic exhaustion, depression and sleeplessness due to the oral frigging antibiotics is infuriating.

'What do I say to Dr Bob?' I ask.

'Tell him I'm trying to salvage the situation. Use the word *salvage.*' Another hug and she's off and I sit there, unable to stop watching the couple opposite. The lovely husband has just brought his wife another pillow and keeps smiling as he rubs her arm.

I call to give Dr Peg an update and she says I should just dump Dr Bob. 'I'll call him now. You don't have to ever speak to him again,' she says very matter-of-factly. A tough breed, these surgeons, but it's like getting a friend to break up with your boyfriend for you. I tell her to hold off. It's not as if she's recommending anyone else. Indeed, when I ask who she thinks I should switch to, she doesn't come up with a single name. I quickly hang up because I can see that Dr Bob is calling in. Well blow me down if he doesn't sound all hurt and offended that I've cancelled Monday's appointment. I explain that I will be seeing the ID doc again to see how the IV drugs are working. If I'm hoping for an apology and mea culpa, I'm sadly disappointed.

'Well, then you need to come in on Tuesday or Wednesday and if the redness is still there, I'll open you up and wash you out and take out the expanders for a day or two and then put them back.' Even as I feel shocked that he's so infuriatingly casual in the way he talks about cutting me open, I politely promise we'll speak soon and click the phone off as he's still speaking. I can no longer cope. What to do with my anger?

Five days later, I've just had my eighth IV antibiotic session at the oncology centre and been to see my third reconstructive surgeon in hopes of finding someone who 'feels right' to replace Dr Bob. I've yet to even fire Dr Bob on account of I'm a pathetic, guilt-ridden moron and also because I want to keep my options open. What if I don't find anyone better who takes insurance?

They all have different plans of attack but on one thing they agree. Things have gone horribly wrong and unless there's some kind of miracle and we can get the flaming-red infected tit to calm down, the surgery will have to be undone. Not a good thing. Because to be on the safe side, the expander would have to stay out for a month, at which point the crumpled skin will shrink and shrivel. My best bet might be to lop everything off and do skin grafts with skin taken from my back.

I receive an email from Dr Bob. It seems that the one I sent to him two days ago—where I pleasantly but pointedly remarked on his not noticing my infection or treating it aggressively enough—has gotten his attention. Playing hard to get by not going to see him this week has also proved effective. He insists on coming to see *me*, the next day. At *my* place. I feel very conflicted—is this a version of Stockholm Syndrome where you feel a need to see the surgeon who's ruining your life? But I say yes to this mighty unorthodox visit. I mean, when did a highly paid west-side surgeon last pay a home visit?

Dr Bob's pleasant enough. Although anyone who thinks they might be sued is bound to be pleasant but also very careful not to apologise in any way, shape or form. He sticks to his upbeat spiel of, 'Well there's less redness and I think the antibiotics are working,' and then even ventures a, 'Well I understand that you felt safer with IV antibiotics,' which is a bit much given that at this point at least six other doctors have said that was the *only* way to go. Why I can't say those very words to him makes me feel like a battered wife who can't confront her abuser.

And so when Dr Bob calls on Thursday and asks me to email photographs, I send them off. On Friday he calls begging me to come in to his clinic on Sunday evening. He adds, fairly dramatically, that he's worried my breast might *explode*. I kid you not—that's the word he uses. I drag my friend Sheila with me to meet up with Dr Bob. She makes a valiant attempt at asking some of the questions another friend has emailed to her iPhone … but they soon become redundant in light of the fact that Dr Bob has taken the liberty of booking me in for surgery the very next day at 5 pm. Either he's a genius clairvoyant who knows I'd like to dump him and wants to scare me into pre-emptive surgery quick smart—or he genuinely thinks I need to be under the knife. I wonder how to arrange for Nick getting to and from school but my darling daughter, despite her crammed schedule as both college student and coffee shop manager, will make it happen. She's the best.

Could there be anything more aggravating than a 7 pm surgery and an entire day without food, water or coffee? Crossing town with my pal Brooke Adams at peak hour means we're late for the 5 pm check-in time. Sure enough, by 5.20 pm everyone at Admitting has clocked off for the day. The place is a ghost town. Two other very sweet friends, Sheila and Joyce, meet me inside the hospital and we wander up and down, take the elevator to different floors and resort to calling out, 'Hcllloooo?' trying to find some humans who might be appropriate to the situation.

Finally we come across two nurses sitting at a dimly lit admitting desk in an inner lobby straight out of *The Shining*. They're not wildly welcoming and when they realise there's no pre-op blood work, I find myself explaining that as my breast was about to explode there hadn't been time and besides, I say, 'I was here a few weeks ago. I'm very healthy.'

'Except for the exploding tit,' snickers one of my pals and they both collapse in hysterical laughter. The now-hostile nurses hustle me into a pre-op cubicle. Vitals are taken and the usual dull questions are asked about allergies and crap, and then I'm asked who'll be driving me home. I say that I'm to be admitted for two nights and all hell breaks loose—they insist they have no knowledge of a sleepover whatsoever!

They're cranky and I actually scream as one of them, who may or may not be trying to emulate TV's drug-crazed Nurse Jackie, inserts an IV with all the finesse of a panda bear wearing snow mittens. My two pals appear in the doorway as the other nurse repeats there is no paperwork that will allow me to stay the night, and I keep insisting that Dr Bob said I was to stay! It's farcical but terrifying too and both pals are now suggesting that perhaps, 'We should leave and come back another day.' I'm sorely tempted. And then I'm asked the dreaded question, 'What procedure are you having?' and I have to say in my own words, 'Well they're taking it all out—the expander, the Alloderm and leaving me … empty.'

In the nick of time, here comes Dr Bob—or God to the nurses—and they relax. One of my girlfriends, a New York toughie, demands to know why it all seems so chaotic and disorganised. Dr Bob is unruffled as he tells us it's all 'under control'. He confirms to the nurses that I'm definitely staying and that's that. Dr Bob has bags under the bags of his eyes, and I ask him when he last ate.

It's so late in the day, no one bothers with the niceties like putting me 'under' before I'm wheeled into the operating room, which is scary and messy with boxes piled in one corner and dingy white tiled walls. It's certainly not as gleaming and groovy as on *Grey's Anatomy*. Where are my drugs? Ah, here's the drug man and all I can think about as he chats wearily to me is that it's nearly 8 pm and aren't all these folk tired and hungry and desperate to get home? They must hate me. And I'm out. But only till midnight as this was a comparative 'quickie', just a two-hour surgery. I don't feel so bad—the usual searing pain— but then I remember, and like some tragic amputee, I feel for where my left breast was … nada. Flat as a pancake. Great! Even though I knew it was coming, it *sucks*. Less than twenty-four hours later and a day early, I decide I'm done. I pack up and schlep past the nurse's station. I don't bother to say goodbye or get checked out—no one cares. I arrive home, rush to pick up Nick from school and am careful, shrinking back slightly when he leans in to give me a big hug, in case he feels the absence of breast on one side.

I'm still thinking of changing surgeons, for all the obvious reasons. Because Dr Bob failed to notice a vicious infection. And because when I visit Dr Bob a few days later, he announces he wants to book me in for surgery the following Wednesday to open me up *again*, put in more Alloderm and replace the expander. I guess surgeons have to stay confident and cocky, but given what I've been through, the fact that he talks of slicing me open so casually is fairly upsetting.

Then, having heard of yet another great breast surgeon, I head off to Beverly Hills to meet him, desperate to hear if he thinks my breast skin will survive if I wait the month—or will I need skin grafts? This good-looking young surgeon—Dr McDreamy—tells me I should wait and insists that he has seen skin come good again once it's inflated with the expander, but I do not believe him. How can I wait another six weeks? My stress levels are through the roof and I feel I will go crazy. Like a phantom limb that people claim causes pain, this lack of breast actually hurts. It's disturbing and so, within days, I'm back to Dr Bob. 'Let's get the show on the road, Dr Bob. Can we go back in and do surgery at the end of the week?'

But blow me down if someone hasn't got to Dr Bob, and he's now changed his tune and says we have to wait for six weeks at least. He claims that he's sure the skin sticking like glue situation is not irreversible. I wish I believed him. He's now playing it safe and the truly upsetting thing is that because he doesn't want to be up for malpractice, having already failed to diagnose a staph infection, I may end up having to have tons more surgeries—skin grafts, flaps and endless opportunities for infection. I'm fucked. Whatever. Life goes on.

My darling pal Brooke Adams comes over next day and whisks me off to a pot pharmacy on Western, having convinced me that I'm in dire need of some good soothing edibles and whatnot. I already have a pot prescription from my new, wonderfully evolved holistic OB/GYN, Dr Cynthia Watson (who has been giving me some vitamin infusions to try to help restore my immune system), and so, after explaining that I'm an exhausted insomniac with anxiety, some very precise strains are suggested, with insane names like Green Crack, Girl Scout Cookies, Trainwreck and Alaskan Thunderfuck. Within about forty-five seconds I'm thoroughly confused and beg Brooke to make the deal, to get me something very, very mild to help me sleep, along with a few cookies, and suggest we call it a day. She happily obliges. We head back to her place for just a few puffs; I feel nicely mellow and she drops me home. I stash my bag of goodies in the very back of the fridge, where I promptly forget about it for a good six months, and when I do remember—what a shock—it's gone! (Nick pleads innocence but Lola finally gets him to admit his pals found it and they all partook. Great mother I am—supplier of weed to my teenage son.)

Time for a divine cup of tea, but ten minutes later, having opened the *New York Times*, I'm feeling very straight and, well, it's downhill from there. Within moments I'm in a white-hot blaze of anger as I read yet another horrendous story about how the chief medical officer of the American Cancer Society now admits that the advantages of mammograms have been greatly exaggerated. I'm so angry I have to get the stepladder, reach up to the top of the kitchen cupboards, find the American Spirits and light up immediately before heading off to pick up Nick from school. Mammograms and mammogram machines are big business and make radiologists and then oncologists a lot of money. So much of cancer detection and treatment is just about money.

Since, alas, none of what I've done to myself is reversible, I feel I must carry on in the quest to restore myself to a two-titted person, so it's back to Dr McDreamy for a second visit to see if I still like him. One visit's not enough when sharp knives are involved. What he's suggesting, to minimise the risk of re-infection, is taking both triangle-shaped latissimus muscles from my back—the ones you use for pull-ups or a mighty golf swing—and putting them into my breasts to support the implants. And to make it look symmetrical he wants to do both breasts, which means two incisions under my arms, another two further down for the camera to enter my body and two more incisions where the muscles are slipped in. A four-hour operation and four drains for a couple of weeks. Two drains were charming. Four really sounds like fun.

Dr McDreamy's cute but not that cute.

Let's leave my back muscles where they naturally reside and pop in an expander and wait three months till I might be ready for the permanent implants and life again as I once knew it. That's Dr Bob's plan and it's sounding good—especially when I discover that Dr McDreamy, contrary to what his receptionist told me, is not contracted with Anthem and thus it would cost me a good deal of cash.

Dr Bob starts to seem like an even more appealing option when I go to see yet another surgeon, Dr John. I'd seen him in my initial quest for Mr Right but he didn't take my insurance so he was out. However, I'm now so determined to educate myself and get it right. Or as right as you can get it. At our first meeting he'd concurred about expanders and finally implants as the way to go and now I'm curious, in light of the ten-week staph infection, to see if he suggests staying on the expander/implant path or might he be on the same page as Dr McDreamy, recommending the latissimus muscle removal.

Well, this time round, the good surgeon takes one look at my breast area and visibly winces. He seems bad-tempered and I instantly blurt out, 'Please don't hate me—I went elsewhere for the surgery because I couldn't afford you,' but it doesn't seem to appease Dr John. He acts like a war general, telling me to man up and to jolly well 'live with it' (meaning the lopsided uni-breasted phase) for about six months to 'completely minimise the risk of re-infection' and stop worrying about the way I look.

He then demands—with not an iota of the charm he showed the first time around, that I sit and bend slightly forward from the waist so he can grab the subsequent roll of fat. He concludes that in six months or more a 'flap' would be the way to go. He could take skin and muscle from my lower stomach, making an incision from hipbone to hipbone and use it to make a breast from scratch, nipple and all. Somewhat stunned, I ask if he doesn't agree that I could just try having an expander put in again. No, there's too much risk of re-infection he insists, like some know-it-all, celebrated surgeon, and besides, he bitches, 'That's all they know how to do at St John's—you need to come to UCLA where we know how to do flaps.'

Only one tiny problem … I don't want a fucking flap. And by the way, I do not use the term 'know it all' lightly. I've asked all eight surgeons I've seen and they give educated guesses *all* the way, with half saying, 'Go ahead and fill 'er up in six to eight weeks' and the other half saying, 'Wait six months before putting back the expander.' So, let's be frank—it's a crapshoot. And grudges against other hospitals are not my business, Doc. Of course I don't say that. I truly don't know how to respond to this doctor who doesn't look me in the eye or ask if I have any questions. In short, he shows not a whit of humanity.

As Bette Davis might have said—having cancer, without a partner, ain't for sissies. Making every decision alone means there's no other poor bugger but me to blame when it all goes hideously wrong.

CHAPTER 12

The '80s

W HAT A DIFFERENCE a decade makes. Although dreadfully homesick when I left Melbourne, I wasn't scared. Ten years later I was utterly terrified of leaving London and my new 'family' of Michael and the three kids as well as so many dear, dear friends. Thus, leaving my psychological options open, I found I could just about handle my traumatic departure from London if I pretended it was just a quick trip—so off I flew with just two suitcases, leaving most of my belongings behind, to New York, a city I'd always adored whenever I was lucky enough to visit. So very different and definitely a place that suited my temperament.

It meant disciplined, spartan days writing a spec script called *It's Only Rock'n'Roll* in a friend's almost empty spartan apartment in midtown Manhattan, discovering the joys of speedy sandwich and coffee delivery but still wondering what on earth I'd done. I didn't miss the perks or my huge walk-in closet or the Harrods charge card but I truly missed my pals and familiar routines. Something had drawn me to America, however. After years of feeling like a second-class citizen as a woman in London, I truly believed that it would be different in America and that as a female director, I would find more equality.

And, to be perfectly frank, I did have a bit of a crush … about twelve months earlier on a trip to LA with Michael, I'd met Al Pacino at director Tony Richardson's pad during one of his weekly Sunday lunches. Tony had a house above the Sunset Strip (having sold his fabulous Egerton Crescent house to Michael several years before when he announced he was leaving the snobbish confines of London for good) and he loved to entertain. Preferably the rich and famous. Anyone from Princess Margaret, Jack Nicholson and Sir Larry Olivier to his ex-wife Vanessa Redgrave, or Jessica Lange or Gore Vidal. Plus any number of young, up-and-coming good-lookers, usually male and rarely straight. And if Tony, an inveterate tease with a wickedly perverse sense of humour, could stir up some trouble and get people arguing, he was happy as a clam.

Al had come with Robert de Niro and we met as we both stood in line to serve ourselves roast chicken and potato salad at the buffet lunch. Al flirted like mad and jokingly asked me to dance—and was literally ready to waltz me round the room—but I declined, having no idea who he was. He was very attractive but I didn't recognise him and I suspect my casual attitude was a challenge. We exchanged a few glances and I found myself mesmerised by those wonderful eyes. Over dessert I finally realised who he was. On my very first trip to LA with Michael in 1973 we drove up La Cienega, that rather grim drive past the bizarre oil pumps and right on Sunset Boulevard and along to the Chateau Marmont. Michael had somehow wangled a wonderful top-floor suite with a balcony overlooking the Strip. I walked out and took my first Hollywood snap—a picture of the huge billboard below us of a bearded Al Pacino as Serpico. I have the picture in my album. (Behind the billboard Sunset Strip looks quite bleached out and bare. Compared with New York and London, LA then felt to me like a sleepy country town.)

The morning after Tony's lunch, Al and I happened to meet up again by the pool at the Chateau Marmont, where Michael and I were staying again, and later that evening we somehow contrived to have a jolly rendezvous in his bungalow for an innocent hot chocolate. I took my Aussie girlfriend Honey with me—and Al had his oldest best pal Charlie Laughton staying with him in the bungalow. And no, I don't believe I mentioned that I had a long-term live-in boyfriend. He didn't ask. And that was that. But we exchanged numbers and a few weeks later he called me in London. He was there to see a director about a play and was staying at the Athenaeum Hotel. We went to a museum and then had lunch at San Lorenzo. We sat in my VW Bug outside the Athenaeum and talked for hours. But we didn't hold hands. We didn't kiss. He left town. On quite a few heart-stopping occasions, he had subsequently called me for long phone chats but at such distance, it had all seemed hopeless. Or was it?

I'd been agonising about leaving my 'British family' for about two years already and suffered the same guilt I'd had about leaving my parents. I didn't know what to do. The idea of leaving and heading off to America was terrifying—but the thought of staying put was just as unacceptable. I wrote a letter to Al saying that I was thinking of coming to New York for a spell but tore it up and threw it in the wastepaper basket in the bedroom. Uncharacteristically, Michael must have been on the lookout for evidence because a few nights later he sat up in bed in the middle of the night and shouted, 'Get Pacino to pay for Pickford's!' and stormed off downstairs. (Pickford's was the name of a big moving company, and having seen the note, he was suggesting that Al pay for my move!) I explained that I hadn't even kissed Al and that we were just friends—true at that point. I had hoped that things would now be out in the open, though a real heart-to-heart with Michael was still basically out of the question. He refused to ever discuss things or make an attempt to revive our romance—and the concept of shrinks and couples therapy was yet to arrive in Britain.

So a couple of months later I summoned the strength to pack two cases and leave everything else I possessed behind. I told Michael I'd be back in a month or two—but I think we both knew that was unlikely.

Yes, I did call Al the minute I was on the tiny island of Manhattan and I did spend time with him. Our first kiss, one hot summer night as we strolled along Fifth Avenue right outside the park, was possibly the most romantic kiss I've ever had … and we did get on incredibly well. Why? We couldn't have been more different—a dropout bad boy from the Bronx and an all-girls school graduate from Brighton—but sexual chemistry is a wonderful thing. I felt like Al could barely grasp where I was from but, very winningly, he seemed fascinated—if a little incredulous—when I told him I was a runner. He kept asking me about it and one day, as we went for a walk in upstate New York near his out-of-town house, he suddenly challenged me to a race. He pointed to a bench about a hundred yards away and, very serious suddenly, said, 'On our marks, get set, go!' And we were off! Neck and neck for a few seconds and then I shot ahead, beating him big time! Al was absolutely stunned. He loved baseball and football and truly fancied himself as very athletic. He just couldn't get over being beaten by me. But sweetly, he was genuinely impressed and would boast about my sprinting prowess for years to come.

But this first time around, only about three or four months passed before things between us became weird and tense and not terribly amusing or fun. At that time Al was the antithesis of today's media-savvy, *Access Hollywood*-friendly actor. He was very invested in the 'tortured, shy, fame-hating movie star' role and liked to hole up in his horrifyingly claustrophobic, tiny windowless apartment just off Madison watching TV or reading some well-thumbed copy of *The Iceman Cometh* or *Richard III* as he ate cold pasta or Jell-O left fully prepared in the fridge by a morning maid.

And when he did venture out, it wasn't easy. He would dart into restaurants like the Left Bank or Joe Allen's—sometimes through back doors—panic if he saw a gaggle of fans or even one lone photographer waiting outside and generally draw so much more attention to himself than necessary by dashing through restaurants with a beanie or a bandana or a big old hat pulled down over his head and just two dark darting eyes peeking out. People would suddenly stop and stare at this oddball character acting like a madman.

Sometimes one of his coterie of round-the-clock drivers would be sent in to check things out. I would ask, 'Check out what?'

'Well you know, just take a look …' and sure enough the driver would pop back to the car with the riveting news that 'It's pretty full in there but they've held your table at the back' or 'It's half empty and they've got your table in the back …' or … 'Liz Taylor's at your table in the back. She's paid the check but she wants to wait and say hello to you.' It was laughable—but also sad because it was just so clear that here was someone with the world at his fingertips having a fairly miserable time. Al seemed to think it would jinx his talent if he had some fun. It was if he equated misery and angst with talent and success. Just my take on it all. But he definitely took himself very seriously, and frankly, it was a bit of a downer.

On our own—or with just a few people up at the distinctly non-lavish and down-home house he'd bought on a nice piece of land by the Hudson River, he might finally relax enough to be a normal bloke and we'd all just sit and chat over endless cups of coffee. Or play some paddles. Or play a great game of 'tell', which took me years to work out. Al was like a little kid who got such a kick out of insisting to me that he was psychic and could figure out which object I was thinking about. I'm clearly a bit thick because it just didn't occur to me what was going on … Al would run off to the kitchen so I could pick an object as the 'thing', and then he would come back, sit and study the room and walk around sizing up various objects, waiting for the 'feeling' that would tell him he was at the right spot. One of his cronies—and they were very much cronies, always loyal out-of-work actor pals whom Al had known for years—would be doing the 'tell', either chewing gum or pulling on his ear when Al was near my chosen object. Now, I knew there must be a trick but I couldn't work out what it was. Al was tickled pink as I would gasp every time in shock and awe!

But back in the city, he would become weird and paranoid at the drop of a hat and make things upsettingly dark, gloomy and complicated. So after a few months I was 'over Mr Misery Guts' as I wrote in my diary:

> I think the final straw was waking up yesterday morning on his sofa, after creeping out of his bed at about 5 am cos I couldn't sleep in his miniscule double bed with him about two inches away snoring. When I woke up he was standing there staring at me and he finally said, out of nowhere, 'What do you want from me?' Well I wasn't used to men asking such ridiculous and slightly hostile questions at dawn. I got on my high horse, said, 'Absolutely nothing Al,' quickly dressed and took off.

I was very ready to look up old pals and feel some joy and a sense of the camaraderie I'd been lucky enough to have in London. I found it a huge relief and incredibly satisfying to realise that once you have this invaluable foundation of a bunch of international pals, you can

Sandy Gallin, mega-manager to the likes of Barbra Streisand, Cher, Whoopi Goldberg and Nicole Kidman at various times in their careers, seen here with one of his all-time favourite clients, Dolly Parton, and his great pals Kelly and Calvin Klein. Dolly was sweet and very friendly—but very keen to retreat indoors. 'I'm no sun worshipper ...'

Lola looks at my albums sometimes and crankily demands to know if I ever stayed in. Yes, of course, I respond defensively—but not when in New York for a lightning weeklong visit. Another night in Manhattan and another Andy Warhol rendezvous, this time with Rachel Ward, Andy's PA Catherine Guinness, publishing maven Shelley Wanger and her friend Steven Aronson.

Back in the day, when Jack Nicholson thrived on being out and about as one of the world's biggest movie stars—a long way from the Mulholland Drive eyrie he now rarely leaves. Here Jack and his Saturday Night Live *pal John Belushi, the troubled comedian who just a year later overdosed at the Chateau Marmont, attend Lorne Michaels' wedding to Susan Forristal in the couple's backyard in the Hamptons.*

actually go lots of places and whip up some fun. So before too long, the invites started to trickle in … Days would be spent eating Vegemite on toast and instant coffee alone and lonely as I typed—but nights were soon spent at Elaine's or 21 or Studio 54 with Diana Vreeland, Rachel Ward, Bianca Jagger, Nell Campbell, Andy Warhol and Fred Hughes along with tons of Londoners like Hercules Bellville and Gael, Sabrina Guinness and Ben Gannon, cos let's face it, in those days we were total gadabouts who didn't know a savings account from a hole in the wall and we went everywhere all the time and thought we should!

I also spent a huge amount of time and energy trying to interest someone in American television in the idea of doing a half-hour TV show based on my thirty-minute short film *Hobbs's Choice*. I hate to sound immodest but it was a great idea, very ahead of its time, putting fabulous girls into fabulous frocks in great locations and putting it all to music and interviewing designers and making it hip and witty and fun and accessible. But I was trying to flog this idea all on my own and no one could quite wrap their heads around it. I came very close and at one point I met people at Revlon who wanted to back it, but that's when you need deal-makers, a crack agent or a killer lawyer. I had none of the above or the wherewithal to keep up the momentum. As a lone chick I simply wasn't taken seriously. It was my first inkling that America might be tough to crack. But I definitely had not the slightest inkling that things would heat up again so massively with Al.

CHAPTER 13

Go West Young Woman

ABOUT SIX MONTHS after arriving in New York it was time to get serious, head west and hit Hollywood. I was still nostalgic for London but realised that to do more directing, I needed to explore LA, so my two suitcases and I headed there. (I still hadn't properly moved out of Egerton Crescent in London and to this day have no idea what happened to my clothes, most of my diaries and belongings, but fortunately you don't miss what you forget.)

At first I stayed in the fabulously kitsch Tropicana Motor Inn on Santa Monica Boulevard—inspired by my dear friend Hercules, who had lived there in one of 'the insanely roomy' bungalows decorated with his collection of postcards and orange crate labels for several years. Herc loved to entertain and had many cocktail-hour soirees at the Trop in his suite with the plaid sofas and the fake wood panelling. Jack Nicholson and Anjelica Huston, Bob Rafelson and Buck Henry, Teri Garr and Michelle Phillips were all regulars.

A few weeks later I bade farewell to Herc. I spent a few nights up with Rachel Ward, who was at the height of her movie-star fame and living with fellow thespian Darryl Hannah in a fabulous, remote house at the very top of Coldwater Canyon—it had a Jacuzzi with the best view ever and rattlesnakes in the heat of the day. She'd just begun her love affair with a very dashing Bryan Brown, and on the

Saturday night she decided she'd better try to impress him with a bit of a bash—a Saturday night barbecue—with several of her new Hollywood friends. We ran around all day, buying supplies and flowers and incense and candles, and then zipped back up the hill to prepare. This was nab-a-man time and Rachel marinated meat and baked potatoes like her life depended on it while I made salads. By about seven, we were very overexcited. A new romance is always thrilling and her enthusiasm was infectious. We opened up some champagne and put on our favourite music du jour: Bob Marley's *Kaya* album. We decided to see if anyone would notice if we played it over and over the entire night. No one did. It was a great success—Rachel and I sang along every time 'Easy Skanking' came on—and it took very little savvy to predict that this was a match made in heaven. Or on a Hollywood backlot, anyway. Bryan's innate swagger and sense of humour were clearly winning and the posh English gal was smitten! I do know I secretly envied her finding a true-blue decent Aussie bloke.

Up in the hills, high above Coldwater Canyon, just a few weeks after finishing the shoot for The Thornbirds, *the stunning young Rachel Ward and Bryan Brown are already very much a couple. I suspect BB was daydreaming of how to spirit his well-bred British beauty back to his lair down-under, away from all her Hollywood admirers.*

My director pal Jamie Foley, now directing the next two instalments of Fifty Shades of Grey, *had a dinner party one night and everyone chuckled when Cher walked in, having just gone blonde. I told her it was a bit much that she had copied me in the hair department and she graciously apologised, laughing and insisting that she felt it would not stay that way long—the upkeep was too gruelling. On the left is my dear friend, actress Carol Kane.*

Despite both of us being working girls it was still a madcap carefree time, and looking at photos of Rachel and I acting like juvenile fools in the Jacuzzi in the middle of the day, having actual fun with pals like Hercules and Susan Sarandon and Brit photographer Johnny Rosza, just makes me smile. At least it wasn't all stress and hassle trying to impress idiotic Hollywood execs.

Days later I moved back down the hill, having found a very teeny guesthouse on Miller Drive just above Sunset. It was like a cute cave, the guest pad underneath a house that was perched precariously on the side of a hill. It had a big deck with a fantastic view and a huge 'walk-in cupboard' at the back of the apartment for storage, which was really just a few planks on the dirt of the hillside. Same routine— writing a script, a musical called *Tropicana*, by day, and then trying to work out how to network my way into getting an agent. A couple of days after dropping off *Dead on Time* to agent Jeff Berg's office at ICM, I met one of his agents, John Burnham, at a party. I told him I was looking for an agent and his eyes lit up. I'd like to think it was because he was impressed when I told him about my three cinema shorts, but when he took my number and asked me out for dinner twenty-four hours later I realised that my youth and reasonably good looks might be involved.

I was never very good at saying 'no', and besides, as my director friend James Foley told me, 'I take meetings and dinners with agents all the time—it keeps my current agent on his toes, you never know when you might want to switch and you can't ever know enough agents.' So I went to dinner with John—but I've really never been a great schmoozer, I rarely had witty comebacks or put-downs when aggressive guys bombarded me with silly sexual innuendos and I was always stunningly bad at hiding my feelings, especially when indignant in nature. By the end of the evening I could tell he reckoned I was a dud, especially when I said no to his suggestion of coming in for the proverbial nightcap when he dropped me home. It was the first of many occasions when I felt I'd blown it by being an indignant prude incapable of canny diplomacy or schmoozing long enough to at least try to get my way.

But this time it didn't stop his boss, the powerful Jeff Berg, from starting to call me over the next few weeks—even going so far as to come to my tiny guesthouse on a Saturday morning to insist I sign with him immediately. I'd been hoping to meet some other agents first to weigh up my options, but terrified I might not meet anyone else, I signed with Jeff and within a few weeks I realised that with some agents it's all about the chase—and from then on I barely heard from the guy. I should have taken my time and signed with a female agent, one who perhaps actually liked women and wanted to see one succeed.

The fact is that as a female director, it's unbelievably bloody hard and even though women are really infiltrating and outshining men in the rest of the workforce—especially in middle management— not enough of us are getting nearly far enough in the world of

My dear friend, director Jamie Foley ... talented, yes, but judged entirely differently to me—a female director. The bias against women was so prevalent and pervasive then ... and the shocking news is that working women directors are just as scarce today! It simply hasn't changed. Possibly even worse now than then. This was at the opening of one of his early films, Reckless.

With my two big brothers, David and Geoffrey, on a trip back to Australia after I'd recently met Chris Thompson. He had not proposed yet and I had no idea we would marry and I would stay on in America. One of my big regrets, of course, is not having spent more time with my parents and my brothers over the years.

157

film directing. The Directors Guild of America (DGA) says that there are fewer women directing today than there were thirty years ago. The Sunday *New York Times* just did an alarming three-part series on the lack of women directing in both film and television. I found that the industry was sexist in really old-fashioned ways. For instance, as eager-beaver ambitious directors, Jamie Foley and I would go to DGA or Academy screenings or premieres of movies—to see and be seen and hopefully meet industry folk who might be helpful to us. Well, Jamie would work the room, and I would try to do likewise—though I knew far fewer folk so I would either trail behind him or chat to anyone I was lucky enough to know. But one morning, a producer called me and remarked that he'd heard I was seen 'partying up a storm' the previous night after a screening of a film a female friend had directed. I was horrified and angry and remember saying, 'No, I wasn't partying. A friend of mine made a movie and I went to see it!' But it dawned on me that as a woman, the *perception* was that I was 'partying' whereas Jamie was seen as 'networking', when in fact we had done the exact same thing, spoken to the same people and behaved in similarly sober fashion. You couldn't win.

But it was really no easier with female studio execs or the few women producers around. One felt they were determined to prove they didn't have a whit of extra sympathy for women for the very few showbiz openings, and indeed, I think there was so much jealousy and rivalry among women that secretly these gals who had the power to hire had no intention for the most part of giving a fellow female a break! One night Jamie and I had dinner with the powerful Paramount head Dawn Steel. I'd just finished directing two music videos back to back with Chaka Khan and one was pretty cool. Shot in black and white by cinematographer Michael Ballhaus and with lots of dancing extras, it was like an old Busby Berkeley musical with fabulous top shots of the kaleidoscopic dance sequences (I was the first to revive the Busby look—though many others followed). They were both made in New York, with the second video shot with the hilarious and sassy hip-hop group Fat Boys over one long night till dawn on the streets in the Village. Throughout the dinner, Dawn sat with her back to me, facing Jamie, peppering him with enthusiastic questions and finally, as the bill was paid, turned to me and said, 'You know, I'm off to New York and London next week and I really need some new clothes. Do you have any favourite new stores?'

Excuse me? I wanted to slap her but instead simply replied, 'Dawn, I really only wear vintage.'

She looked at me, frowning. 'You mean … ?'

'Yes, other people's old second-hand clothes.'

And with a slight shrug, I was dismissed. She turned back to Jamie and that was that.

A couple of weeks later, according to a diary entry I happened upon recently, I came upon another powerful woman in the biz. This time, at a dinner party, it was the super agent Sue Mengers, who remembered me well because she'd liked the *Sunday Times* interview I'd done with her several years before, when I was still with Michael White. I wrote in my diary:

Sat night—Dinner party with Jonathan Demme [director of *Silence of the Lambs* and *Philadelphia*] … I wear the beige dress and in some weird self-destructive way I put on pink diamond earrings and bracelet and don't look remotely like a serious-minded director. But as Demme later points out, his friend Joan Tewkesbury looks as serious as they come and can't get arrested, so surely once people talk to me they'll realise I'm a lot more than a blonde head of hair. Sue Mengers then comes up to me and gives me a 'healthy dose of advice' that leaves me utterly depressed.

'Forget it Lyndall, nothing's changed in this business for women, the same prejudices exist. And you're certainly not making life easy for yourself by looking like this. You look much too sexy. Dye your hair till you can get a job or at least buy a wig and put on a sack. You won't get anywhere looking like that—especially with the Frank Prices of this world running things. Jeff and Jim (my agents, Jeff Berg and Jim Wiatt) won't tell you this. They think you look too cute.'

She went on to suggest I pop back to London for a few months so that I don't get 'stale, over-exposed and in a rut'. The last bit of advice was odd for a struggling, penniless director—but the rest of it was all too true. A thoroughly sexist town then, *thirty* years ago—and *now*. Jeez.

And then one fateful day about three months after arriving in LA, I met the first of the many 'sons of powerful men' I was to meet. Jeff Berg sent me off to meet John Davis, the son of Texan oil billionaire Marvin Davis. Marvin had recently bought 20th Century Fox and John had just installed himself there as a producer. John was a fresh-faced kid of twenty-nine, who looked ten years younger, and at our first meeting at the 20th Century Fox commissary I could tell John was sizing me up to see if a chick with a hip new white-blonde crew cut might be pliable enough to be bossed around. I'd read the script he wanted to make—a coming-of-age story—and it needed work. With endless confidence I told him how it could be improved and made hipper and cooler.

After several meetings, it became clear that he thought he could have all the control with a female first-time feature director. I didn't listen to my gut, which told me I should hold out for something better with an experienced producer who wouldn't be threatened by my every suggestion or teasing attempts at humour, and foolishly, I took the job. But this son of the owner of the famous Fox lot had some definite control issues—a few weeks later, when a bout of bad food poisoning incapacitated me one night, John took it as a personal affront and hounded me with calls till I showed up, pale and weak, in the office a few hours later.

However, I became very invested, got on a creative roll and really grew excited as I worked with the screenwriter on a whole new draft, turning the lead character into a singer/songwriter and setting it in Miami. When we went on a location recce to Miami, I was more gobsmacked than I thought possible by the colours and the beach and the Art Deco buildings—and a fabulous outdoor dance hall, open to the stars, that I found. It was totally thrilling. This was '83, before the

A hideous peek into being a female director trying to find her way in the preposterously chauvinistic Hollywood world of the '80s. Rather than screaming, I thought I might try to make a joke about how John Davis, son of the owner of 20th Century Fox at the time (and who had never produced anything in his life), insisted he knew everything. Wildly frustrating.

TV show *Miami Vice*, and no recent movie had exploited the fabulous Art Deco side of Miami as a location.

But John was resistant to our changes and thought the film should still be set in the very middle-of-the-road Midwest. This was not a match made in heaven in terms of collaboration. Quite the opposite, and in retrospect, I don't believe I handled it as well as is crucial in these situations. But I had no support system as he was refusing to hire production designers and key personnel who could support my ideas and stand up for me, and I remember feeling incredibly alone and isolated. So on the odd occasion when I could get him on the phone, I would moan and groan to my agent Jeff Berg. Big mistake!

Now, I've been known to be overly dramatic in my time and I believe I may have said something to Jeff like, 'John's so controlling and difficult. He's a nightmare! This can't go on!'

Well, the head of a Hollywood agency is a busy man and likes to take care of business quick smart, and he apparently took me very seriously one day and called me back the next day to say he'd taken care of it. 'You're off the film. But I've gotten you a first-look deal at Fox and you get to have an office at Fox for two years …' and that was pretty much that.

I was speechless and started to say, 'I didn't ask you to get me off the film!' but he had to take another call and it was a done deal. I was in a complete state of shock for days and could not sleep—and even writing this now I feel just as upset and traumatised as I was when it happened.

In fairness to Jeff, I can only assume that John was ready to dump me anyway—but he may have simply been taken by surprise when one of the most important agents in town called and said, 'My client isn't happy. She wants out.' What if it was simply me bitching and complaining to an agent who took me way too literally? I took it very badly and was horrified and guilt-ridden for the longest time. And angry that Jeff and I had not had a conversation where I said I wanted to be *off* the film. But there was nothing to be done. Jeff dismissed me with a hurried, 'You're better off,' and that was that. A horrifying lesson that I truly had not learnt the art of the schmooze or how to handle insecure producers. I had the emotional intelligence of a gnat, took everything way too personally, and quite simply, I had blown it.

But had I? I wonder if it might have gone down differently with an opinionated *male* director who had strong creative views? I wonder if he might have garnered a tad more respect and support from his

On the Fox lot, in preproduction for a movie I got fired off … looking probably a little too glamorous for my own good. Barely a day goes by now when the scandal of the dearth of women directors in the biz is not mentioned in the papers, and the talk of all the unconscious biases against women is deafening. Makes me realise it wasn't just me they banished!

producer? I wonder whether the big-time agent might have done more to back up his male client, persuading the producer and studio execs that they'd hired him for a reason and to back off? Women directors are often treated like crap, like whining, complaining bitches instead of focused, highly motivated people who are just as capable as men, if not more so, of having an original creative vision and the confident chutzpah it takes to direct a film. Ah well … it could be explained away as sour grapes if the statistics of how few women film directors there are did not tell the true story.

The New York Film Academy's recent investigation into gender inequality in film found that only 9 per cent of directors are women and that there is a startling five-to-one ratio of men and women working behind the scenes in general. A male director whose movie gets excellent reviews and does well at the box office—despite no money spent on marketing the film and a blackout on personal publicity by a vengeful producer and studio—would still get another job in a New York minute and go on to thrive. When that situation happened to me, on the other hand, I was shut out and never directed another feature. A radio panel on this very subject came on recently as I was driving and I had to pull over as my blood started to boil. Everyone on the panel agreed that a woman with an unsuccessful movie, no matter how good it is, rarely works again, whereas men can have a string of flops and continue to work. There's a big movement to try to change the statistics and get women back in the saddle, but it's slow going. The asinine perception in the movie business is that men are better at handling big budgets and a big crew. In fact, it's often the absolute reverse, as women excel at multi-tasking and almost always come in on time and on budget, unlike their male counterparts whose egos get in the way—and they're great at being kind and considerate to crews!

And let's not start with ageism in Hollywood—and indeed everywhere. As Charlize Theron so brilliantly put it in a recent *W* magazine interview: 'Women, in our society, are compartmentalized so that we start to feel like we're cut flowers and after a while we will wilt.' But things will slowly change, right? They have to!

CHAPTER 14

Hollywood Hustle and a Home Birth

S O I ENDED up doing what directors on the hustle do in Hollywood—took tons of meetings to pitch cunning 'high concept' ideas that might be developed into a script. And to pitch oneself when there was a 'go' project and they were actively looking for a director. These took days to prepare for—rereading the script several times, making notes and getting ultra-prepared to persuade them I had the ideas and the balls to take it all on.

One meeting with the then head of Universal Studios, Thom Mount, seemed to go incredibly well. I felt I was on fire—witty, snappy and quick with ideas as the conversation took sharp turns hither and thither. I'd been persuaded to take a slightly off-the-wall male friend with me, Blaine, who I thought could help do the rewrites the script needed. We sat there together in a very deep soft sofa and as we finally left the meeting to high fives and convincing promises of, 'We'll be in touch,' the two of us felt pretty darn pleased with ourselves. But suddenly, as we waited for the elevator, Blaine started frantically patting his pockets. He'd lost something but it wasn't till we were in the car and driving back towards Hollywood that he had the guts to fess up—it was a vial of coke he'd bought the night before. He'd felt the need for a quick hit when he hit the men's room just before the meeting.

To my horror, he told me he had a feeling it must have slipped out while we were on the sofa! And sure enough, a day later Thom Mount's secretary called and discreetly asked if I'd 'left something on the sofa' when I was at the meeting? Great. Thanks, Blaine. And yes, that was the only call I received. Nothing from Mr Mount himself, naturally, as they don't tend to hire coke-toting directors.

So I just kept working … writing three different scripts at once. Endless networking. I managed to get some more music videos to direct, with one being particularly memorable: a ten-minute extravaganza for Warner Bros called 'Ocho Rios'. I recently found the clip on Youtube and watched it for the first time in nearly thirty years. Whoa! Talk about politically incorrect. It starred an eccentric gay singer/songwriter called Paul Jabara and was one of those 'story' videos with dialogue, a dozen dancers, extras and actors speaking lines! As I write I am gobsmacked by how campy and over the top it was—with a chorus (that I completely forgot about) that went 'Oh that negro, oh that negro!' as Paul, in full drag, drooled over a six-foot-eight, good-looking black man we cast. There were typhoons and stabbings and simulated boat rides and it all began with Paul stepping into a travel poster that came to life and became a Jamaican beach. I can't even recall how we did that, but I know it took a lot of thought! And there's my brother Geoff, who has extraordinary rhythm, as one of the fantastic dancers—along with my brilliant yellow Caddy with massive fins, used as a prop in a smoke-filled alleyway!

These videos were such fun to do, especially if you were fully prepared. (Although Chaka Khan's drug habits were anxiety inducing and once, before a shoot, when I went to discuss the storyboards with her, she opened the door to her Manhattan apartment stark naked and looking just a tad worse for wear. She proceeded to sit and listen, naked, to my now hurried description of what the shoot would entail as I tried to look everywhere but her big, busty naked self.) Yes, a wonderful diversion, but I was starting to have some odd, unsettling feelings. Firstly, much to my horror, I'd started to become alarmingly fascinated by babies and, having never before given two hoots for them, suddenly found myself staring into passing strollers, squeezing any bare, fat baby feet I could find and actually longing for a big, fat-headed one of my own.

I had one very cute boyfriend, a lawyer turned manager turned producer called Nick Wechsler, who was very cool and had great taste in movies, but when it ended he told me I had 'chunky thighs', so I decided I did not really like American men—until one fateful Saturday night I met a clever, very funny TV comedy writer, Chris Thompson. I was very reluctantly out on a date with a humourless young producer dude and a bunch of film folk at the old original Spago up on Sunset Boulevard. Chris sat there, radiating cool, and immediately got my attention with his stunningly quick and witty remarks. He was cryptic, dry and cynical and really made me laugh. Most of the guys I'd been out with were serious, ambitious and dull in a corporate goody-goody way. They played it safe and talked of wanting to get to bed early on a 'school night'—which covered every night except Friday and Saturday—and frankly, they bored me stiff. But did I really have to develop a crush on someone on the complete other end of the spectrum? A real 'bad boy' who openly admitted he'd just got out of St John's after a month-long rehab stay for cocaine addiction. A boy who'd run away from home, had been in juvy and had lived on Hollywood Boulevard with a stripper. I mean, seriously—was that strictly necessary? He was a high-school dropout who'd done a spot of plumbing before being discovered doing stand-up by comedy writer Garry Marshall, who thought he was seriously gifted and gave him a job writing for *Laverne and Shirley*. A few years later he created *Bosom Buddies* and cast an unknown Tom Hanks in it. But he partied hard and, like all addicts, didn't know how to put the brakes on.

He took my number and we started to hang out. Oddly, and I'm far from the type to have premonitions, the very first time I walked into his house I had the strongest feeling we would become a couple and I would live there. When I flew off to Australia a month or two later to work on a film musical project called *Cappuccino Boom Boom* that, alas, did not come to fruition, he followed me three days later in an impetuous but very romantic move that I found utterly compelling.

He loved all my Aussie pals and that seemed a great sign. My parents flew up from Melbourne to see us and they seemed to approve, though one meeting hardly suffices. Back in LA just a month or two later he proposed and I said yes. To my surprise, he was desperate for a baby—and was over the moon when to my shock I discovered I was pregnant. It was a complete mistake and it took me a few weeks to get used to the idea, but Chris was delirious immediately, running out to buy baby clothes and white booties the very day the pregnancy sticks turned a positive pink. It was a heady time with things moving at lightning speed, but despite some initial misgivings, I became a true Pollyanna, convinced I could 'make' the perfect life with this nutty but charismatic guy. We had a great engagement dinner with friends at a very hip, now defunct club called Helena's—and we were toasted all night by the likes of Jack and Anjelica, my Aussie director pal Maude and the actress Carol Kane. I was happy and proud and endlessly amused by my good-looking, sexy, quick-witted fiancé. Friends liked him. I adored him. We went to London and again I showed off my new fiancée. He went to a fabulous jeweller in Burlington Arcade who specialised in vintage rings and bought me a beautiful diamond ring. But funny people often have a very dark side.

I married him five months later in a lavish Hollywood wedding with a gospel choir and lots of London pals like Gael and her husband, Francesco, and Hollywood buddies like Tim Leary and Jack Nicholson as well as Mum and Dad, my sister-in-law Liz and her daughter Alex, who was a bridesmaid. Honey, my dear pal from Melbourne, was there in the wedding party, her daughter Angel another bridesmaid. Mandy, my darling Firbank friend, flew in, as did a wonderful London girlfriend, Charlotte. Geoff was there, but alas my other brother David did not come. I was blessed to have so many wonderful pals in attendance! I was deeply grateful I could still fit into the stunning cream satin gown designed by Hollywood costume designer Marlene Stewart as I was already three months pregnant. And frankly, it was amazing that Chris even made it back from the booze and drug-fuelled Las Vegas bachelor party that the fascinating Timothy Leary had organised with such exuberance, adding several hookers to really make for a memorable night (something I only found out months later). Chris was late for the church rehearsal, looked like death warmed up and could barely speak. I recall that my mother, who with Dad had flown over for the wedding and who never missed a trick, was not impressed by his late appearance. The wedding itself was just gorgeous with a full-blown gospel choir who sang both spirituals and something new— 'Waltzing Matilda'—and my darling dad walked me down the aisle after first stepping on my dress and nearly sending me flying. But the wedding bash was *really* fun, despite so many disparate groups, including the Aussie contingent, the friends who'd come from London, the local friends *and* 'the buddies of Chris'—mainly comedians and funny TV-writer friends. Just a few months ago Lola found the wedding video and popped it into an old VHS machine I still have.

The official wedding photo. Top row, from left to right: Liz Hales, Barry Diamond, Tom Hanks, Gael Boglione, the groom and bride, Honey Bell, Scott Banac. Middle row: Geoffrey Hales, Mum, Dad, Mitza Thompson, Mandy Zachariah, Kaya Bell. Bottom row: Alex Hales and Angel Bell.

Despite—or perhaps because—he was such a 'bad boy', I was nuts about the good-looking writer Chris Thompson. When he proposed marriage, just 5 months after a 'meet-cute' at Spago, I immediately said yes. He was sexy, funny, talented and wanted a baby at exactly the same time I'd shocked myself by becoming clucky! Not a hard decision to make … even if I had met him a few weeks after his first trip to rehab for coke. Here we are at our engagement dinner at a club called Helena's.

Wow! What a party. I was stunned to see the likes of Bill Maher, Tom Hanks and Garry Shandling all competing to be the funniest as they basically did stand-up for the videographer. I had never watched the video as the first few minutes were shaky and completely dark, and I assumed the entire thing was like that. But no, there it all was—a massive hoedown and to see my mum and dad and brother Geoff and so many friends all talking to the videographer or making speeches was just too weird and touching, and I had to run out of the room and leave Lola to watch alone!

Back to being pregnant. So, I had a deep mistrust of doctors and what I determined were their interfering ways with childbirth, and after a few visits to an OB/GYN and talk of amniocentesis, epidurals and the higher chance of a C-section at my age, I started thinking about taking back the power and having a home birth. I know, I know. I'm an idiot. But to my surprise, Chris was totally on board with this idea and we went to some home-birth classes, found a midwife and felt invincible. Thus, with not even an hour of morning sickness, feeling utterly brilliant and adoring being pregnant, I went about my business, directed a couple more music videos and impatiently waited, convinced it was a boy, for Tiger Thompson to arrive. Things were lovely for a while. Chris was a great cook and we entertained and had dinner parties and Christmas lunches—and Chris went along with it all quite happily, buying me a husky puppy for Christmas and trying to play just a little less golf.

The labour began one late summer afternoon when my brother Geoff and I were sitting in Olivia Newton-John's new store on Melrose, Koala Blue (which had opened a few weeks earlier with a big party and Dame Edna declaring it a true-blue Aussie outpost of style), enjoying a delicious chocolate milk shake. I started to have a few odd rumblings and since I was already a week overdue, it seemed wise to head home. We zipped back over the hill to Studio City and with a ludicrous amount of confidence, I called Chris to come home then popped on sweats and ran around turning on music and taking a few more photos of the gorgeous, newly decorated spare room all set up as a nursery, with shiny white crib and changing table, toys, sock monkeys and a gorgeous wooden four-foot-high Pinocchio. I lay on the bed to relax and the contractions seemed to have stopped. I called the overly casual midwife and she said to call back when the contractions were a few minutes apart. Well, the night wore on at a tedious pace and by about midnight I hit the huge Jacuzzi in the back garden, hoping it would both relax me and hasten the labour. Luckily, it was all going so slowly there was plenty of time for Chris to pop down to the local 7-Eleven when some guy called to say he wanted a $300 ransom for Molly, the wicked escape-artist husky dog. A few weeks earlier he had handed her over for just $200.

Suddenly the labour began in earnest. I was in utter agony and despite a very high pain threshold, finally began screaming so loudly that the neighbours called the cops, thinking someone was being murdered. When the police arrived Chris ushered me back to the bedroom and quickly tried to summon the midwife, who seemed to be possibly sleeping very soundly. As the pain now reached epic heights I longed for drugs and epidurals—the whole nine yards. Indeed, I began to panic and begged to be taken to hospital but just then the midwife finally arrived, announced it was too late for hospitals and that it was imperative I started to 'breathe'.

'Fuck breathing. Where are the drugs?' I screamed and just then my darling pal Honey, who had successfully birthed not one but two babies at home, arrived. Honey's arrival calmed me down and soon the midwife demanded that I get up and try squatting on the floor with Chris supporting my arms so that good old gravity might accomplish what doctors, drugs and forceps would otherwise be doing. To my astonishment, it worked and within just a couple of minutes, with Honey snapping some utterly extraordinary, quite discreet and miraculous pics, out popped a gorgeous and perfect baby girl. In literally seconds I was pain-free, filled with energy and utterly ecstatic as the champagne was opened and I realised that drug-free, bedroom childbirth was not remotely advisable but definitely a huge high with its wild, back-to-nature sense of accomplishment. I had deliberately not told my mum that I was planning a home birth as I knew she wouldn't approve—and indeed when I fessed up a few days later she was livid. I don't blame her. I'd feel the same if Lola was to try it.

Things were idyllic for a couple of weeks, maybe three. I remember one summery day in July, just ten days after she was born, swimming

Moments after squatting on the bedroom floor, out popped Lola Rose. It was that easy when the time came, but beforehand—a long and painful labour. I felt like an invincible pioneer woman, utterly ecstatic to find we had a gorgeous, healthy girl. Chris was so moved but it was only when I saw this photo that I realised he had wept. So thrilled to be a dad; so proud and besotted by his beautiful daughter.

in our huge grotto-like heated pool right after breastfeeding her. As she slept in a cute woven basket under a leopard-skin cover a few feet away under a tree, I thought, Wow, I'm really so very happy! To this day I remember that swim and the feeling of joy.

Then Chris got a very welcome green light on a TV show he'd written. In other words he was back in the stressful saddle as show-runner of another sitcom, so he'd begun boozing again, which he always did under pressure, and would rarely come home before midnight, if at all—sometimes it was a day or two later. It was a swift, cruel descent into feeling like a stranger, almost like the enemy. Many years later I was casually informed of an affair that began right then on that particular show but at the time it simply didn't occur to me. I just know that once, desperate because I hadn't been able to get hold of Chris for a day or two, I showed up at a Studio City bar called Residuals that I knew he frequented after work, along with lots of other TV folk, as it was just across the road from Radford Studios on Ventura Boulevard. I'd been driving round for hours with Lola in the back, looking for our dog Molly, who'd disappeared again, and Chris had responded to none of my calls. Carrying our 'bundle of joy', I went to the door of the bar, crept in a few feet and quickly spotted an animated Chris chatting up some girls at the bar. I'm afraid to say that I just felt too lame and pathetic to even bug him and I silently backed out of the joint. Any attempts at discussing our situation went nowhere.

I knew this marriage was not going to last. But I was in denial. What could I do with a tiny baby but hope that some miracle would occur and he would stop drinking and start behaving. We were growing apart but I had no idea what to do about it. He would not communicate and occasionally made references to the fact that he didn't feel he was good enough for me or my swanky pals. And since I was breastfeeding a baby I could hardly spend 'quality time' at his favourite bar. Such a strange time. I was never happier, with my ridiculously good-looking baby, but never feeling more alone. And then I got a feature film to direct.

CHAPTER 15

'SOBs' ...

ABOUT THREE MONTHS after Lola was born I was summoned to Paramount for a lunch meeting with Frank Mancuso Jr to discuss a film called *Back to the Beach*. I had read the script—a parody of old beach movies—and despite years of four or five writers toiling away, it was mediocre and unlike the brilliantly campy old beach movies. No one even broke into song. Frank had seen my Rowan Atkinson short and my *Saturday Night Live* short called *Hollywood Mom* starring Tracey Ullman, loved them both and it was clear at our lunch meeting (being taken to dine was always a positive sign) that I had a shot at getting the gig. When I mentioned the meeting to Chris, he told me that by some bizarre coincidence, he too had been approached—to work on the script. Now, in his heyday Chris was a highly paid script doctor who could pocket a ton of money for a complete rewrite—and sometimes just as much money if the movie had a green light and they were simply desperate for a quick comedy 'punch-up'.

So he was considering an actual offer whereas I had no offer, wasn't passionate about it and had already made plans to go to London to show off my Lola Rose to Gael. Chris was already working on a sitcom pilot and so off I went on my own to have a dose of London life and reminisce with old friends. Well, blow me down, if a few days into

174

the trip, the frantic calls started coming in from the coast, offering me the job and—oblivious, of course, to the concept of a long-awaited pleasure trip—asking if I could come back the next day! Ain't it always the way? You leave town, not caring less, and they offer you your first feature to direct. At this point I still had serious doubts but Chris called to encourage me and it's hard to resist the chance to direct a green-lit feature when your confidence has already suffered such a blow at the hands of a 'son of the boss' (SOB).

What I didn't quite realise was that *Back to the Beach*'s producer was another SOB. Frank Mancuso Jr's dad was not the owner but the chairman and head of production at Paramount. And it turned out that Junior was more neurotic and insecure than one could have thought humanly possible. In fact, he made John Davis look like a mensch! But it was definitely a 'go' picture—it was being fast-tracked to make a specific release date and so a few days later I bundled up Lola Rose and off we flew back to LA to a job, a dysfunctional marriage and, as it turned out, a gruelling six months dealing with a producer with whom I had zero rapport.

I soon met the preordained stars of the flick—Frankie Avalon and Annette Funicello—who were both utterly adorable and thrilled to go along with everything, especially my concept of turning it into a musical with retro beach outfits for dance numbers on the sand. Alas, we had to shoot in the middle of winter in Malibu. But the work environment was hostile from day one and most of my creative ideas were smacked down and obliterated. I persevered, however, and they agreed to turn the film into a musical. Soon the musical numbers alone were worth the price of admission—with Stevie Ray Vaughan and Dick Dale performing 'Pipeline', Pee Wee Herman singing 'Surfin' Bird' and Annette Funicello doing a fabulously upbeat version of an oldie called 'Jamaica Ska' with Fishbone. The number of old stars signing up for cameos was growing every day—from Don Adams (*Get Smart*) to Eddie Byrnes (*77 Sunset Strip*) to Bob Denver and Alan Hale Jr (*Gilligan's Island*) to Jerry Mathers and Tony Dow (*Leave It to Beaver*). Connie Stevens, Annette's nemesis from the old beach movies, was also a 'yes' and—I hate to say it—we even hired OJ Simpson, still a beloved sports hero at the time, to spoof a popular TV commercial where he jumped over a huge pile of luggage at the airport in his hurry to catch a plane. It was a couple of hours' work and he was gone. He was polite and professional if a little reserved.

But they foisted a First Assistant Director (AD) on me whose job, it seemed, was to do very little of a helpful nature but instead to spy on me and report to the brass in long meetings behind closed doors with Frank and his production manager, Marty Hornstein. Well, there's one hard and fast DGA (Directors Guild of America) rule—namely that a director gets to choose his or her own First AD, who will be supportive, empathetic and an advocate when cost is an issue but the director feels strongly that something is crucial for the film. A good AD will come up with solutions—either by scheduling things differently or suggesting something else can be eliminated to save time and money. Chris was being very slow to hand in pages—much to everyone's annoyance—but I was too busy with casting and dance rehearsals and finding locations and looking at costumes and designs for beach shacks to deal with a non-communicative husband who was still asleep every day when I took off to work. One morning at a meeting, with Chris still a few days behind turning in pages of the script, this First AD suggested in front of everyone that I try 'not fucking [my] husband for a few days' in order to inspire him to write quicker. The straw that broke the camel's back.

I'd had enough of this creep. I told Frank and Marty I wanted him replaced with an AD of my choice. They protested with tight-lipped fuming stares and more closed-door meetings and clearly didn't think I would go ahead with my threat. But I found someone, brought him in and they had no choice but to give in. However, there's no doubt about it, I had cooked my goose. Had I been a dude my actions would have been seen as tough, macho and completely justifiable. But I was female so I was instantly labelled a 'difficult bitch'. I had won a battle but was about to lose the war.

The next AD wasn't much better and feeling, as the director inevitably must, very alone, I lost about seven kilos over the next two months. We started shooting with only half the script finished, and as everyone from the production designer to the costume designer to the choreographer agreed, this was the shortest pre-production for a studio movie musical ever! It was daunting. Ever since the AD episode, Frank did almost everything humanly possible to avoid having to speak to me and instead let loose his grim production manager to deliver bad news at every turn. The highlight of the day was when the nanny appeared with my darling Lola Rose and I would continue directing with Lola on my hip. But even if I'd had lots of support, it was quite simply an incredibly difficult shoot—with, at one point, over a hundred extras, a reggae band, kids, surfers and Frankie and Annette all having to be wrangled on a wintry night shoot on a windswept Malibu beach. Nightmare! But quite honestly I did a great job and was proud of my efforts.

A questionable decision to turn my own helpless daughter into a punk extra for my movie Back to the Beach. *But it was a chance to have her on the set and she loved any excitement.*

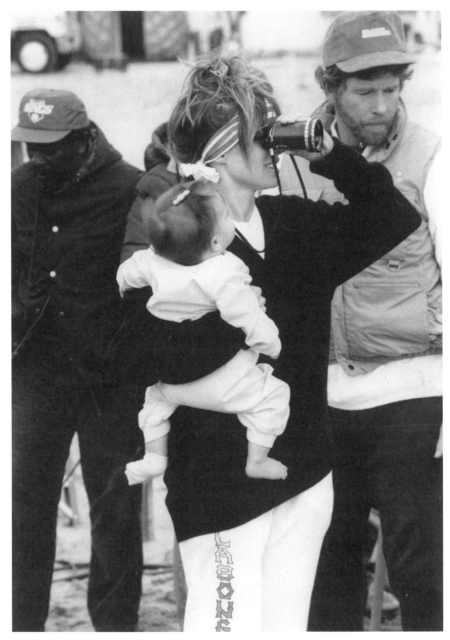

On the beach in Malibu for Back to the Beach *with seven-month-old Lola—a gruelling shoot in the middle of winter. With a very short pre-production period I still managed to turn it into a musical and complete it on budget and on time with no support—indeed, hostility— from the producer.*

About halfway through the shoot, Chris slipped off to Hawaii for a week of golf—and returned about five weeks later. Quite the adoring father and supportive husband—*not*! Week after week he promised to return but never showed. My birthday came and went—I'd told folks on the set that Chris would be back for it ... and as the birthday cake finally appeared at the end of shooting at Malibu that day, I could see the sympathetic looks and hear the crew's whispers as it was clear he was a no-show. The one person I could rely on for a good chat was my dear brother Geoff, who was working in the art department and designed everything from surfboards to bongos and beach shacks.

The film came in on time and on budget—a miracle, but I got no, 'Well done, Lyndall,' from Frank or Marty. I was given very little time to edit and at one point Frank simply re-edited scenes at night without me. I was shut out of the advertising campaign completely and Paramount's publicity office made sure not one single solitary interview was organised. It was as if the film had directed itself. Yet it still got dozens of genuinely excellent reviews, with Siskel *and* Ebert both giving it a big thumbs-up! Roger Ebert called it a 'wicked satire'. He wrote:

> This movie absolutely blindsided me. I don't know what I was expecting from *Back to the Beach*, but it certainly wasn't the funniest, quirkiest musical comedy since *Little Shop of Horrors*. Who would have thought Frankie Avalon and Annette Funicello would make their best beach party movie twenty-five years after the others?

But wait. Whenever someone is considering hiring you as a director, the custom is to call the last producer he or she has worked with, and so whenever anyone called Frank for a recommendation—*fuggedaboutit*. He trashed me completely. But worse than that, he and Marty made it their mission to actively put the word out all over town that I was a nightmare and not to be hired. Sometimes in meetings people would unwittingly say, 'Wow, I've heard some things ... but you seem so great.' Once on a plane ride to New York, Frank and Marty were sitting next to a writer friend of mine and out of nowhere, apropos of nothing, they launched into a vicious tirade against me—and they didn't even know this guy.

About a decade later, Marty had finally gone to AA for his very obvious substance abuse problem, and as one of the steps is to make amends, the man had the guts to call me out of the blue one day and apologise. Sounding genuinely remorseful he said, 'I'm so sorry for all the unpleasant things I said about you. You didn't deserve it.'

'Well thanks Marty, but it's all a little late,' I replied and hung up.

I'd like to be able to say that it was better to receive his apology late than never, but I'm not sure there's a way to make up for the damage he and Frank did to my career. They were bullies, and I was a woman, and that's just how things were. And, I'm sad to say, things are still this way. The best I've been able to do is accept the reality of my life. Acceptance is vital, and I'm trying my best to forgive.

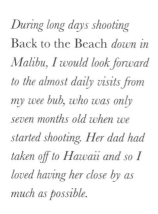

During long days shooting Back to the Beach *down in Malibu, I would look forward to the almost daily visits from my wee bub, who was only seven months old when we started shooting. Her dad had taken off to Hawaii and so I loved having her close by as much as possible.*

CHAPTER 16

Hollywood Mom—and the Marriage Is Over

T HE COMEDIAN Tracey Ullman and I met at a party at Peter Asher's house in the Colony in Malibu when we were both pregnant. We instantly became fast friends. A few months later we both had baby girls. Mabel was born just eight weeks before Lola and we really bonded seriously over a mutual determination *not* to let 'these needy, hopeless bloody babies' interfere with our fabulous careers. But of course we were actually completely nuts over them, and even though we tried to keep up and read *The Hollywood Reporter* conscientiously every day, we had to admit that we could barely think straight for a few months with the fun and excitement of our new bubs. I shared lots of laughs with the very witty Brit as we had endless play dates together, took the girls, and our pooches, to the dog park on Mulholland, strolled around Lake Hollywood or pushed the girls on swings in sunny playgrounds all over LA, gossiping and planning projects. We even went on a golfing weekend with our husbands— both golf-mad—in Palm Springs.

Although it's always a risk working with a friend, we had a lot of fun and no arguments at all when making a short film I directed for *Saturday Night Live* starring Tracey as a wildly ambitious TV star obsessed with fame and the size of her trailer! When she hears that a rival star has a slightly bigger trailer she suggests, 'Well, put one on top of the other then. That would work wouldn't it?' A hardcore harpy, she shrieks at her agent on the phone even as she's in labour and her husband's shouting, 'Oh honey, it's crowning, it's crowning' … Then there's one huge blood-curdling scream, which could either be childbirth agony or, more likely, ecstasy at the news she's just been given, 'Oh my God, I don't believe it! My *own shoooow*!!'

In the film she proves, while telling us what a caring mother she is, to be the most frighteningly distracted mum of all time—chatting on the phone to a producer while her daughter, Mabel, plays with knives on the bed next to her, flirting with the pool man as she ignores

My dear pal Tracey Ullman and I bonded over our two bubs, Lola and Mabel, who were born just a couple of months apart. This particular weekend—about a month before I directed the Saturday Night Live *short with Tracey—we went to a golf resort so our husbands could play golf while Tracey and I hung with the girls. It was definitely Tracey's idea to hang them upside down. (Tracey's producer husband died in 2013 after a long battle with prostate cancer and Chris tragically died in June 2015 of an accidental drug overdose on the eve of a comedy writing comeback.)*

Mabel, who actually falls into the pool. The babies, about three or four months old, had been precariously lying on a floating pool mattress— a questionable directing decision, but it still makes me chortle every time I see it. She then forgets that the car seat containing the baby is still on top of the car as she drives off. *Saturday Night Live* loved it and it had several airings. It was my favourite kind of black humour.

I raved about Tracey to Michael Fuchs, head of HBO, and told him he must do a TV show with her. He did. And it was a huge hit. I should have been on board as a producer or director but, as usual, I was a bit of a dope and simply happy to recommend friends, put people together and help get things going. I didn't have the killer instinct to get myself attached or compensated in any way.

Tracey and I hung at bashes given by veteran party-giver Penny Marshall and Carrie Fisher and met everyone worth meeting in Hollywood, especially the older stars and writers, whom I loved. George Axelrod, for instance, who wrote *The Seven Year Itch*, was as funny and entertaining as it gets.

Though I missed London and all my saucy, sophisticated friends every day, I felt at home in LA, with lots of other fabulous transplants from London like Eric Idle, Tim Curry, Tony Richardson, Ken Tynan's daughter Tracy Tynan, a Brit stylist named Sharman Forman and a fellow Aussie director, Evelyn Purcell. I reconnected with American folk I'd met in London like Lorne Michaels and of course Jack and Anjelica and Peter Morton (co-founder of the Hard Rock Cafe). Stylist/art director Michael Roberts was often in town and it was great to discover that Sabrina Guinness had just moved here to LA, along with some new Brit pals like dapper Charles Finch—who entertained constantly and gave a brilliant pyjama party where everyone acted like kids and donned their PJs—as well as the lovely good-time gal (Lady) Anne Lambton, who gave intimate Brit-style dinners in her Laurel Canyon eyrie. I could still throw a fabulous party with twenty-four hours' notice—and did, often with two friends who were now successful Hollywood managers, my ex-beau Nick Wechsler and Keith Addis. One big bash in Whoopi Goldberg's honour—she was looking for a manager and I told her Keith Addis was the answer, and she signed with him—went on later than most in LA, where folk like to be in bed on the early side. At least two hundred showed up, everyone from Barbra Streisand to Ellen Barkin and Winona Ryder to the very lively and adorable Robert Downey Jr, who, like 50 per cent of the guests, spent half his time in the bathroom getting mighty pepped up. People always showed up in droves as we made sure our parties were very light on agents and business, and heavy on pals and plain fun.

Other directing work followed—of more *Saturday Night Live* short films as well as TV commercials, music videos and episodic TV. One *SNL* short, starring the late, great Phil Hartman, revolved around Elvis still being alive and well and going to AA meetings with Art Garfunkel and exercise classes to lose weight before trying his hand at stand-up in a New York comedy club where the MC was a youthful-looking Larry David! I was attached to several films but after months of work they could disappear into the ether overnight due to lack of financing or not being able to get the right casting—or was it my reputation, thanks to Frank Mancuso Jr and his henchman Marty Hornstein? I was still looking for a great comedy script I could direct that would establish me as a comedy director. I came across one script that I instantly loved, a black comedy about a guy, a serious commitment-phobe, who falls in love with a girl once he finds out she has a terminal illness and it doesn't mean a lifetime together. Of course, only once he's moved in and proposed marriage does he discover that the diagnosis was wrong and she'll likely live a long and healthy life. I was wildly enthusiastic and my agent set up meetings for me and the writer to pitch it to a couple of studio execs.

The writer—single, depressed and rather dishevelled—was broke and didn't have a working car so I picked him up and drove him to the meetings, feeling so sorry for someone without transport in this sprawling metropolis. I shouldn't have fretted too much. It was Larry David and about six months later the show he co-created, *Seinfeld*, hit the airwaves and he's now worth—what? A billion bucks! Our project didn't get off the ground and the carless Larry and I lost touch. Damn!

When Chris walked out, Lola was just a tot. Very kindly, Jack invited us to jump aboard a private plane to get away from it all and enjoy summer in Aspen. He has a couple of houses there—as you do—and we stayed in one with my dear Aussie pal Honey and her daughter Angie. There was stunning fresh air, hikes and tree hugging—and it was a lovely break. No, she wasn't a shy child …

By this time my marriage was in big trouble. Yes, of course, it takes two to tango and I take responsibility. I wasn't coerced or drugged and forced to marry the guy. But I didn't know how to fix it. Chris simply wasn't interested—in me or in going to AA for help with his addictions to booze and cocaine. I did talk him into giving therapy a try. Just one visit about six weeks before the end to see some vile misanthropic excuse for a therapist in the Valley, who dismissed the whole marriage with a shrug and the charming statement, 'I have developed something I call "The Toilet Theory of Relationships". I believe people get together simply to dump their shit on each other.' Hardly surprisingly we never went back.

And so, one morning just before Lola turned two, the charismatic and talented addict I had married announced—with no fanfare at all—that he was 'no longer in love with me' and was 'outta here' … and two minutes later he'd packed a small bag and was gone. No explanations or apologies. It was brutal and quick.

His relationship with Lola became fractured and very inconsistent—but like all little girls, she adored the father she infrequently saw.

Perhaps I should have seen the light a little earlier, not been as desperate for commitment, a family and a sense of belonging—and to be rid of the feeling of being a disenfranchised Aussie. But, despite being an expert at it, why persist in heaping blame on oneself? Hooking up with Chris was a great move. I got one of the best daughters a mum could ever hope for and I'm now very good friends with her still-witty dad.

Chris, when he put his mind to it, was very handy! He could cook extremely well (and enjoyed it), unblock a toilet (having worked as a plumber in his early twenties)—and he could carve a mean pumpkin, much to our daughter's delight!

CHAPTER 17

Yet Another Move

For my sanity, I decide to move out of the teeny box apartment I've been subletting during the months of chemo and into a lovely Spanish apartment with a third bedroom for Lola and a double garage, which means I can get rid of my insane storage fees. In the last two years in LA alone, I've moved four times. And there were six moves in the four previous years I spent in Australia. The urge to nest somewhere is strong.

And so I've talked Lola into coming with her mother to the San Fernando Valley storage joint where I've had crap in storage since I sold my 6000-square-foot Spanish Hancock Park house eight years ago. I bought it when I split up with Al. It was a mess—but an original, untouched house split into two for different families but with amazing light fittings, fantastic Malibu tiles, double hand-painted ceilings, a *Romeo and Juliet* balcony and a panelled library. I did a number on it and it was just a sensation. Stunning but huge—with a guesthouse, a pool house and two huge basements that had all been filled by yours truly. And so furniture and baby clothes and boxes of photos that I refused to part with had all gone to a ten-by-twenty unit in the Valley eight long years ago.

When I returned from Australia I had all the stuff shipped back that I had optimistically shipped there, thinking I would find home back in the wonderful Land of Oz, but alas … it just didn't feel right once my dad had died. Four years of hanging out at hospitals, rehab centres and retirement homes had left little time to make a life again there, and besides, Lola was back in America. And so, at vast expense, my stuff came back to join the stuff that had stayed behind in the Valley. They loved me at All Aboard Storage.

And so, there we were, in blistering heat, unlocking the units for the two bad-tempered moving men, who stared at the boxes covered in about an inch of dust. As they piled it all onto the truck I tried to imagine where the big pieces of furniture would go—the lovely old green velvet armchair my dad had sat in for fifty years, the black velvet bed from my days with Mr Pacino in the stunning apartment I decorated from scratch on Central Park West, the gorgeous red mid-century sofa I'd found in Sydney, my granny's favourite old china and the hand-carved bench her grandmother had made … where exactly would it all fit in the new apartment?

I felt like my head might actually explode as I frantically opened boxes, hoping I might find some priceless gems I'd forgotten I owned. But no, apart from some nifty Dolce & Gabbana and Comme des Garçons clothes that Lola quickly spirited into the car, it was mainly just bedding and kitchen crap like Target tea towels and sad old spatulas—that has now become *the* most expensive crap of all time after travelling from New York to LA to Sydney to Melbourne, back to deep in the Valley and now to Hollywood. Yep, that's the kind of tight ship I run! I realised the full extent of my sickness when the guys informed me that a second back-up truck was needed.

The double garage at my new apartment was already utterly full and when I tell you that discovering I'd managed to hang onto two large filing cabinets filled with phone bills from 1997, along with letters, treatments and faxes sent to about two thousand producers and studio executives, was one of those major self-loathing moments, I think you know what I mean.

I find boxes of thirty-seven different drafts of *Mad about the Boy*, the romantic comedy script I'd spent seven years of my life on—a script that was two weeks from shooting in Vancouver with Melanie Griffith and famous DJ Howard Stern, who'd actually taken two weeks off his prime-time radio show to come and play a sleazy record producer, with me and Lola and Nick and the entire crew all there in hotels, totally overexcited as sets and locations were all locked! And then the producer had a meltdown and pulled the plug for no good reason. It's so sad seeing those shooting scripts and music cassettes of all the fabulous gospel music that Richard Perry and I had selected for the film … years and years of my life down a very disappointing drain.

Being the demented mum I am—with undertones of hoarding, more than a hint of sentiment and a dash of 'utter moron'—means there are the boxes of Nick's heavenly baby clothes plus an entire box of all his Batman costumes (he was a truly obsessed Batman and called me 'Robin' for a good two years), and photos of my dad in his Spitfire and stupendously sad and brave letters from his days as a POW on the Burma railway that seemed to come hurtling at me like missiles out of the dust. And old passports of my mother and postcards she had sent me from Crete on her way to join me for the European holiday of a lifetime back in the days when I had it all … and Beta tapes of me on my TV spot 'Hobbs's Choice' in London and huge one-inch cassettes of the short film *Dead on Time* that I'd directed—but no machines in existence to even play them any more. They have to go …

But not the twenty-five boxes of fantastic albums from my former life. Photos of Jack and Anjelica and Michael and me, and Mick Jagger and all of us at the Red Ball in Paris or lying on the beach in St Tropez or going to see Bob Dylan with Diana Vreeland or at the bull ring in Ibiza on acid watching Bob Marley or interviewing Andy Warhol for the *Today* show … these memories rushing at me, as we stuff yet more boxes into the garage, take their toll. In all, I've moved about eighteen times in thirty-two years. It's too much. And the unpacking is gruesome. I feel ill and hot and sweaty and still toxic and poisoned after a year of mammograms, missed diagnoses, botched biopsies and waiting and being told I'm fine and then being told I'm not fine and then another biopsy and a lumpectomy, chemo, steroids, a double mastectomy, four general anaesthetics, three subsequent surgeries, ten weeks of antibiotics, the electric sessions, the oxygen treatments, the Vitamin C infusions and the expanders being expanded and the needles and IVs—so many needles … there's not a lot of zip in my step right now.

As far as the surgery decision is concerned, I have no more energy to give it and so I decide to continue with Dr Bob. He schedules the surgery to try and restore my breast for one week hence. But I'm so deeply tired that three days later I put the surgery off for two weeks so that it will be eight weeks from the last surgery, and I can be uncommonly *sensible* and rest, do yoga, eat well and go to bed early and meditate. None of which I do, naturally. I feel compelled to unpack every last idiotic possession and get the new place totally together for my kids. How can I come back home from yet another surgery and fight my way past boxes full of things I forgot I had?

I consciously try not to stress my kids out too much with all this moving I put them through, but I do drag Nick to Ikea once. A mistake. He's taken to acting like his very sensible, miserly sister and thinks he can bitch about my spending. Realising he makes some good points I angrily take a few things out of the trolley as he says deeply irritating things like, 'It may be only ten bucks but it all adds up, Mum!' And so by the time we're in the car I scream, 'It's funny how you didn't mind me spending *seventy* dollars on your brand-new purple suede skate shoes yesterday, Nick! Funny about that but I'm not allowed to buy a genius paper-towel holder to help me stay organised!' and then we scream at each other for a while and I say, 'You need to take some responsibility and do your share of the homework on your own without tutors!' and then he screams that he doesn't care about school and tutoring and he'll 'just live in a sewer' and we don't speak the rest of the way home.

But, ten days and six trips to Home Depot and Ikea later, I've bought yet more extension cords and picture-hanging hooks, hammered and assembled and glued and stood on ladders and hung mirrors and made everything, especially the kids' bedrooms, look pretty darn great. I do sometimes wish there was a good man who would appreciate my manic ability to make a wildly stylish yet cosy home. I mean it's not everyone who has the foresight to bring their Aussie electric pizza maker and seven fabulous old lamps to America and then find the cunning store that sells Oz-to-US converter plugs. Am I right? Frugal and a connoisseur of good lighting! (Seriously, I'm actually very good at this and have a business and website to flog my decorating skills.)

So on Sunday night after hitting the Cactus Taqueria on Vine for our dinner and after barely stopping for two weeks straight, the lovely '40s Spanish-style apartment is looking pretty together, and I relax for the first time with my kids in the living room with a fire blazing and hit the hay by midnight. Next morning I take the heavenly teenager to school and *insist* on a kiss in the car because he's staying the night with friends—as his silly old mother has her *fourth* surgery for the year coming up in a few hours.

So here I am back at St John's for the late surgery to put the expander back in and give me a semblance of two breasts. The tedious admissions procedure again … the taking of the vitals, signing many, many forms I never read and remembering with guilt that I have yet to make a will!

Dr Bob's late again and I run to the toilet to drink from the tap just cos I'm thirsty and a rebel and it's 5 pm … and here's the shocking truth. I look forward to being put out because I *need the rest*. I wake up at 12.30 am, and there's my divine, smiling daughter, who's been waiting for hours for her mother to wake up and be brought back to the hospital room. My hand goes to my chest and yes, there seems to be something resembling a breast there.

'A chilled glass of good French champagne would go down well right now,' I chirp brightly. But after a few minutes I see that my poor angel, who started her day at 6 am at the coffee shop and then had a full day at college till 10 pm, looks shattered and I wish I'd come round sooner. I kiss her goodbye and she's gone. I lie there feeling guilty that I left home in Melbourne at twenty and never went back.

I didn't ever just get a chance to hang out with *my* mum, help her out or have this kind of closeness with the dear mother I adored. I did my best from afar—and when I did a Qantas commercial in my early days in London, I gave the two first-class tickets I received to my parents to visit me in London, fly to Paris with me, stay in the South of France with us, hit Monte Carlo and generally have a wonderful time. 'The trip of a lifetime,' as my mum put it as we said a tearful goodbye at Heathrow. And I flew to Australia almost every year to visit. And I sent tons of letters and postcards and albums I made them along with weekly phone calls. But if you live over sixteen thousand kilometres away, the distance takes its toll. For me, the guilt is monumental and seems to be fade-resistant.

I go to sleep wishing to goodness I was capable of following orders and sleeping on my back, especially as I just read in *Us Weekly* that Tom Cruise sleeps on his back to avoid wrinkles around the eyes and neck.

By 7 pm the next day the angel posing as my daughter brings delicious salad from Wholefoods with tuna and mint and beans and I feel better immediately. A note to hospitals all over the globe—good healthy food makes you feel better! Even Lola nearly gags when she takes a bite of my hospital turkey dinner and agrees that it's beyond inedible. I soon send her home to hang with Nick, who's been shockingly sweet on the phone and has told me he made himself pasta for dinner and is doing his maths homework. It's amazing how easily kids just straight out lie (I know this because the maths teacher later emails to say it was not done!). I give him many, many instructions for packing as he's being collected tomorrow at 10 and taken to LAX for a flight on his own to New York to spend Thanksgiving with his godmother.

He suddenly says very sweetly, 'I'll miss you Mum. Will you be okay?' I know it's a worried tone. I can only imagine how worried he's been this past year. It's hard to tell how much fear has swirled around the brain of a gorgeous thirteen-year-old who's growing like a weed, has size-twelve shoes and who shaves, speaks with a manly deep voice but still gives very big hugs. He's moved nine times, been to five different schools (two in Australia), has tutors three times a week to help with failing grades and a mother who swears like a trooper. But no boy has ever had a more doting mum or a more fantastic, loving sister. We give and demand more annoying kisses than most, so he knows he's loved and gives tons of affection back—but it doesn't stop the guilt for all the drama I've dumped on myself and my kids with my insane choice to have a double mastectomy.

By 9.30 pm Dr Bob shows up after a day of surgery, helps me off with the bra contraption and I suddenly realise it's the moment of truth as he takes off the bandage—not completely but enough to see that it could well be a minor miracle. He didn't lie. My breast skin seems to be uncrumpled, it looks like a normal breast and I'm happy!

My darling, good-looking dad in Canada, about to go on a training flight in his Spitfire. The RAF boys got to name their planes and Dad's girlfriend before the war was Shirley—an absolute shocker, who, unhappily married, would call drunk on a Saturday night during my parents' marriage, and who finally nabbed him once my mother died.

This is a good outcome. Some of my deep, deep anger towards Dr Bob subsides as he swiftly disappears and I start to tidy my room and make my bed again. I collapse into bed in a lot of pain and press the buzzer, hoping I can rustle up some pain meds quick smart.

Yes, I'm very thankful that I have a smooth breast but grow weary as I remember that both breasts have just temporary expanders and so this is not my final spell in St John's.

It was bi-coastal living and bi-coastal entertaining: in retrospect, pretty darn wonderful, and of course there were so many fascinating folk to see in Manhattan. This was one of many evenings at a great house we rented on the Upper East Side. From left: me, my great friend screenwriter Buck Henry (of Catch 22, The Graduate *and* Heaven Can Wait *fame) new pal the legendary Lauren Bacall and my dear pal and Nick's godmother, talented casting director (*The Sopranos*) Sheila Jaffe.*

CHAPTER 18

A Single Mum ... but Not for Long

T HE DAY AFTER Chris packed his ridiculously small gym bag and left the Studio City house for good, I found myself sliding to the kitchen floor and dissolving into a sobbing heap as I tried to load the dishwasher filled with brightly coloured melamine baby plates and bowls, and fat spoons and forks for chubby little fingers to hold. It had just truly sunk in that I would be raising my daughter as a single mother. *It wasn't the plan.* And whatever came to pass, the dream of Lola growing up in a warm, cosy, tight-knit happy family had gone up in smoke. I knew he wasn't coming back and that even more importantly I shouldn't want him back. But the pain and guilt seeped into my very bones where it has happily lodged ever since. Jack Nicholson invited me and my girlfriend Honey to get out of town and come visit him in Aspen with our respective daughters. It was summer, so no snow—just beautiful walks in the fresh air, some tree hugging and Jacuzzi time. I happily accepted.

But if the pain of losing a husband felt bad, it was nothing to the pain of losing my mother a few months later in Melbourne. She'd been chronically ill for years and on my parents' last visit to see me in LA just months earlier, she had been horrifyingly thin and weak and seemed to be fading away before our very eyes. I took her to doctors and we tried to work out what was causing her complete lack of appetite and general malaise, but she didn't want to have a battery of tests and would say, shockingly, that she felt fine. I believe she was stunningly depressed and yet her Australian doctors, who rarely if ever prescribed antidepressants, did not seem to see it—nor did they do enough in my opinion to work out the root causes of whatever was making her so sick and tired.

I flew out to see her when she was already in hospital and slightly 'away with the birds'. Were they pumping her with morphine? I didn't have the gumption to really get into it with her doctors at that point. She was just so sad and ill. But then I did the unthinkable. A few days later I booked a meeting with some bigwig I had been waiting to hear from, and with Lola back at the house with a nanny and Chris, and the prospect of a job, I decided to fly back. Mum told me I 'had been a good daughter', and weeping hysterically, I left her in a hospital bed and flew home. I arrived back in LA to find the meeting had been cancelled, and two days later my dad called to say she'd just died. I will never forgive myself for leaving and to this day don't know what possessed me to do it. The guilt is as keen today as it was then. I flew back that night with Lola and my brother Geoff and that was that. I dreamt about taking her to doctors and getting her better for years to come—only to wake up and start sobbing when I realised I had *not* done that and she had gone.

Divorce proceedings began, and soon enough I was sent packing from the Studio City house Chris had owned before we met to look for a rental. The first one I decided to go and look at sounded perfect—a '50s house in the hills with spectacular views. By a bizarre coincidence, it turned out to be the very location I'd chosen for Frankie and Annette's nifty Midwest house in *Back to the Beach*. Built by and for the architect who designed wonderfully kitsch, stylish things like the Cup and Saucer ride at Disneyland, it was divine. Pink brick with a flat roof, a cactus garden out front, rock walls, terrazzo floors, a stunning kitchen, curvy ceiling with concealed lighting to make it glow and floor-to-ceiling windows looking out over the entire Valley, it became one of my favourite houses of all time. It was glamorous, but intimate, cheerful and a fantastic party house. Indeed, it became party central on many a night over the next few years. Lola loved it and had lots of sleepovers with multiple girls from her kindergarten class at Campbell Hall, her new school, in the giant living room. After feeling so shell-shocked by recent events, I started to see the light at the end of the tunnel. I dated a couple of dudes and realised that while I wasn't totally washed up, my heart *still* wasn't in it.

One Saturday night, I called Judy the babysitter, and after a gruelling farewell to Lola—who had a complete wailing, flailing melt-down when I tried to kiss her goodbye, clinging to my legs begging me not to go—I finally, after reading her three more bedtime stories, forced myself to head out on my own to a party. I'd been invited by the host, a relatively new friend, the good-looking composer Richard Baskin, who I'd met when I had my office on the Fox lot. A truly good, kind person and a total doll! I walked through his front door with that sick, nervy feeling I always have walking into a party I'm not giving. I'm basically a shy person, not good at small talk, and thus wouldn't dream of approaching strangers at parties—instead making a beeline for a familiar face, no matter who!

Well, I looked around and there standing by the fireplace was Al Pacino. We hadn't spoken in about six years though I had seen him twice in that time. Once I was crossing 57th Street in New York and he called out, 'Hey Lyndall,' and waved from the passenger seat of a passing car driven by his trusty driver Marlon. I waved back and he drove on. I also bumped into him, literally, in the crowded hallway of Bruce Willis's house at a Labour Day weekend party as I arrived with Chris, cradling a two-month-old Lola in my arms, and Al was following a begloved Diane Keaton out the door. We said 'hi' and smiled, he didn't seem to notice the small human I was schlepping— and that was it.

But here he was, smiling at me from a few yards away, so I sauntered over only because I could see no other familiar face in the crowded room. We started chatting and the six-year gap melted away. I felt like we'd seen each other just a few weeks ago. There was no awkwardness at all—and anyway, he was with Diane Keaton as far as I knew. As if reading my mind he asked, 'Where's your husband?'

'It's over—he left me,' I replied.

'Really?' he asked almost skeptically, and for the first time I replied quite happily, 'Yes. It's very much over.'

As always happens at parties with Al, folks were lurking feet away ready to pounce and I wandered off, determined to play it cool and give him space. But about twenty minutes later he found me, took my hand and said, 'Come with me.' He led me outside to a courtyard and said, 'I'm just so happy to see you. There's chemistry between us still. Can't you feel it?' My stomach lurched with a rush of romance-induced adrenaline and I felt positively giddy but quickly pointed out that he had a long-time girlfriend, Diane Keaton. 'We're through,' he insisted emphatically and with a smile added, 'I'm available!'

'Well I'm sure there's tons of females around who'll be thrilled to hear it,' I cheerfully responded, attempting to be flippant and winningly casual.

'Are *you* happy to hear it?' he asked solemnly, those gorgeous dark eyes boring into mine. He hadn't let go of my hand yet.

I smiled and shook my head. 'Absolutely not!' But I suspect my idiotic giggling-schoolgirl demeanour gave me away since I was happy to hear it. Very happy.

He pursued me over the next few weeks and all hesitations were soon abandoned. Firstly, he seemed so much lighter and happier and less invested in being the tortured artist. This was a new and improved, way more upbeat Al. And secondly, it's lonely on your own in LA—or anywhere else for that matter. I craved romance and affection and pretty soon we were madly in love and back together. It was fun and incredibly exciting. He could tell a great yarn, whisper sweet nothings and generally be as amusing and seductive as any human being I've ever met.

There were just one or two teeny-tiny drawbacks. For one, since he lived in New York, he only came to LA to shoot movies—this first time round it was *Frankie and Johnny* with Michelle Pfeiffer—and he would then turn round and go right back to his beloved New York, where he had an office/hangout in the city and a home base thirty minutes up the Hudson River. And so less than four months after we got back together, Al was packing up—not literally, of course, as there was a bevy of 24/7 drivers to do his bidding in two cities—to go back east. After a couple of weeks of phone calls, talk of my joining him began and I was all in favour of it as I realised that the relationship had no chance of surviving unless we were in the same town. I fretted that Chris would not want Lola to leave California. No need. In exchange for a big reduction in child support, we were free to go.

It started with a couple of exploratory trips to New York to look for apartments in the city and find a school for Lola. On the first count, Al couldn't care less about his surroundings and should have left it all to me, but ever careful with money, he wanted a reasonably priced rental and refused, over the years, to ever contemplate buying his own apartment in New York. Utter madness as I eventually found him a couple of absolute gems that were a total steal. Anyway, once I settled on the posh Upper East Side Hewitt School for Girls (where the headmistress quaintly shook hands with each girl on the school steps each morning) and we found an apartment not far away, Lola and I moved to New York.

In many ways it was thrilling and certainly endlessly entertaining to watch folks' reactions to Manhattan's very own living legend of an actor. Realtors showing us apartments would be in such a state of excitement they could barely breathe or speak, the elevator man would beam maniacally and thank Al for all 'the joy man, you're a genius man' while any devoted *Scarface* fan would virtually genuflect and kiss Al's hand. The outpouring of love and sometimes downright grovelling in the streets, restaurants, the park or at Broadway theatres was endless and exuberant, and unlike in LA, where interaction with the public is limited, life in Manhattan provided a constant meal of adulation and compliments for a hungry actor. Al was always very friendly and gracious to his fans.

He was pretty much the King of New York and, like royalty, he didn't care to shop or deal with money. He liked to sign for the bill and several of his favourite haunts like Joe Allan's or Orso's were happy for a quick signature on the bill at the end of a meal, but many waiters at other places were utterly nonplussed when Al would take the bill, produce his ever-present Sharpie (which is the stars' pen of choice to autograph shiny 10 × 8s) and make his signature squiggle. I would immediately recognise the confused, embarrassed stare and remind Al that he didn't have an account at this particular establishment and to hand over the plastic. He would invariably express shock that his signature was not enough, and indeed some managers would scurry over and be very happy to just get an office number and leave it at that, but if pressed, Al would produce a credit card with good humour,

Depending on the year and the movie, Al and I moved back and forth between Los Angeles and New York. But as soon as we moved back to LA there'd be a reason to go for a quick trip to New York and then we'd stay in big suites in fancy hotels like the Carlyle. Buying an apartment would have made sense, but Al's business manager, Ken Starr, now in jail for fraud, discouraged that …

often get me to add up a very generous tip and charm everyone within listening distance.

But shopping was out. Only twice in eight years did I get Al into an actual shop. Once we were down in the Village about to see an off-Broadway show and a temporary cap came loose on my top front tooth—anyone's idea of absolute living hell but having always had teeth problems, it was something I had nightmares about regularly! In an effort to keep Al fit, I'd been my usual tedious nagging self and talked him into playing squash in a Midtown health centre with me but during our very first session he managed to whack me hard in the face and send my front tooth flying. The sight of a big, dark gaping hole where my front tooth had been was nothing short of shocking and utterly traumatising. Al sweetly took me to his dentist, who saw us immediately, and stayed with me as I lay in the chair while the cavern was filled, hoping he would quickly forget the horrifying sight. So when I stupidly chewed some gum and felt the temporary cap come loose a few days later I practically fainted on the spot. When I suggested that he go into the drugstore on his own to get the dental glue for me, he looked at me like I'd suggested he jump into a pit full of snakes or take over as commander of a space ship! I imagined him thinking, 'What about "National Living Treasure" do you not understand? I'm an icon. I do not go into stores alone. Ever.'

But when he did finally agree to come into the drugstore *with* me to find the glue, I realised that a grown man, my boyfriend—like many other movie stars—lived in a world where he didn't have to shop, cook, clean, get gas, pay bills or do any of the things that take up so much of we mortals' daily lives. So, after expressing utter amazement at the variety of shampoos now available, he admitted it must have been a good ten to fifteen years since he'd last actually been inside a *shop*, and while it was tempting to slap him across the kisser, I needed to be very still in order to keep my loose tooth in place with my tongue, so I simply smiled, bought my tooth cement and dragged him off— rescuing him from a gaggle of gasping shoppers who had spied him lurking in a corner studying aftershaves. By the way, I was just as guilty as anyone of keeping him in the bubble and catering to his needs. I'm definitely in the caretaker category—and as such felt compelled to always pamper and soothe him, from the Kiehl's moisturisers I would buy him to eventually dragging him to have fancy Midtown facials and detoxifying seaweed masks—and once a seaweed bath! Some things were short-lived, like the house calls from manicurists and yoga instructors, but I was persistent and bugged him to work out and try to drink less coffee—especially as he was such a bad sleeper and I thought both would help. What he really appreciated was someone to share a late-night bowl of ice-cream with or a little chocolate treat, and frankly, a sexy smile from Al and a growled, 'Thanks, honey,' in that wonderfully low, gravelly voice, kept me happy for years. Let's face it, I'm a sucker for charismatic, entertaining and witty guys. With a strong dash of narcissism.

The only other shopping sortie involved my birthday one year, and as we were already in Soho one lovely summer Saturday afternoon, I convinced him to come with me into Comme des Garçons—one of my favourite stores of all time. Unfortunately, in that never-ending caretaker role, I'd already spoilt him rotten by getting the fabulous store to deliver suits and shirts and waistcoats and shoes to the apartment for Al to choose from—with a lot of guidance from me—and so along with other items of clothing I organised and bought for him, he truly had no need to actually go to any establishment to peruse or purchase. But on this one day, with the chic, young but very discreet salespeople in awe at the sight of Al in the flesh, he stayed long enough—approximately four minutes—for me to try on a long navy-blue skirt (which Lola wears to this day), buy it and that was that. The one big shopping spree. Al didn't do gifts. Never bought me one. Nor did he expect them, but I was an incurable romantic and idiotically over-generous gift-giver who spent an inordinate amount of time and money thinking up fabulous gifts of paintings, rings, photo albums, cashmere sweaters and such. On his birthday, only a couple of months into our reunion, I had music and flowers and gifts sent to his trailer on the movie set—with instructions to listen to a particular number on the Bob Dylan CD—my favourite song of the moment and one I thought so apt, 'Tight Connection to My Heart'. Barely a peep from Al. I don't think he ever listened to the CD. He was shooting a film and that took precedence.

So anyway, here we were in New York, everything hunky dory, except that actors get offered jobs at odd, unpredictable and very random times. And so, no sooner were we settled in than an offer for another movie in LA would appear and it was time to up stakes, pack every single thing for me and Lola (Al did not want the expense of keeping the apartment on so they were always let go) as well as Molly the dog, and all head off in a limo to the fabulous but now sadly defunct MGM Grand Airlines terminal where, once on the plane, a lovely 'booth' would be reserved for us with two lots of seats facing each other and a table in between. Molly the very well-behaved escape-artist husky dog preferred the window seat to look out of and would gently nibble at treats on a plate provided by Lola. Al would sit with a pile of scripts he rarely looked at but instead would ask me to read for him—though he was always happy to open up a well-worn copy of *Richard III* or *Salome* and contemplate a return to his first love, the theatre. There's a reason his career, especially in the theatre, has lasted so long—he has a true appreciation of great writing and relishes any chance to hit the boards and portray some of the classic larger-than-life characters in literature.

Once back in LA, Lola and I would return to the pink house and I would drag out the cute little pale pink uniform so Lola could return to her LA school, Campbell Hall. Al, always keen to have his own space for poker games and meetings, would usually take a hotel suite or rent a house, depending on how long he planned to stay. There was also the matter of his phobia of anything resembling a permanent, cosy domestic scene and old habits die hard. He was always jealous and proprietorial but obsessed with his independence and his image of himself as a 'lone artiste'. It meant a permanent sense of chaos and impermanence for me—but a woman in love can put up with an awful lot.

My career? I was in a panic. It had lost momentum and being with Al and mixing with lots of famous, powerful folk did me no good at all. In fact, looking back I think it was counter-productive since it's often the case that an attractive 'unknown' woman on the arm of a movie star is not taken seriously. I would run round trying to get meetings in an attempt to get *Jane's Turning 39*, an older woman/younger man romantic comedy I'd written, financed and made, but during meetings I found that the conversation always came round to Al! What was he up to, was he attached to this or that movie project? Even, shockingly, how did we meet and was he a romantic boyfriend? It was wrong and depressing and I doubt very much that a male director dating a female star would have been asked these questions. And then would come truly annoying suggestions that he should play the part of the older record producer *or* that he should exec-produce the film. As it happens he would have been perfect to play that part, and certainly, having Al attached as exec producer, even just in name, would have made all the difference and led to a green light.

But of course I didn't dare ever mention such things to him and instead just tried to be the best girlfriend I could be—sending multiple faxes a day to his various assistants in New York and LA making sure that his trainer was booked, that he had vitamins, healthy foods and scented candles in his trailers, and had massages, facials and paddle-tennis games booked for some weekend fun by the beach in Santa Monica. Playing paddles down by the beach in Santa Monica, with his old friends like Ken Sylk (a divine writer and funny sweet guy, married to Denise Crosby—granddaughter of Bing, and who has become perhaps my very best friend in LA) and Richard Baskin, was one of our favourite outdoor things to do. Al, looking madly clown-like in big baggy shorts worn over his favoured black silk pants, and I made a great doubles team. Afterwards Al would lie on the sand in the sun with Lola and life would feel normal for a short but lovely spell. Short because Al has extraordinary energy and rarely relaxes for long. Two of my favourite mini breaks with him (always mini—five or six days max!) were a road trip to Santa Fe—where we listened, en route, to Robert Hughes's *The Fatal Shore* on tape, which he found fascinating—and a trip to Venice. Just divine, when we finally got away from crowds, awards and the paparazzi and were taken on long cruisy open-air boat rides along the canals.

And the parties continued, as Al deserved, in my opinion, to be feted whenever nominated for Academy Awards and such. Or any old time really. I loved to surprise him with birthday parties. A fabulous joint one the first time with Ken Sylk, who shared a birthday, and I could tell Al was just very chuffed by the elaborate cake and lots of mad decorations. Dinner parties. Game nights where we played Celebrity, a mad Hollywood version of Charades which Al at first, feigning shock, said he would not partake in, but of course I told him not to be a party pooper and he obeyed from then on in. I tried to make him do things slightly out of his comfort zone and was often, but not always, successful.

And one party, given at my house in LA, may have surpassed all others in terms of the 'glam' quotient. Al had been quite rightly nominated for his fabulously witty and electrifying performance as Big Boy Caprice in Warren Beatty's *Dick Tracy* and, as I've said, was leaving behind his 'mystery man', antisocial phase and entering his amiable, outgoing period where he really enjoyed people and the praise they heaped upon him. And he could really make a party pretty special with his amazing and irresistible brand of charm and humour. He's a very, very funny man and, alas, has not often had the chance to showcase his comedy 'chops'.

People turned out in droves to this party I whipped together single-handedly in a few days. Despite his having been superb in so many great parts, Al had never won an Oscar. This was his sixth nomination, and it definitely seemed appropriate to celebrate. (Once more, he did not win, but two years later he won a Best Actor Oscar for *Scent of a Woman*.) No fancy invites, just phone calls. (Today, it would be a studio affair—corporate, staid and probably not in a private home.) Guests included Whoopi and Warren, Barbra Streisand and Madonna, Phil Spector and Michelle Pfeiffer, Richard Harris and Andy Garcia,

Robert De Niro and Jack, and Ellen Barkin, to name a few. I hired a wonderful Sikh vegetarian chef, Akasha, to cook delicious food and made sure, as usual, that there were tons of desserts and chocolates for my sweet-tooth, teetotal boyfriend. It was a huge hit—a real doozie. Agents and managers would call and angle for an invite and if I'd had a brain in my head I would have used my 'juice' as the hostess to parlay it into some meetings but I was far too concerned with keeping Al happy and keeping the fetes strictly non-business. It means they were pretty special and chic and a sought-after invite. Al really loved this particular bash.

The once shy and retiring Al was thrust into party mood by yours truly, who felt he should be feted for all his work and, in this instance, his nomination for an Oscar for Dick Tracy. *He would generally say it wasn't necessary to have a party—but after a while he plain loved them! Why the heck not? It was fun to see him enjoying the fuss, especially as they were intimate gatherings devoid of agents or execs.*

Backstage with Barbra after a concert she gave at Madison Square Garden. I'd known her for a few years and was just utterly gobsmacked by her skin, which was flawless with not even a hint of a line to be seen. I would sit and stare at her, demanding skin care tips. Her best? 'Don't make too many facial expressions!'

One of the all-time great parties I gave for Al—for his Best Supporting Actor nomination for Big Boy Caprice in Dick Tracy. *It was a big ol' megastar turnout: Jack, Warren Beatty, Richard Harris, Barbra Streisand, Madonna—and in this photo we see Whoopi Goldberg, Michelle Pfeiffer and Ellen Barkin. He was stunned by how many showed to congratulate him.*

Madonna came with Warren and was riveted to meet my clever chatty daughter, who was in her best dress, immediately announcing that she *loved* the name Lola, and if she had a daughter would call her Lola too. Copycat! She and my Lola were inseparable, discussing fashion—Lola's Mary Jane shoes and her dress—as well as 'dishing' the guests for ages as Warren looked on forlornly waiting for his date to rejoin him. Lola was very adult for a five-year-old and wouldn't dream of missing a party—especially one for Al, whom she adored.

Lola and Madonna really hit it off at the party I organised for Al's Dick Tracy *Oscar nomination. Madonna was thrilled to meet the very chatty and sophisticated Lola, who had small talk and repartee down pat. They hung for ages, discussing shoes, fashion and hair.*

Another night, another Oscars: off to the big ceremony with Al to see if he might finally win for Scent of a Woman. *It was his eighth nomination, and he was also nominated for Best Supporting Actor for* Glengarry Glen Ross—*so, surely to goodness, he would win for one of these excellent performances. Phew! He did: his first Best Actor Oscar.*

It's no secret that the official events—the Academy Awards, movie premieres and Broadway first nights—are not as much fun as private evenings ... but certainly one pretty thrilling exception was when my icon of a beau finally won his first Oscar. After being mobbed by hundreds of well-wishers at the Governor's Ball, Al actually seemed excited as we drove up in the limo to the waiting swarms of paparazzi outside the *Vanity Fair* party. It's quite heady stuff to know that you will be the centre of attention in a sea of other famous actors ... and I could almost sense that after the twenty-minute drive alone in the car with just me, it was time for another hit of mass adulation as he eagerly jumped out of the car holding the gold statue. The place erupted in

Al and I rented a house on the beach in Malibu for a couple of summers when Nick was a baby and Lola was nine. At a big day bash we threw, Mick Jagger spent a lot of time on the phone to London, clearly trying to placate Jerry. The phone was right by the door out to the deck and Mick spent a good hour smiling at everyone walking past as he sweet-talked the patient mother of his children.

cheers and applause and it seemed as if the entire room was engulfing us. For about an hour we didn't move from one spot as they lined up to pay their respects—Warren and Whoopi, Sharon Stone and Michael Douglas—till finally he whispered, 'Honey, help me, I've got to sit down.' I led him to a nearby table and about ten seconds later we were joined by Michael White, my old boyfriend. They'd never met but this was a good time to make the introduction. They eyed each other warily and exchanged pleasantries before photographers interrupted and I could see neither planned on becoming pals.

We travelled back and forth between New York and LA all the time, so when not at a Malibu summer rental giving parties for Robert Altman and Mick Jagger and Warren Beatty and Annette Bening, we were entertaining Lauren Bacall and Buck Henry and Paul Rudd and Edna O'Brien in a five-storey house on the Upper East Side. Al had become a bona-fide extrovert by now—a fun, gregarious party animal and a far cry from the shy recluse who wouldn't dream of attending a party when I first met him.

And so, without realising what I was giving up, I had jumped onto the runaway train that was Al's life and realised way too late that it made no stops for anyone, was a very expensive ticket (emotionally and every other way) and was headed in just one direction. A direction determined by Mr P—according to his career, which was what he cared most about. It meant that when asked where she grew up, Lola now responds, 'LA, NY, LA, NY, LA, NY and then back to LA.'

CHAPTER 19

The Prince and the Movie Star

OVER THE YEARS Al, in his quest to stay busy and engaged, began making his own films—financing, directing and starring—and since it was his dough, it meant he could edit, have screenings and re-edit till the cows came home and stay, happily, *very* busy! It really made sense since unlike other rich men, he had no interest at all in the usual—like acquiring real estate, summer cruises on yachts, investing in restaurants or fast cars. His 'experimental' movies starring his own good self became an unusual but passionate and costly hobby. It began with *The Local Stigmatic*, about a couple of crazed and violent working-class Englishmen, by the writer Heathcote Williams, and after acting in the play Al bought the rights and actually had the riveting 56-minute film directed by his old theatre friend David Wheeler. Al tinkered with this one for about a decade and it was never released theatrically (although it was included in a boxed set of all three of Al's self-funded movies called *Pacino—An Actor's Vision*, released a few years ago).

Then with his 1996 documentary, *Looking for Richard*, Al directed his first feature-length film. Al both played Richard III in various scenes from the play with the likes of Alec Baldwin, Winona Ryder and Kevin Spacey, *and* himself, as the Shakespeare buff, guiding us through the play's plot and historical background mainly by heading to the UK and talking to scholars and actors famous for performing Shakespeare—including Vanessa Redgrave, Sir John Gielgud, Kenneth Branagh and Derek Jacobi.

Al is genuinely fascinated by Shakespeare's continuing relevance to popular culture and his enthusiasm for it becomes quite infectious, and after countless screenings—dozens of which I faithfully attended—and extra shooting, it was, I have to say, utterly engrossing and entertaining, not to mention innovative. A labour of love and he was justifiably very proud of it. The screenings provided a whole social life as well, with friends and friends of friends invited to come and give their two cents' worth after the screenings and often on into the night at dinners that Al presided over, always in engaging theatrical form.

I never ceased to be impressed by his tenacity and at the same time his incredibly casual, shoot-from-the-hip way of getting footage. There was rarely a shooting schedule or a shot list. He made it up as he went along for the most part. But his knowledge, experience and charm made it a legitimate way of working, and out of the countless hours of footage he extracted gems—some really gripping scenes from the play itself and a sense for the audience that they were flies on the wall, witnessing behind-the-scenes rehearsals and goings-on that they rarely have a chance to see. As director, he welcomed collaboration but was definitely in charge. Most of his direction was spontaneous and as long as the camera was 'turning' or the Avid (editing machine) was humming, Al was a happy camper. He even had two or three editors working at times, on different versions, unaware that they had competition.

The first dozen screenings held my attention and I religiously gave notes like the supportive girlfriend I was, but I'll be honest, by about screening number seventeen, I was slightly burnt out and disappointed when I realised that a scant few of my suggestions were being heeded. And yes, I was feeling a mite unfulfilled. Al's career was so completely consuming our lives while mine had stalled, badly. All the moving back and forth to remain at his side, keeping up with his exhausting schedule and his tendency to rarely hit the hay before about 1 or 2 am, while still having to get up at 7 to take Lola to school—along with mounting career frustration—was leaving me perpetually tired and quite dispirited. To stay busy and because I'd long held secret ambitions, I started classes with an acting teacher, Marcia Haufrecht, and one of the most enjoyable things I ever did was perform in a play at her tiny theatre on Eighth Avenue. Al came to the opening, with much anticipation by members of the cast who hadn't known of my beau till a few days before—and I think most of them thought I was a lying hound until they saw him with their very own eyes on the big night, moments before the lights went up. Backstage was pandemonium. They were stunned and totally overexcited, terrified they would forget their lines, and I almost felt bad that he'd come.

'It's fine,' I reassured them. 'This is his favourite thing—seeing off, off, *off*-Broadway plays. Don't even think about it!' For some strange reason I was hardly nervous at all. It was just such fun, but pragmatically I knew I'd left it too late to make it a financially rewarding career. And my belief was reinforced that very night when Al took me to dinner following the play—after very kindly telling the cast they had all been 'fantastic'—and said that he thought I was great but that he wished he'd met me ten years earlier because then he 'would have made sure I'd become an actress'. I had indeed left it too late.

I then began re-setting my romantic comedy in New York and got together a cast for a reading in the loft space Al had rented for rehearsals and the endless script readings he had for potential films and plays. When he was offered a role, unless it was something like *Godfather III*, he would generally consider a part only once he'd had one or two or perhaps even three readings of a script. He had to 'hear the part', he insisted, and then, if not convinced there was quite enough in the part as written to sink his teeth into or if it didn't resonate, he would often quite happily decide to spend his own money and hire writers to work on his part, and by extension the other parts, since it's almost impossible to change one part in isolation. The directors and writers of the projects would all be happy if it meant Al was signing on to do the film.

But back to the loft and the one reading of my script I was given permission to hold there. I had become friends with Mia Farrow, my new neighbour a little further down on Central Park West. On my second move back to New York with Al, we had rented an apartment in a brand-new building at 96th street. It certainly didn't have the old-world charm of the Dakota or the San Remo but it had fabulous views of the park and I was deliriously happy to be able to put my stamp on it—I have to say I did a pretty great job of turning it into a chic but cosy place. With no movie to direct I threw myself into it. Luckily, Al could not have been less interested if I'd been doing needlepoint, so I had free rein.

I had the foyer painted a fantastically brilliant red, and covered the walls of the living and dining rooms with an amazingly cool mouse-grey wallpaper. I don't usually love wallpaper but this one gave instant 'Central Park West' character to the glaring white walls. I'm loath to use the word 'eclectic', but I did put together a witty mix of my brother Geoff Hales' fantastic art, bamboo floor lights, black velvet sofas, mid-century lamps and great rugs. The master bedroom was a triumph. I decided to be bold. Black walls, black carpet, black velvet curtains over dark brown wooden venetian blinds and a beautiful bed with a simple low black velvet headboard.

Okay, I was a little nervous. The painter thought I was off my rocker insisting he paint the walls black. But it worked! Not remotely gloomy, it was one of the coolest rooms of all time with a simple white cotton bedspread over hot pink Pendleton blankets and the most divine twinkly vintage flower lights on the walls. And Al did love it and particularly appreciated the blackout curtains—as he was a chronic insomniac but a recovering alcoholic and so he refused to even take a herbal sleeping pill.

But Lola's room was sweet and girlie—pale green and pink, with an Adirondack-style bunk bed, a big pink armchair and assorted stuffed animals, including koalas and a favourite kangaroo with a joey in its pouch. Each morning Lola and I would wait for the Hewitt school bus, which picked her up at the corner of 96th Street and

Central Park West, and then I would rush back, briefly taking on the role of domestic goddess by taking Al a tray of coffee, fresh OJ and whole-wheat toast or bran muffins.

Unlike me, Al was always in a surprisingly good mood in the mornings, but after some telly and a quick read of *The New York Times*, he would be up and out and off to his office in an apartment on 57th Street to make calls and take meetings, or to the Actors Studio, or to the Village to have coffee with a friend—often his best pal and mentor for thirty years, Charlie Laughton, or to meet a director for lunch at Joe Allen's. And when he ran out of meetings, there was always a posse of cronies—out-of-work actors he'd known for years— he would summon for poker games.

I would take off downtown and scour vintage furniture shops for my next project—his country house about thirty-five minutes north of New York on the Hudson River. Almost devoid of furniture, I fixed it up and made it bloody fabulous in record time. Many week-ends were spent there and both Lola and Molly the husky loved it. A pool, a paddle-tennis court and a huge front lawn. Most Sundays I organised big lunches—with help from the 'house manager' who lived there full-time and looked after Al's dogs—for lots of people who would come up from the city for the fresh air, bike rides and hotly dis-puted games of paddle tennis. Occasionally Al and I would have yet another race to see who could run the fastest across the huge stretch of front green lawn. He still hadn't gotten over that time I'd beaten him in a foot race, and he gamely tried time after time to beat me— but never succeeded!

So I worked like a dog to make the atmosphere—indeed, as much of his life as possible—fun, interesting and filled with friends, booking dinners and theatre tickets and rustling up companions on a daily basis—and I know Al enjoyed it all up to a point—but it never really ceased, in my mind, to feel like we were 'playing house'. He seemed to have a horror of anything that smacked of permanence or domesticity and, unlike me, was happy to move from coast to coast at the drop of a hat.

And so, back to Mia Farrow, who had yet to move to her idyllic country compound and was still down the road on Central Park West. I was mesmerised by her beauty, wit and absolute calm in the face of the whole drama that was playing out in the media—namely her break-up and custody battles with her long-time boyfriend Woody Allen, who had run off with Mia's adopted daughter Soon-Yi after taking naked photos of her.

Mia was an incredible mother and the fabulous old apartment full of kids felt like something out of a Jimmy Stewart movie. It was massive, with slightly worn and faded old furniture but utterly full of charm and filled with books in neat piles everywhere. But it wasn't chaotic. Quite the opposite. It was organised and completely awe-inspiring. The kids all pitched in to help each other, older ones reading to younger ones, able-bodied helping the blind and disabled. I was wildly impressed, both by Mia's being so committed to her kids and virtually saint-like in her patient, loving handling of the brood and then by what charismatic, scintillating company she was when we hit the town.

She hated to spend money on herself and would wear the simplest cheapest clothes—blue jeans and cotton thermal tops under a jacket she'd picked up from the army surplus store and clogs. No makeup. But she would be the centre of attention (no mean feat now that Al was such a 'chatty Kathy' raconteur) with that radiant, smiling face of staggering beauty, her brains, her fascinating stories and insights and just a ton of innate charm. She would discuss Woody with me—but never out in public. Luckily pretty much all else, including tales of Frank Sinatra, Roman Polanski or even her days on *Peyton Place*, was allowed at parties. And of course she could discuss politics or books or plays with total ease, and we'd all sit entranced by this marvellous woman who would suddenly have to slip home as she never employed a live-in nanny, and she'd be up again at the crack of dawn to get seven or eight kids up and dressed, fed and then packed off to various schools with bagged lunches before she faced the day and dealt with her Woody woes.

I had endless arguments with people who would announce that Mia was 'clearly nutty' for having adopted so many kids, but what few people know is that the last few kids weren't sought out by Mia. Instead, adoption agencies around the world would relentlessly hound her, begging her to take these unwanted kids who would otherwise rot in an orphanage if she didn't come to the rescue. Mia would refuse but a couple of months later they would call again, pleading with her to change her mind. And on three occasions she did. In my opinion she's pretty amazing and someone who is not just 'hot air'—she truly cares about children in need. And she acts on it to this day, with her work in Darfur.

So I gave my romantic comedy script, *Jane's Turning 39*, to Mia, who agreed to become attached to the project, and I organised the reading at Al's loft—with Mia reading the lead role of Jane, the song-writing mother of a teenage daughter who discovers that her song-writing partner and husband has been cheating on her. Then despite being wooed by an older successful record producer who can restart her career, she falls for a younger man. Her teenage daughter does not approve. It was ahead of its time then. Anyway, I fear my agent invited too many people. Certainly too many came—probably just so they could say they went to a reading at Al Pacino's loft, with Al there to boot! And of course his very presence distracted people no end. You could see heads swivelling and eyes endlessly darting to him. I was a nervous wreck. Of course, people were complimentary afterwards but as a complete cynic, I believed very little of what I heard, but I did know it would make a good movie.

Mia, Al and I went to dinner afterwards—just the three of us, and I was completely horrified when, as we finally got round to discussing the reading, Al suddenly piped up, out of nowhere, that the part of Jane 'needs a lot of work'. Now this was a script that had gone through at least thirty drafts by then, and for all its faults, the part of Jane was pretty solid. I felt energy levels drop, the air went out of the conversation, and frankly, the project went downhill from there.

Al was simply thoughtless but if I'd said the same thing about a script he'd written, in front of an actor he wanted for the part, he would have been livid beyond belief. So when we got home from dinner, I brought up his comment to Mia, but he refused to concede for one moment that he might have been out of line or could have kept it to himself.

Never sure, as a movie star, who was truly a friend or a phony, Al valued loyalty above all else and got weird and paranoid at the drop of a hat. He was wildly angry once when I invited him to a big party a British girlfriend was having and then when he realised that it was a charity event—and that conceivably his presence *might* be used to lure others—he went ballistic and refused to go, and was very angry with me, convinced that either I or my friend was using his celebrity to impress others, or that somehow he was being used. It was all deeply upsetting as he ranted angrily, simply unable to believe that there were no ulterior motives, other than we might have fun and it was a great worthy charity. Al's behaviour could be very hurtful.

It finally occurred to me that my unswerving loyalty wasn't necessarily sensible or indeed reciprocated. I mean, in what now seem like the actions of an idiot in love, I went way beyond the call of duty. It was not unusual for me, after listening to Al, to call his agents and lawyers to complain that deals and offers were not what he deserved. I even called Mike Ovitz once when he was supreme commander of the Creative Artists Agency to say that since Al had been 'pay or play' on an Oliver Stone film about Noriega, he should have been paid when the plug was pulled. Mike insisted that Al had been happy to quit the project. 'No, that's not at all true,' I said as Al hovered nearby listening to the call. 'Oliver quit the project and called Al to tell him and Al simply said, "Okay, fine." He still should be paid.' But I could tell it was a tad unlikely that Mike would concede the point with me and he soon announced he had to 'jump off to take another call'. I encouraged Al to get his lawyers to make the call—but he was loath to ever make a fuss.

Once, when his original manager and the producer of films like *Serpico*, *Scarface* and *Dog Day Afternoon*, Marty Bregman, got up at a gala night honouring Al at the Museum of the Moving Image and made an outrageous speech that did nothing but belittle Al and put him down, he was truly devastated and I was simply furious. But of course Al is actually the ultimate politician and diplomat. I'm the hot-headed impulsive Aussie jerk who had to send out a letter blasting him for such disloyalty and then for good measure copying his agents and publicists. I endeared myself to no one—not even Al. I was an idiot. But all my doing and I must and do take full responsibility. I was clearly looking for a man who cared deeply and could take care of me, and I know that my childhood insecurity about money and employment was deeply embedded and someone like Al seemed like a 'provider'. But that should include really caring about what I needed and craved, and these were not issues Mr P could grapple with when he had such a 'big life' as he often put it.

When *Looking for Richard* was finally bought by Fox, there was talk of a movie premiere in London—perhaps even a royal one. And so, through my dear, clever and deeply charismatic friend the writer Candida Lycett Green—who Michael White and I had spent so much time with in London and at their country homes for weekends—the introduction was made and a letter was written by Al asking if Prince Charles would take the time to look at the film—and then hopefully give the go-ahead for a royal premiere—if we brought it to London to show him.

'Yes, happily,' came the prompt and enthusiastic response. So we flew to London, stayed a couple of nights at the Dorchester and then motored up to Norfolk in a chauffeured car to stay the night at Sandringham with our precious booty—the cans containing Al's film. We weren't sure what to expect but the sight of Prince Charles beaming from the doorway as the car drove up put us instantly at ease, with His Royal Highness greeting us like long-lost buddies. I'd said to Al, 'Don't forget—a slight bow when you first meet him and call him "Your Royal Highness" the first time and then you switch to Sir, not Prince Charles' etc. etc … I could tell Al had no intention of trying to remember and figured that movie stars can pretty much get away with anything.

Well the darling Prince pretended to remember me with an incredibly smiley 'Lyndall, how lovely to see you,' and thus it fell to me to introduce Al, who did manage some kind of very subtle head nod as they shook hands and grinned at each other and it suddenly seemed clear that it must be as much fun for princes to meet movie stars as vice versa.

There were lots of jokes and Prince Charles very swiftly suggested that Al might like to perform a bit of *Richard III* after dinner. Sensing Al's horror at such an idea I quickly reminded him that this was a royal command and he *had* to do it, but there was lots of laughing as he politely declined, begging forgiveness for such insolence in the face of a royal request.

Bidding farewell to Prince Charles after visiting Highgrove. Thanks to my dear, recently departed friend Candida Lycett Green, we made contact with HRH and had driven up to Sandringham to show him Al's documentary film Looking For Richard.

After a quick drink we were shown upstairs to our rooms by a butler and yes, of course, our overnight bags were already unpacked, with cosmetics and such already neatly lined up on the dressing table, and when I popped back upstairs to get a cardigan after dinner, noting that our beds had now been turned down, curtains drawn and my men's cotton jim jams put out on the pillow.

Then came the horrifying news that the *Looking for Richard* tape we had brought was incompatible with the royal video equipment! It would not play. The trip might have all been for nought. How could this have happened? Al and I went into panic mode and calls were frantically made to agents on the coast and the Fox people in London. Promises were made that a film version could be sent *if* there was the right equipment to show it. More discussion between butlers and film folk. Nail-biting time as we waited to find out.

Meantime, dinner must go on. It was a cosy dinner with just two other guests and no sign of Camilla. We ate roast lamb and organic salad vegies, some very yummy little roast potatoes and then a rasp-berry fool along with some very tasty organic wine, and it was relaxed and jolly but very much over by 11 pm, when we also found out that there would indeed be a screening tomorrow morning of the film. The cans of film *and* the equipment to show it would be chauffeured up by 8 am and ready to go.

As we headed back up to our suite of predictably old-fashioned, conservatively furnished rooms we looked at each other, slightly horrified at the prospect of the long night ahead without the delights of the Dorchester Hotel—that is, room service and all-night TV. Al and I always got into a terrible habit of staying on New York—or sometimes even LA—time when we came to London, rarely getting to sleep before 5 or 6 am, and thus wasted most of the day sleeping. Once we didn't get out of our hotel room till around 5 pm and we rushed to the Royal Academy to find it closed—an awful feeling—but Al's insomnia and refusal of any prescription sleep aids played havoc with changing time zones and shut-eye.

On this trip we'd come from LA and so it was incredibly early for us—mid-afternoon—and the long night loomed ahead of us. We undressed, got into bed and looked at each other, not remotely sleepy, and in my case, ready to resort to my stash of emergency sleeping pills. We read for a bit and Al did what I found very soothing and pleasant— read a little of what he was reading out loud. Then I jumped up out of bed, remembering with glee that I had some chocolate in my bag in the other room. We were both chocoholics who had similarly serious sweet tooths. I told Al I thought it was a Kit Kat. But just as I was feverishly rummaging in my massive handbag for the treat, I was suddenly plunged into darkness. Ghostly 'oohing' sounds were coming from the bedroom and I realised my boyfriend had decided it was time for a game of hide and seek in the dark. I literally couldn't see a foot in front of me, and my loud whispering for Al to turn the light on and not be a silly bugger was simply met with more ghostly groaning and a few rustling sounds. As my eyes adjusted to the light I finally saw a crack of light about ten feet away, signifying the door out to the corridor.

I tiptoed over, groped for the door handle in the dark and quickly opened the door to shed some light on the proceedings and there was Al, almost bent over double as he crouched behind a big armchair, his bare bum suddenly exposed by the stream of light. It was a fabulous image. I wished desperately I had a camera to record the moment but I've found it's a hard one to forget. We both started laughing hysterically and I almost hoped a butler or Tiggy might pass by right at this moment—just for fun—but he was safe. It was just after midnight and all seemed to be sleeping except for the folk from Hollywood.

Wide awake and nowhere to go till a quiet knock at the door at what seemed like ten minutes later but was in fact 8.30 am. The curtains were opened and a tray of coffee, toast and marmalade—and *The Daily Mail* with a headline about Lady Diana—was put in the sitting room next door. We staggered up, as we had agreed the night before to meet Prince Charles downstairs for a proper breakfast before showing him Al's film.

So thirty minutes later, feeling absolutely shattered and facing the world about six hours earlier than we were used to, Al and I headed downstairs to join our host. Let's be frank—even movie stars don't keep royalty waiting. There he was, sitting alone in a rather modest and sparsely furnished breakfast room, already eating muesli and free-range eggs. I feared we were in fact a few minutes late and quickly ordered kippers and scrambled eggs as I knew they would be ready and waiting in the chafing dishes. I'd had enough weekends in stately homes to know the drill. Prince Charles seemed very perky and spoke passionately about the environment and sustainable farming but in a way that was entertaining and understandable for the uninitiated. He truly has proved to be ahead of his time—progressive and committed as well as far more knowledgeable than most politicians and a leader who should be applauded for so many of his efforts in raising money, preserving beautiful old English architecture and showing the rest of the world how we all need to focus on local, sustainable and organic food. He was an unfaithful husband but I'm still a fan.

Right after breakfast we retired to a large room out near the kitchens where a screen had been put up and the film was about to roll—for just the three of us! Having seen it countless times and feeling so deeply tired, we both had to fight like crazy to stay awake. We had cups of coffee at our feet but they were soon cold and it was sheer hell to keep our eyelids open—but finally, *finally*, it came to an end and His Royal Highness was full of what seemed like sincere enthusiasm and praise and said he would be 'absolutely thrilled' to attend a royal premiere whenever he's needed. It was just after 11 am and he had another appointment—thank the Lord—so we swiftly took our leave. He even came to the door to see us off. Many heartfelt thank yous and fond farewells followed and we were off. We slept almost the whole way back to London. Mission accomplished.

About six months later we headed back to London for what had become a grand and glamorous opening at the Odeon Leicester Square. This trip was quite thrilling as I'd gotten to invite some pals and would get to see them in the precious couple of days prior to the big night. I always felt so happy to be back in Blighty near my best friend Gael and her darling generous husband Francesco and their four kids (the eldest, Lara, being my lovely goddaughter) as well as the wise and wonderful Candida, and for years I'd been encouraging Al to try and find a movie or play to do in London that would take us there for a stretch of several months. Fortunately, we had gone to London a few times over the years and it was always my idea of heaven—being with my best pals and Al in the city I loved the most. As soon as we were installed I rushed out to try and find a dress to wear at my favourite, now non-existent shop called Voyage on Fulham Road. Al couldn't believe I needed a new outfit but I truly didn't really like dresses and always preferred tailored, somewhat unfeminine suits or a simple pencil skirt and a great jacket. Pretty, sexy clothes didn't suit me but it seemed my favourite pinstripe suit was just a tad underdressed for London where, unlike in LA, people still dressed to the nines. I really did not like the dress I ended up buying and wearing, and should have spent more time before we left for London—but no matter. It was clear that trying to look as glamorous as I once had was a losing battle and it was time to work on being a good, kind person. But wait, I was already good and kind. Okay—time to realise that ageing sucks and vanity will cost you plenty. At least I knew enough not to slather on the makeup and that less was definitely more as we grow longer in the tooth.

Much to my relief, the fabulous Leicester Square crowd was out in force waiting to see the movie star so Al happily posed for lots of pictures outside, and then we were ushered inside for pre-show drinks with just our besties—Gael and Francesco Boglione and Cand and Rupert Lycett Green. We were highly excited and Al was definitely nervous about the British reaction to his attempts to deconstruct Shakespeare. Once again he voiced his fears, 'They may think I'm just an American jerk trying to prove he can do Shakespeare …'

'I'm sure they will,' I responded, teasing but anxious as always to put Al at ease. It was times like these that I wished Al could join us for a glass of champagne but he sipped his coke and lemon, and we soon headed back to the lobby for a few more photos—before being given the word by all sorts of royal security staff to quickly line up in an upstairs lobby to officially greet Prince Charles. We had made a list of people who should meet and greet the Prince, including Al's long-time agent Rick Nicita, Kevin Spacey, a producer of the film Michael Hadge, and several Fox executives who were distributing the film. We were lined up in strict order with Al at the head of the line.

A beaming Prince Charles suddenly materialised and greeted Al like a long-lost buddy—very politely saying he was 'really looking forward to seeing the film a second time'. Al missed just half a beat but then quickly pointed out that several changes had been made and it was all smooth sailing. Turning to me, His Royal Highness said, 'Ah Lyndall, what a treat to see you again. And how many times have you seen the film now?'

I quickly rolled my eyes and said, 'A few too many, Sir!' and grinned. He winked and grinned approvingly. 'Ah, a supportive girl-friend … I'm sure he appreciates it.' He truly could not be sweeter or more adept at putting folk at ease and pretty soon it was time for him to move on down the line. No matter how lovely it was to chat, one did heave a sigh of relief as he left—it's still hard work talking to a royal.

The screening met with huge applause and many, many plaudits for Al as we left the Odeon and headed off to the Middle Temple Hall for a post-screening black-tie reception. The Middle Temple has stood since Elizabethan times and is one of the Inns of Court where English barristers now have their chambers or offices. The great hall is where they still gather for lunches and meetings.

It was, predictably, a little stiff and formal—and not as much fun as one would hope but the whole evening went off without a hitch and the reviews were incredibly warm and uniformly good.

The real treat of the visit was an unexpected invite a few days later that came through to our hotel room from the Prince's secretary to come and visit the Prince at Highgrove for the night and take a private tour of his magnificently understated gardens. His Royal Highness

Lined up with Kevin Spacey in the foyer of the Odeon Leicester Square for the royal premiere of Al's documentary Looking for Richard, *waiting for HRH Prince Charles to walk down the line, charming one and all with his suave patter and smart, witty questions.*

Few can resist a royal / Hollywood invite when it appears in the letterbox, and Mick and Jerry were no exceptions. It was a fun, star-studded night. I found it a little stressful and I know Al was a mite nervous, but all went off without a hitch and Looking for Richard *was very warmly received by the British press.*

gave us a blow-by-blow of the fabulous plants—all grown of course without any fertilisers—and the importance of organic gardening and composting. But he kept it so fabulously entertaining and was infectiously proud of his accomplishments—like the meadow filled with wildflowers, including thirty-two native and endangered species. And the walled kitchen garden, he pointed out, giving us a green bean to try, kept the estate self-sufficient in fruit and veg! I felt it was a complete triumph and the Brits should be so incredibly proud of their caring and forward-looking heir to the throne. I do think it may have been Al's one and only conversation throughout the course of his life about gardens and composting and rare native plants, but he was a trouper, feigning avid interest. When it was time to take our leave, I asked the butler to take some snaps and off we drove, through stunning, summery, overgrown lanes, back to London. Al and I agreed that Prince Charles was a gent, wonderful company and we felt privileged to have spent more quality royal time with such a good sort.

CHAPTER 20

My Fabulous Kids

Lola was nine when 'we' adopted Nick and she definitely adored my idea that we were adopting him 'together'. I guess a combination of failing to get pregnant again along with a long-held conviction that adoption was a wonderful way to go, very much rekindled once I met Mia Farrow, led to me deciding to adopt.

I had tried once before while in New York. Lola and I flew to Minneapolis for the birth of a little girl we called Adelaide. We took her from the hospital back to a hotel and had her for a few wonderful days before her mother changed her mind and the grandmother came to take her away. It was devastating. We flew home with an empty baby carriage and all the paraphernalia and took a break before I decided to go with a lawyer in LA for a private adoption.

I get chills every time I remember the excitement as Nick's birth mother's due date arrived. We were on *high* alert. Forget the anticipation of Santa, Disneyland, the Tooth Fairy—or even her *Little Mermaid* fifth birthday party. Waiting for her baby brother (we knew it was a boy) to be born beat everything. She was deliriously impatient and a joy to watch. Every time the phone rang we both screamed. Even Molly the husky ran around in circles like a maniac. Lola didn't want to go to school in case she missed something but I swore on everything holy that I would swing by Campbell Hall on the way to Valley Presbyterian. It was before GPS but I had my route worked out. Fortunately Nick came into the world at about 8 pm on a Friday. We were standing by but still imagined it would be a few days away.

I had just made Lola and her friend Ally from school—who wanted to be in on all the excitement—mashed potatoes and lamb chops, and since I detest cooking I'm not keen on any effort going to waste, but once we got the call at about 7.30 saying, 'We just wanted to inform you that they're about to do an emergency cesarian—you should come now,' that was it. Dinner was left on the table. We shrieked, screamed, panicked, laughed, ran around in circles and tore out the door to the Valley. Driving very swiftly down Sunset and over Coldwater Canyon, we arrived in record time, taking a good fifteen minutes off my timed practice run. We arrived at the maternity ward and were naturally sent to lots of wrong places before we ran down a corridor and bumped into a nurse carrying a swaddled baby.

'Is that ours?' shrieked Lola. The nurse looked up wide-eyed as if we might be crazed baby-snatchers.

'Is that the Hobbs baby?' I smiled politely. She confirmed that this was the baby for adoption and we all cheered. But she was a humour-less human and was having none of our glee, and she promptly marched off to the newborn nursery, not even slowing down as Lola and Ally ran behind, desperate for a peek. Unfortunately children were not permitted in the nursery and I sent the girls around the corner, where they frantically jumped up and down to try and see through the glass window.

I was still carrying the huge camcorder bag which I hadn't had time to open … I followed the nurse as she put the drops in his eyes and rather roughly checked and measured him, and with shaking hands I tried to get out the camera. He started to howl and I was desperate to pick him up but wasn't about to grab him for fear of being sent out with the kids … I guiltily waved at them as they madly gestured for me to bring the baby over to them. I did finally get to hold him for a few precious moments and weepily took him to the window so they could get a glimpse. Their faces were beaming. All very touching, so very sweet. Al was the first person to hold him when I brought him home. Adopting Nick was absolutely the best decision I've ever made.

The adventure began and not an ounce of jealousy ensued. Lola relished the thought of Nick as 'her baby' from the moment she held him two days later in the hospital as I signed papers and we prepared to drive him home with us. From then on she would rush in from school, sneak into his room and pick him up even if he was asleep, against strict orders, to 'watch over him'.

'But he's asleep, Lola. Go and play in your room, honey.'

'He was awake, Mum—he was crying,' she would bald-faced lie, thirty seconds later, having wickedly woken him from a deep sleep.

And baby makes three! This was taken by my pal Sheryl Lowe just two days after Nick was born. Ever since Chris had left, Lola's words had rung in my ears: 'We're just half a family now.' I felt we were so much more complete now—and Lola was deliriously happy. Indeed, adopting my darling Nick was the best thing I ever did, for both myself and Lola.

Gazing at my gorgeous new baby boy, just two months old, on the sand in front of the Malibu beach house, summer of '96. Nick was a great sleeper until Lola and her friends started sneaking into his room and waking him up to play with him. She was totally crazy about her new brother, but also very naughty. Not surprisingly, Nick became a terrible sleeper.

As he got older Lola and her friends would spend hours fussing over him, giving him bottles, bathing him and dressing him up (often in dresses, like a doll, sometimes with lipstick—he didn't mind) but always with extraordinary maternal finesse and expertise. Our place was a favourite hangout and understandably—they got to play with a real live baby who left the long-begged-for American Girl doll and myriad outfits for dead. All her pals adored him. Especially our fabulous next-door neighbour who was exactly Lola's age. Lauren, also adopted, was mad for Nick as well and would often appear, pretending she had permission, to help Lola give Nick a bath and then stay for dinner—often her second.

Like Lola, Nick had to get used to travel pretty darn quickly and before he was two he'd had way more than a dozen roofs over his head. He'd been to London, Melbourne, Sydney and LA, learnt to crawl and walk in a five-storey East Side Manhattan house where parties and dinners were the norm, been in more limos than is decent, dined regularly at Orso's in the midtown theatre district and flown on the Concorde with Al, who would panic at the sound of a whimper and nervously rush him right to the back to quieten him down and not disturb the well-heeled Concorde clientele. Along with Lola, he'd been to tapings of *Saturday Night Live* where Lola and her pals happily met the Spice Girls, and, like his sister, he'd been introduced to the English countryside as well as room service in many swanky hotel suites. He even lived for several months at the Chateau Marmont hotel in LA with me and Lola, where he would run through the foyer naked in the summer the moment he could take off his own clothes so he could splash in the pretty terrace fountain. There's even one alarming photo of Nick in yet another hotel suite in New York watching cartoons in a diaper as he's given a relaxing reflexology foot massage by a woman as he lounges on a sofa! Wait—I'm pretty sure it was a one-off because Al had failed to show for a massage due to rehearsals. Besides, Nick was a very poor sleeper and I was always trying to find ways to relax the bub!

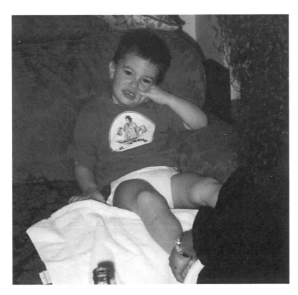

Toddler Nick gets a reflexology foot massage as he takes it easy and watches cartoons in a Manhattan hotel room. It looks crazier than it was—I swear. A massage was booked for an insomniac Al, but at the last minute he bailed. Since Nick's sleeping was equally fitful, I figured we should try it on the bub.

With Nick still small enough to bathe in a kitchen sink, Al and I split when he was two, after seven years together, and I bought the run-down but stunning huge original old Spanish mansion in Hancock Park where Nick happily played in packing boxes for at least six months as I did it up. In fact we all went from the lap of luxury to living—so happily—on a king-size mattress on the floor of the huge double height 'ballroom' with hand-painted walls and ceiling for several months before having the mattress relocated to the floor of the guest house while I happily had the house painted (though I did a lot of it myself and really enjoy painting!) and restored with fabulous old light fittings that matched the remaining ones there. Yes, we camped out for half a year, we ate like very bad campers and we all loved every minute of it.

Six months later I had the most wonderful housewarming Christmas party ever with about 200 people and a huge Christmas tree that Lola and Nick loved decorating and something, like with my wedding, that really left people spellbound: a superb eight-man gospel choir! They were a huge hit and everyone clamoured for more. I found some rather silly posh Beverly Hills friends in irritating shock at my glamorous surroundings now that I was no longer with Al. But if they'd seen the house six months earlier when it was still a two-family home, they would have run a mile. I have a knack for whipping places into shape and will work till midnight for months in a row to get it finished in record time. Hancock Park was yet to become fashionable again after having been chic in the '30s and '40s and many were stunned by how fabulous both the house and the area were ... Many friends soon moved in to the area and now it's a highly sought after hood.

I remember coming back down the stairs the night of this Christmas party after checking that my kids were asleep—Nick was in my bed of course and Lola and two friends, having a sleepover, had made a camp with blankets and my new velvet pillows out on one of the balconies upstairs! I was set to just turn off lights but discovered that the famous music producer Phil Spector (who developed the 'Wall of Sound' formula) was *still* in my house, standing by the bar mumbling maniacally to himself and clearly not ready to call it a night!

I was a huge fan of his music and loved the sound of literally every song he ever produced. Classics like 'Da Doo Ron Ron', 'Be My Baby', 'River Deep Mountain High', 'My Sweet Lord', 'Unchained Melody' and 'Let It Be' were all produced by Phil. I invited him to my parties and at one soiree I excitedly introduced Barbra Streisand to him. Shockingly, Barbra had no idea who he was and I found myself sputtering an explanation as she stared at me blankly. Seriously. She'd never heard of any of his songs. She then confessed with not a whit of embarrassment that she barely ever listened to music. Ever!

Anyway, I was more than polite to a drunk and now somewhat belligerent Phil. I was desperate to get him out the door but recalled another party of mine where he'd dragged anyone he could, including Jack Nicholson, out to his limo parked in my driveway to show them his huge stash of guns in the trunk. I made up a story about having to take a bottle up to Nick—whom he'd sent a gorgeous Tiffany's cup and saucer set to when I adopted him—but after listening to several incoherent stories, started to panic, thinking I could see the bulge of a gun in his pocket. He insisted I sit and drink with him for another hour that felt like six and I simply didn't quite know what to do. But finally I did hear Nick crying and I said Nick had night terrors and I had to go to him! It worked and I ushered him out and closed the door, very relieved. Phil is now in jail for second-degree murder for the late-night shooting of a girl in his house.

But I digress. My darling daughter turned out okay. More than okay. She's a gem. But I wasn't so sure how it would all play out—as evidenced by this article I wrote for *American Vogue* in '97:

In three months my only daughter, Lola, turns thirteen. It's a horror story. A terrifying experience. For me, not her. Look, I may be a mother, but I'm not a moron. I've seen *Dawson's Creek*. I've listened to Eminem's lyrics. I know what they do. First it's sex, then drugs, then sex on drugs.

Perhaps I'm being melodramatic, but this whole entry into the teenage years is making me pathetically sentimental, sad, upset and often angry. Angry at her. Angry at myself and my shortcomings. Angry at the passing of time. I feel short-changed; it's all going too quickly. Lola asks me to tell her childhood anecdotes—things she did that were cute and funny. Who can remember? As a single mom I have no husband to jog my memory. Stressed out and guilty ever since she told me, when she was three, 'We're just half a family now,' I remember little of her precious, already vanished childhood.

But it's the ongoing sense of loss that's so draining. Yes, she's still physically here, but in the pit of my stomach I feel I'm losing her. She now tells me she's leaving home the minute she turns eighteen. It's like a stab wound to the heart every time she says it, mantra-like. Is it so bad living with me? She certainly doesn't need me the way she used to; it often seems she's nice only when she wants something, and the unexpected love notes in childish scrawl that used to warm the cockles of my heart are a fading memory.

Now it's late-night phone calls with angst-ridden girlfriends and gruff, deep-voiced boys, desperate requests for a second ear-piercing session ('Mom, it's so retarded having just one hole'), and endless screaming matches with me over, generally speaking, absolutely nothing.

Our most recent episode of preposterously high drama involved penne pasta. In a frenzied attempt to bond and spend more 'quality time' with my daughter, I suggested that every Monday we follow a recipe and make dinner together. On the appointed night for our new culinary venture, we were merrily cooking away when Nick, my three-year-old, dragged over his little red chair and insisted on helping cut the tomatoes. That did it.

'Oh great, Mom,' Lola said. 'This was meant to be our time alone together, but no, Nick has to get in the way. You love him more than me. You are so mean! I'm going upstairs—goodbye!'

'Good riddance, bad-tempered little brat,' was on the tip of my tongue, but remembering the bonding theme of the evening, I called out sweetly, 'Honey, come back. We'll pop in a video for Nick.'

She stomped back in and began chopping up basil ferociously with a huge knife. I was tempted to suggest that gently tearing the leaves would be simpler and safer but decided to keep my mouth shut. When it was time to chop the garlic, I began to pleasantly tell her the trick to peeling a clove of garlic. 'Crush it slightly with the back of the knife and it'll be much easier to peel.' Big brown eyes rolled heavenward. 'Geez mom, I know that.' I placed a saucepan next to her in the sink. 'Put the tomatoes, garlic and basil in here, darling,' I said. She ignored the request, swung over to the stove, and hurled the tomatoes into a skillet full of hot oil.

'Sweetheart, that's for the fried asparagus. Tomatoes go in the saucepan,' I said, only the teeniest bit reproachfully.

'I can't do anything right! Forget it, do it all yourself. You hate me, and I'm never cooking again as long as I live!' she screamed at the top of her lungs. With a final quick glance at her own furious little face in the mirror, the hormonally challenged one hurled herself out the back door and into the courtyard.

Well, the dogs started barking, Nick actually tore himself away from *Toy Story*, and I expected the neighbors to come running at any moment. (Scratch that. LA neighbors never come running.) Carefully plucking the tomatoes from the scalding oil, I tried to think of an appropriate punishment for such colossal rudeness. A father could probably come up with a few choice words for a wicked daughter right about now, I thought wistfully. Then Miss Theatrical skulked back in, sidled over to hug me, apologised dramatically, and promised to clean up everything.

'Manipulative little monster; I've failed completely as a parent,' I tell myself, until I hear her moments later as she says to her best pal on the phone, 'Can't talk now. Me and my mom are cooking this great dinner together. It's so fun.' Suddenly she's speeding round the kitchen, whipping up a salad dressing, lighting a candle, and asking, as we sit down to a shockingly delicious meal, if we can do it again next week.

So is there hope? Or will it all end in a torrid mix of sex, drugs, and rock'n'roll due to the fact that just a lone parent (trying to sound like two) clapped and cheered at the countless concerts, Christmas pageants, plays, and basketball games over the years?

I have an intelligent, sensitive, and volatile daughter. And although she's growing up in a culture that still awards women primarily for their looks and sex appeal, I'm hoping she'll one day become a fully realized, free-spirited, loving and confident woman.

Or will she? The big question is, am I really helping to make that happen? Have I given her the strength and common sense to make the right choices? Plato says that education is teaching our children to find pleasure in the right things. Did Plato realise how little power parents would have in this day and age? ...

When exactly did it begin to dawn on this doting single mom that the apple of her eye, her pride and joy, her most treasured possession, was no longer her actual property but instead a formidable, maturing person in her own right, a foul-tempered, mother-hating, back-talking, tit-growing little alien who's already planning to abandon her old mom and fly the coop?

Was it when, with some misgivings I was driving her to see *There's Something About Mary*? As I timidly started to explain that apparently there's a masturbation scene in the film, the sweet little pony-tailed seventh grader interrupted, and with one petite cupped hand making the appropriate up-and-down motion, said dismissively, 'Oh you mean the scene where he jacks off?'

Or perhaps it was the moment, just a couple of days later, when my polite query over breakfast about the health of her twelve-year-old friend from New York was met a bit tentatively with, 'Uh, she had sex last week with her sixteen-year-old boyfriend.'

Or was it a week later when I pulled up outside her school and thought to myself—as I gabbed frantically on my cell phone, trying not to bore some agent in the unspoken but strictly allotted forty-five seconds one has with a power player—who is that stunning young vamp in the low-rider, navel-revealing jeans, the baby-pink tank top pulled taut over stunningly high little breasts, the wrap-around black shades, and the amateurishly-dyed pink hair? Just who the hell is that little Lolita, leaning against a lamp-post, rocking back and forth seductively in three-inch black mules as she chats to a lanky, baggy-trousered guy? I donned prescription glasses for a better look. That's no teenage tart, I realised, that's my Lolita, my very own little Lo, the heaven-sent bundle of joy I'd squatted on the bedroom floor and given birth to twelve and a half years ago. My Lola Rose.

I honked the horn, pointed to the passenger seat, and with the fiercest expression I could muster mouthed, 'Get in!' She smiled at the boy, kissed him on the cheek, and then bopped over to get her backpack. Once inside, she giddily announced, 'That's my new boyfriend; isn't he cute? He's in eighth grade. My hair? Oh we did it at lunchtime—it washes out. Doesn't it look rad, Mom?' I was apoplectic. Demanding she take off the black mules I recognised as mine, I sanctimoniously announced that she was grounded. 'For what? Having a boyfriend?'

She was right—not exactly a crime. Wearing sunglasses and tight jeans, I guess that's not against the law, especially at a school with absolutely no dress code. But, by golly, being a twelve-year-old sex kitten seemingly aware of her own allure and totally at ease with it—well, it should be punishable. Somehow. And can someone tell me why I've been setting aside a couple of hours a week to read *Reviving Ophelia* with her in an attempt, as all the psychologists quoted in the book insist is vitally necessary, to build the self-esteem that should be suffering in a girl this age? Her self-esteem is just fine and bloody dandy.

Does it get any worse? What about the recent morning I walked into the kitchen and noticed my boyfriend gazing at Lola, seemingly mesmerised, as she picked at her passionfruit. She was wearing a face full of foundation ('I have spots, Mom—it's medicated makeup!'), kohl-rimmed eyes ('So what? I'm not allowed to wear makeup till I'm fifty?'), and the now ubiquitous cleavage popping out of a teeny black tank top. I had a choice. Slap his face or act like the grown-up I so clearly am. I ordered her upstairs to remove the makeup and take off the tank top. In a pre-caffeinated state of paranoia, I silently wondered what had been going through the boyfriend's mind. After seeing him for four months, I'd let him stay over for the first time. Now not only did I have misgivings about the sleepover but for the first time ever, I felt a mild but nauseatingly distinct wave of jealousy sweep over me. I checked my wildly natural, makeup-free self in the mirror. Not reassuring.

'The makeup's no big deal … but the top's a little too sexy,' offered the now ex-beau as I rushed off to enforce the makeup and wardrobe changes. Then her carpool arrived, and Lola ran past, wearing my new lilac cashmere sweater over the tank top. 'Bye, Mom,' she called. 'Don't be late to pick me up. I love you!'

As the young boyfriend (did I mention he was younger?) gulped the last of his Cheerios and bade me a frighteningly speedy, unromantic farewell, I slumped back down at the breakfast table. Talk about feeling powerless, pathetic and redundant.(And guess who looked cuter in the lilac cashmere?) I could have wept. I did, about half an hour later, when I checked my messages from the night before and discovered that four out of the five calls were for Lola, from guys.

Why so many calls? I wondered, before remembering that I'd seized the phone from her bedroom two nights before when my polite suggestion that she keep an incoming call (at 10.40 pm) very short met with a muttered, 'God, my mother's being such a bitch!'

'You wanna see bitch?' I shrieked as I tore back into her room, grabbed the phone and hung it up. 'How dare you be so rude and disloyal, Lola. It's nearly eleven o'clock. You're twelve years old and this is not acceptable.'

'Mom, I'm sorry I called you a bitch, but I'm nearly thirteen. When are you going to realise I'm not a baby any more?'

With a 'lights off—now,' I headed for my bedroom and vowed to turn over a tough, strict new leaf. After twelve years with a soft-touch mum and little fatherly discipline, there was no time to lose.

'I'm not a baby any more' kept ringing in my ears. There was an upsetting kernel of truth to it. Although the darling stopped wanting to sleep in my bed at the drop of a hat only a year ago, she can now reason with her three-year-old brother in a far more rational, patient, and maturely clever way than I can. She's amazingly kind and affectionate with kids—making up games, creating 'fun', and still keeping control far more smoothly and capably than her mother. She reads voraciously, she's polite, sweet and entertaining with my friends, she's a computer whiz, she speaks Spanish, and she's far more decisive than I am at the supermarket. As for clothes shopping, I wouldn't dream of it any more without the incredibly stylish and tasteful pre-teen in tow.

Yes, I ventured, maybe she is growing up. I remember how grown-up I'd felt at her age. At thirteen I was wearing white lipstick and mascara, and smoking cigarettes with my girlfriends in the bathroom every morning at school before classes at my strict Melbourne all-girls grammar school. But I certainly knew nothing about boys 'jacking off'. The concepts of orgasms and oral sex were as foreign as ... well, I'd simply never heard of them. I was an absolute innocent. I recall being ten and up a tree when an older girl told me what older men actually do to women during sex. I was appalled.

The schools in my day provided nil in the way of Sex Ed and the information blackout continued at home. My fabulously loving but overprotective parents were utterly tight-lipped about all sexual matters—even when a man tried to abduct me when I was about eight or nine walking on my own to school one morning. He tricked me into getting into his car to push some fictitious button on the floor of the passenger seat, then shoved me into the car and slammed the door shut before dashing round to jump into the driver's seat whereupon he whipped out his willy and proceeded to 'jack off'—as I stared, in total shock. He finished and then, as he started the car, I finally had the presence of mind to realise I wasn't locked in and opened the door, hurled myself out, picked up my school bag and ran like greased lightning all the considerable way to school. But as I explained to the teachers and then to everyone later that afternoon when my parents showed up and carted me off to the local police station, I really just felt bad for the guy. Yes, there were many sideways glances as I explained that he must be terribly ill as some 'weird white stuff came out of his thing'. Did anyone— the teachers, the cops or my parents bother to try and explain what had actually transpired? No sirree! They did not and it was many a long year before I truly figured out that he had ejaculated.

Did the lack of frank discussion turn me into a bit of a prude? Perhaps. I certainly have my own problems facing up to my daughter's burgeoning sexuality. When Lola posed the question six months ago, 'Mom, what's a clitoris?' I succinctly (and priggishly) replied, 'It's a part of the female anatomy, darling,' and promptly changed the subject.

So, a few details notwithstanding, Lola and her friends know infinitely more than I knew at their age. How could they not? They've been force-fed sexual information and images via music, movies, TV and magazines from the moment they could walk and talk. They've grown up with AIDS. They've had stunningly detailed and graphically diagrammed explanations of sex thrust upon them at school, ready or not. They've had dick-sucking interns and horny, hound-dog presidents shoved in their faces for the past eighteen months. ('So he actually put the cigar up her vagina, Mom?' 'Apparently, dear.' 'Why?' 'Beats me.') ...

Already at twelve Lola has moved with me eight times, changed schools five times, lived in New York three times, been to Australia a dozen times, and visited England, France, Italy and Switzerland. She's stayed in countless hotels and lived at the Chateau Marmont. She's lived with a movie star and hung out in his trailers and on the sets, met Madonna, Jack Nicholson, and the Spice Girls. She's stayed up way too late at many of my parties and been to countless

Broadway plays, musicals and, to date, two rock concerts. She's hung at tapings of TV sitcoms written by her talented writer-producer father. She's watched me direct off-Broadway plays, commercials, a movie and TV episodes. She's attended readings of my scripts, occasionally sitting in (around a table with other actors) and reading the role of a kid her age. At one table-read of my script with Ellen Barkin and Matt Dillon, Lola read the part of the young pre-teen daughter and put the two stumbling adult stars to shame with her stunningly fluent, flub-free reading. Am I exposing her to too much? Perhaps.

Am I a good role model for her? Hard to say, especially when we all know that that girls would rather die than end up anything like their mothers. I know she's glad that, despite the lack of a dad, I decided to adopt a little brother for her. She feels, quite rightly, that we did it together, and she's absolutely nuts about Nick.

Career-wise, she's certainly seen me experience a lot of frustration and has sweetly sympathised with my tears more than once. I've told her that being a female writer-director in Hollywood definitely rates as one of the tougher challenges a woman can take on. If nothing else, she's been exposed to perseverance in the face of daunting odds. Is it foolish perseverance? I hope not.

But it's easy to see how growing up in Hollywood might 'ruin' a girl, and I watch myself becoming stricter to compensate for my daughter's environmental influences. One of Lola's best friends recently invited her to a thirteenth-birthday party on a Friday night. It consisted, if you don't mind, of dinner at Planet Hollywood in Beverly Hills from 9.00 until 11.00 pm followed by rollerblading at a Burbank rink until 2.00 am followed by a sleepover back in Bel Air. I said, 'That's great honey. I'll pick you up at eleven.' Despite being accused of trying to ruin her life, I stuck to my guns.

There I was dutifully waiting outside the restaurant at 11.00 pm, longing for a wise and witty male person (in an ideal world someone who was also her father and my adoring husband, but who's picky these days?) to kid her into a good mood. Instead, we drove home silently, Lola fuming and me feeling hideously alone. I later learned that the sleepover kids got to bed at 6.00 am. Apart from not needing an exhausted, bad-tempered child for the weekend, isn't there the question of being jaded? If they're up until 6.00 am at twelve and thirteen years old, what do they do for kicks when they're fifteen?

As the weekend progressed, relations remained strained. I nixed another party the following night because her big science project on AIDS was due a few days later. Saturday night found me sitting at my computer waiting for some research (for her project!) to come up on the Net. I glanced at *Reviving Ophelia*, which was becoming rather compelling reading. I flipped through it, hoping to find a section about single mothers with daughters who unconsciously blame them for not having had a father in the house during their formative years. One paragraph jumped out at me. According to the author, Mary Pipher, 'Mothers are likely to have the most difficult time with adolescent girls. Daughters provoke arguments as a way of connecting and distancing at the same time. They want their mothers to recognise their smallest changes and are angry when their mothers don't validate their every move. They struggle with their love for their mothers and their desire to be different from their mothers—they trust their mothers to put up with their anger and to stand by them when they are unreasonable. This is an enormous compliment, but one that's hard for most mothers to accept because it's couched in such hostile terms.'

Now I get it—it's all a compliment!!! Somehow this doesn't make me feel better.

The article got an amazing response. People came up to me for a couple of years at least, saying how much they'd both enjoyed it and identified. At any rate, most folk assured me that clearly, I was doing a great job of single parenting a tricky teenage girl in Hollywood. If only they knew how things went a trifle downhill very soon after the article came out.

CHAPTER 21

Return to Oz

I WAS OFTEN TEMPTED to do a follow-up article for *American Vogue* about how pretty much the moment Lola hit eighth grade, she started getting naughtier and naughtier—to put it politely. Like many kids from divorced parents who have spent the vast majority of their childhoods with Mum, and travelling in first class with a movie star and complaining bitterly when we didn't take her to Academy Awards ceremonies and the like, she suddenly showed great interest in spending more and more time with Dad—especially those weekends where she knew that a big smile and hug for Daddy would ensure that any thoughts he had of following my rules about just one sleepover a weekend—and only *if* he had checked with the parents—were instantly ditched and thus, come Sunday night or even Monday after school, I would get back a shell of a child who'd been allowed to disappear for the entire weekend. Oh yes, I'd do my detective work and it was just outrageous how many lies she told so well.

So there were fights and dramas, Lola played Chris like a fiddle and I lost a huge amount of power. Chris had moved from Santa Clarita with his second wife, Tracy, and their two children to a huge house just two blocks away from my fabulous Spanish house in Hancock Park. And so, if Lola and I had a fight, over anything, she would simply slam a few doors and march up the street to her father's house, and there wasn't a damn thing I could do about it.

I took her to therapists to try and reach her—none of it helped! She was enjoying her newly found power and the freedom she enjoyed whenever she spent weekends with her dad. I tried to be incredibly vigilant but was generally outsmarted by Lola and her best pal, the next-door neighbour Lauren. They were wicked together—lying, heading out at night after lights out, stealing my booze, my money, any cigarettes I sporadically had—but eventually they got sloppy and I came across 'bowls' and baggies of weed ... and overheard conversations for late night trysts. She and Lauren even ran away to Long Beach for a night ... and well, put it this way, if I thought she was tricky at twelve—by fourteen, she was a teeny bit *out of control.*

Now, Lola is highly intelligent and pretty much got straight As her whole life but, as with many kids her age, there was attitude, resentment and teenage angst to burn. So any chance I had, I took us all out of LA and off to wherever I could manage ... No, alas, I do not mean camping in the Adirondacks, rock climbing in Yosemite or even building housing for the poor in Guatemala. We went to places where friends invited us: to Mia Farrow's idyllic compound outside New York or to the Hamptons, where we stayed with my friend Ellen Barkin and her then-husband, billionaire Ron Perelman, who owns Revlon, in a massive spread in East Hampton. Lola, the budding artist, was stunned by Ron's art collection, and she marvelled at seeing famous paintings by Ed Ruscha, Jean-Michel Basquiat and Roy Lichtenstein. We often headed to my favourite destination, London, to stay with Gael and Francesco at their spectacular place, Petersham House, just outside Richmond. Petersham is right on the Thames, surrounded by flowers, fields and ancient pathways, and the house itself has its own nurseries, café and award-winning chic restaurant. Heaven for Nick: horses nearby, river walks, chickens, a pool, a tennis court and Richmond Park with its thousands of deer just two hundred yards away. Heaven for me, too, with Gael and so many old pals. (It was almost too much fun, since it would always make me so sad to go back to LA.) And heaven for Lola, as Gael has three wonderful girls—Lara, my goddaughter, Anna and Ruby—as well as her son, Harry. One year I took Lola on a 'bonding' trip to Paris. She pouted and sighed her way through many museums, including our favourite, the Musée Picasso, but she now looks back at the photos with joy and loves to tell of my outrageous queue jumping in the face of mile-long summer lines. Another summer we went to Prague for a month, where a friend, Charles Shyer, was directing *The Affair of the Necklace* with Aussie actor Simon Baker, Hilary Swank, Chris Walken and Jonathan Pryce. Lola worked as a grumpy PA, having to get up at the crack of dawn, and both she and Nick were extras in the film. I rejoiced that she would be too tired to rebel, but even in Prague she managed to get her belly button pierced and sneak the local drink of absinthe at late night parties with cast and crew.

Back in LA, the drug-taking may not have been totally rampant— possibly even average by today's standards—but with a father who had been in and out of rehab his entire adult life, I was hyper-aware that she may have inherited her dad's addiction gene and was determined to do everything in my power to nip it in the bud and give her ways to deal with it. For a minute I thought of sending her to an arty boarding school up in the hills above Palm Springs and she and her father and I drove up for a tour. Lola, touchingly, was so thrilled that it was the three of us together and kept saying this was the first time she could remember being in a car with both her parents! Of course I immediately shed a guilty silent tear although it was not my doing in any way. Ultimately, Lola decided she didn't want to go to boarding school and so, with violent opposition from both her and her father, I insisted on a better idea—after-school rehab for the darling at a place called Insight, a long schlep away in Van Nuys, four nights a week after school from about 4 till 9 pm. Parents were in attendance on Tuesdays and Thursdays for two-hour group family sessions. Oh boy, and were they horrifyingly grim little reminders that no good deed goes unpunished—leading me to second-guess my decision to send her there at all. I still vividly remember the very first session, about two

Lola's fourteenth birthday dinner in Prague. I was having a silly fling with the director, a fellow called Charles Shyer, and moody teen Lola was a PA on the movie. I was working on a script but had a huge case of writer's block. However, after-hours gatherings made up for it, especially as Anjelica was in town on another shoot. This particular evening was a lot of fun with Hilary and her then-husband Chad Lowe, Simon Baker, Jonathan Pryce …

Lola and Nick as somewhat reluctant extras in Prague, on the set of The Affair of the Necklace. *There was an odd vibe on the set, and indeed the film, starring Hilary Swank and Simon Baker, was a massive turkey. But the sets were lovely and the costumes, by the deeply talented Milena Canonero, were all stunning.*

weeks after it all began, when I was asked to go 'in the middle'—sitting opposite Lola in a very uncomfortable chair—inside a circle of about thirty or forty parents and kids.

Asked by one of two therapists who were always present to talk about why she thought she was there, Lola, with a very cute head full of dreads at that point, paused only momentarily before announcing that her biggest problem in life was her mother.

'What about your mother? Elaborate please, Lola.'

'I *loathe* her,' she shot back. She narrowed her eyes and stared daggers at me, a horrifying mixture of defiance and hatred, and I felt like I'd been shot in the heart. What had I done that was so evil and vile to deserve actual loathing? Spoilt her rotten? Moved too many times? Yes and yes. But what else? One of the therapists asked her to go on.

Lola returned from a five-day school trip with a full head of dreads! I was initially shocked, but within minutes I realised I actually liked them. I was not so happy (nor was the headmaster at her posh school) when, a few months later, she went to school on Halloween with a flowerpot upside down on her head. She was a 'pothead'.

'She barges into my room all the time. She doesn't knock. I have *no* privacy.'

My mind shot back to the night before when she had screamed at me when I went into her room without knocking. 'Oh you mean last night, when I had no hands free and I pushed open your door with my foot because I was carrying a hot chocolate in one hand and a plate of Vegemite on toast in the other for you? Is that my crime? Oh I am so sorry. Arrest me!'

I was very smartly reminded that the rules did not allow interrupting the other person 'in the middle' but I was appalled. I had sweated blood to find the right place to help my daughter and get her back on track and suffered her tempers and lies for months—only to be blamed for everything? Her father and his wife, Tracy, sat there with arms neatly folded and about seventy eyes bored into me as she continued her tirade about my lack of understanding and hypocrisy. After all, I had parties. I drank and smoked weed. 'Very rarely!' I yelled, almost in tears. But again I was sharply reminded to keep my trap shut.

When finally my turn to speak came, I was too upset to say much in my defence other than to simply state I wanted the best for Lola, I was very worried and that the positive drug test (that Insight had done two weeks earlier), along with her admission that she had indeed taken cocaine, ecstasy and lots of pot, proved she needed to be there. And no, I didn't actually think coming in to her room bearing late-night snacks was a crime!

And then came the feedback from members of the circle. The rules did not allow you to respond to 'feedback'—you could only listen to utterly irritating, sanctimonious claptrap like, 'Well you sound like a very angry person. Are you always that sarcastic?' or, 'You seem very defensive. Your daughter's obviously in pain. Why can't you accept that she doesn't like you?' or, 'Well if you have parties with drink and pot—what can you expect?'

'I drink maybe one glass of wine a week and do not smoke pot,' I wanted to scream! But even the kids could say what they liked to you and you had to sit and 'hear it' and 'own it'. It went on like that for month after month. I definitely loathed pretty much everyone there! But at least Insight took over a lot of the 'disciplinary' measures I had tried and failed to enforce. She was not allowed to see her old friends, especially her boyfriend and her best pal, who were two classes above her, she had to go to AA sessions, undergo drug testing and even sign a contract of rules of behaviour.

Not surprisingly, she chafed against this crackdown and acted out as often as she could. Nothing major … just things like wearing a flower pot upside down on her cute dreadlocked head for the day at school on Halloween, calling herself a 'pothead'. (Secretly, I thought it quite witty.) Her school was not amused, though, and for that, along with cutting classes, she was put on academic probation. At home Lola would relentlessly bait me till I lost my temper and screamed. Sure enough what Lola described as 'my tantrum' would be 'aired' just days later at Insight. I was made out to be the 'monster mother'. But when her dad and Tracy were in the middle, she had very little to say, rarely if ever reproaching Chris for his rehab stints and spotty communication throughout her childhood. Intellectually I knew that she trusted that I wasn't going anywhere, whereas she still craved attention and acceptance from her father and was not about to criticise him.

And Chris, having initially fought me all the way about the decision to send Lola to Insight, insisting I was overreacting like an insane crazy person to her drug-taking, actually started to enjoy the whole process and became quite a star in his own right. He went to AA meetings and clearly enjoyed giving feedback to both kids and parents alike. He was like a wise old guru, knowing the 'rehab speak' as well as he did and making 'sober' jokes like the smart old comedy writer he was. Was he also trying to impress some of the stars who had problem teens as well? Possibly. They must remain nameless but boy did they get an easy ride. Therapists and parents alike did not dare say 'boo' to movie stars—but hey, we were in Hollywood.

At times, both Lola and the therapists as well as Chris were so set against me, insisting that Lola be allowed to live with Chris, that I even got my therapist to come to witness this humiliating and utterly unfair, in my opinion, movement to put me in my place. Yes, he was the favoured parent and was revelling in it till one day, having been stumbling in his sobriety, he fell off the wagon and right down the slippery slope, ending up back in rehab for a month. The attacks on me stopped; Lola calmed down and began to really thrive. She started to express herself in an incredibly insightful and eloquent way and she clearly gained a huge amount from the experience. I gave her a fabulous 'surprise' barbecue for her sixteenth birthday at my house in Hancock Park with all the kids from Insight and lots of old family friends. It was a big success—though I know Lola was upset that many of her old pals, especially her non-sober boyfriend Julian and best school pal Evan were not allowed to come. But she was still pleased with all the attention and it was fun to see sober kids having such a ball as they jumped from the top of the guesthouse roof into the pool below with wild abandon.

But like all programs, it was flawed and after eighteen months both Lola and I agreed that she had gotten as much as she could from it. My dad was unwell in Melbourne. I wanted to be much closer to him for what I initially told friends would be twelve months. We were all ready for a stint in Australia and so I spent months packing up a lot of stuff, storing a lot but shipping many, many things to Australia— secretly hoping it might be a permanent move. I had recently finished a gruelling six months renovating a rather dull nasty house I had bought in the Hollywood Hills off the famed Mulholland Drive—but with one of the best views imaginable! I foolishly sold the Hancock Park house when money got tight and bought a much cheaper house with potential. I knocked down walls, added concrete floors and a fabulous kitchen with custom eat-in booths and made the stunning deck twice as big with huge caissons that went deep into the hillside. Again we lived like camping gypsies as serious chaos began to surround us. Nick slept in a tent in the big living room and Lola and I slept on mattresses as I had the bathrooms and kitchen gutted and several walls removed. We didn't leave—even when we shared one loo with the workmen and had a pile of rubble where the kitchen was … And by the time it was looking quite stunning and I'd entertained there a few times, I changed tack, rented it out and we arrived in Sydney, where most of my pals resided, with lots of trips down to Dad in Melbourne planned. Best not to get too attached to anything, I say …

The thrill of escape slowly waned as we spent six weeks in a serviced apartment and I tried to get my bearings and readjust to being back 'home' after thirty years away. Rachel and Nell Campbell were welcoming—as was the heavenly Charlie Waterstreet—and Mandy down in Melbourne was so happy I was back, but still I felt like Rip Van Winkle waking up from an acid trip as foggy flashbacks from the past slithered in and out of my brain. It's tough to go back. One friend hastily pointed out that I had 'left it far too late' to return. I scoffed but felt very unsettled. And my poor dog Cooper, a divine black cocker–lab mix, was in quarantine about an hour away for three months and I would weepily drag the kids out to visit him once a week and then drive back, very sad.

Some strings were pulled and Lola, without a Catholic bone in her body, was accepted, thanks to a good word from Rachel Ward, at a rather posh Sydney girls convent school—where she saucily sported an adorable short uniform, blazer and straw hat. She would head out in the morning, looking outrageously cute in her 'sexy schoolgirl' garb, with black-rimmed eyes and tanned legs, head to a nearby cafe for a cappuccino and a cig, and attract catcalls and whistles as she made her way to the nearby station for the train ride to school that took her over Sydney's stunning harbour to the North Shore. Nick went to a public primary school and seemed very happy, while I found us a very thin house in Surry Hills to live in and tried to get a gig … not easy after so many years away. They don't take too kindly to gals who piss off for a quarter of a century and then think they can swan back in and find work.

I re-set my romantic comedy *Mad about the Boy* in Sydney and pursued all sorts of different things—but it was tough. Support was not forthcoming, even from friends, and indeed in some quarters there was outright hostility. Then Lola got early acceptance to the Chicago Art Institute and before the year was out, to my total shock, she was gone. I was truly devastated to be losing her and to not even be able to go through the ritual of taking my daughter to college to buy her electric kettles and settle her into a dorm. At the airport I wept bitterly, remembering almost identical scenes of tears whenever I left my parents and headed back to my life in London. She was so excited to be joining the two friends she had been forbidden to see for eighteen months at Insight—Julian and her fellow artist and great pal Evan, who were both already at the Art Institute. For a few months I felt utterly desolate.

Dad's health went downhill and so Nick and I packed up our rented house and drove in the ancient green station wagon I'd bought filled to the brim, with Cooper the dog, down to Melbourne, a big truck filled with the furniture I had already acquired following behind. We stayed on for a total of four years, moving five times to various short-term rentals as I kept imagining I could summon the guts to return to LA any minute—but of course I could never bring myself to tell Dad I was going. I adored him so much and he suffered with such grace.

So life revolved around Dad—shopping in the same shops I'd been to as a kid with my mum, cooking, driving him to doctors appointments, cleaning the house and trying to also be as kind and sweet to Shirley, the woman he'd married a few years after my mum died, as humanly possible. It wasn't easy. For her, in my view, it was nought but a marriage of convenience. She and Dad had been an item way back before the war and Dad went off with 'Shirley' emblazoned on the side of the Spitfire he'd been trained to fly—but just as the Spitfire never arrived, so the relationship was a dud. When he finally returned from the war his brother Charlie told him in no uncertain terms that Shirl had not waited and instead had been carousing with Yank soldiers who'd been stationed in Oz. Dad didn't contact her and instead married my mum a few years later, who then had to put up with many years of a drunken Shirley calling to speak to Dad on the odd

Saturday night to complain about her alcoholic husband. I remember the calls even now and my mother swearing like a trooper for the next few days, cursing Shirley for her outrageous behaviour. A year after my mum died, Shirley's husband died too, and she was on the blower to my lonely father just weeks after he returned from a wonderful long stay with me. They married and I had them come to stay several times in both New York and LA. For the premiere of *Scent of a Woman*, Al generously agreed to fly them in, put them up in a swanky hotel on Madison Avenue, have them out to the country house and then on the night of the movie opening, bring them to the big party afterwards with limos, bodyguards, the whole nine yards. Then in LA, I dragged them to parties and glamorous nights at Chasen's in LA with Al and Frank Sinatra. They were meant to hit Vegas but I'd tired them out. They were beat.

Back home in Black Rock, Dad was put into service as Shirley's personal chauffeur, 'chief cook and bottle washer' as she joked once. But it was completely true and for twenty years, he'd been shuttling her around obediently, completely at her beck and call and keeping the booze flowing as she funnelled as much money as she could to her lazy son. I bought her cashmeres and fresh flowers, paid for annual trips to the Gold Coast and weekly cleaners. Once when Dad was in hospital for three weeks with a staph infection, and Shirley, thanks to Australia's fantastic health service and Dad's gold card status as a war vet, went to one of our fabulous 'after care' joints so as not to have the hassle of making herself so much as a cup of tea, I went and did a massive 'makeover' of the flat—painting every inch of it, dyeing the carpet, adding new curtains, bedspreads and a new drought-resistant pebble-filled garden. I worked seven days a week with help from my dear cousin Jane and an Irish handyman called Dermot and when I brought them both home for the big unveiling, Dad was touched but Shirl seemed distinctly underwhelmed.

As soon as Dad was too weak to drive, Shirl started to become abusive, and once it was crystal clear his health was failing, she bailed. Yes, she actually left him. Stunningly, she sent her lousy old china cabinet off to auction, and despite Dad's endless exhausting entreaties to get her to stay, her weak lump of a son actually arrived one day at about 3 pm, took three suitcases to his car and then muttered, 'Bye, Norm. You ready, Mum?' Dad made his way to the driveway and then, leaning on his walker, watched as she got into her son's car, without so much as a goodbye or a hug, never to see him again. It was astonishing. Tearful, he staggered back to his big comfy chair and stared into space. I knew I couldn't leave him now.

Dad had an enlarged heart and was growing weaker. We sold his apartment and moved him into a fairly decent 'independent living' complex. In Australia, veterans are treated incredibly well and with respect. Dad, as one of the very few living World War Two vets left alive, had a gold card, which when presented to doctors meant 'kid glove' time. No question whatsoever of a bill. And carers to help get him up and dressed at least five days a week, which was a massive help.

After I'd been in England for about three years, I sent my folks two first-class tickets to come to London. We took them to the theatre and I swept them off to Paris and the south of France. One of their all-time top nights was a dinner party we gave for them in the copper dining room followed by a visit to a swanky Mayfair gambling club. Mum touchingly said it was one of the best nights of her life, and here you can see Dad, after several glasses of vino, feeling no pain.

Once Lola was born, I was so happy when Mum and Dad came to visit me again—this time in America. After Mum died, I made sure Dad came over a few more times … We always had a ball and took trips to New York, Santa Fe and up the coast to Big Sur and Monterey. Luckily he was around for a few of the parties! He was such a cool customer with a wonderful, dry sense of humor and he totally charmed all he met, including the likes of Jack, Al and many of my girlfriends.

Naturally I had to come in and paint and tart the new place up no end, with groovy black tiles in the kitchen and gorgeous mocha-coloured walls and a massive flat-screen TV so he could watch cricket and tennis and whatever else he liked. I visited seven days a week, dragged him down for lunch, nagged him to join in the exercise classes and have massages down in the spa and, eventually, just wheeled him out into the sunshine where he would doze as I sat weeping quietly a few feet away.

My dear sweet Nick, after years of watching me tend to Dad, now followed suit and was utterly divine as he helped Dad in and out of his wheelchair and our car, took him for walks, played Uno and poured his whiskies. He even amused Dad no end with his wheelchair tricks and we used to joke that Nick should go for a *Guinness Book of Records* feat of being able to balance on the back two wheels of a wheelchair for the longest time.

But as the months passed, Dad had barely an ounce of strength left. He couldn't walk at all and his quality of life had gone. My brothers Geoff and David, David's lovely and kind wife, Liz, and my cousin Jane and various grandkids would all visit often, trying to will him into keeping going. He was such a delightful and gentle sweet man. Over the years I'd quizzed him about his experiences at the notorious Changi prison camp and then on the Burma Railway— which of course he'd never discussed while we were growing up—and eventually I'd even recorded hours of interviews with him when he came to stay with me in America. It was gripping stuff—especially the way he told it with such modesty and even humour. When ABC's *Australian Story* came along to do a piece on me and Dad, it was sadly too late for Dad. He simply didn't have the energy to take an active part in it and give voice to some of his experiences. Alas, the belief held by the Imperial Japanese Army that men like Dad who had sur- rendered to it were guilty of dishonouring their country and family was something these poor men had to live with for a very long time.

The last two nights of Dad's life, Nick and I slept on the floor of his tiny living room. On his last night Dad called out to me a few times and each time I would help my father, who must have been unbearably humiliated, the few steps to the bathroom and onto the toilet. It was a false alarm. A few hours later, after I'd gotten up and taken Nick to school, I rushed back to his side and he asked for some wine. I gave him a glass of white wine and then he asked for ice-cream. I fed him a few spoonfuls and then he drifted off to sleep. An hour later I was on the phone to a friend in LA saying I thought it was near the end and that I really wanted to tell him I loved him. My father had never really stated things like, 'I love you,' though I knew he adored me. My pal urged me to just go and tell him right away and I said, 'Yes I'm going to.' At that precise moment, this heavenly man who came each morning to help my dad get dressed and tidy up was vacuuming round

Dad's bed when he shouted, 'Lyndall, he's not breathing any more,' and that was that. He had taken his last breath.

The first person I called as Dad lay there was Lola. The second, rather ridiculously, was Al. But he was sweet and sent such lovely flowers for his funeral. That was a devastating day I cannot stand to think of and the more so when I saw how a heartbroken Nick couldn't stop weeping as he sat with Lola—who'd flown out for the funeral—a few feet from the coffin.

I wept for hours and despite adoring certain things about an Aussie life and the comfort of family members nearby, I knew that day I wanted to be back in America near Lola. And so, a month or two later I sold the Beaumaris house I'd recently bought and Nick and I packed up and headed off once more—back to LA in time to give Lola a fabulous twenty-first birthday at my house up on Mulholland, which was temporarily not rented. Maybe if I'd stayed on, I would have found 'a life' in Oz, but I was truly a nomad by now—a 'disenfranchised person' as my older brother David had once told me—and it's the way it is. It's the price I paid for having had all that brash confidence and the chutzpah to have left home to explore the world. But I miss Australia and friends and family and all the wonderful things it has to offer. As Germaine Greer said in an interview I did with her in the early seventies, 'I miss everything about Australia. I miss the light more than anything. And the sky. In England the sky's always like a grey felt hat, but in Australia it's miles away—there's not even a sky. There's emptiness above you and around you. Australians are still my favourite people. They're still the only people in the world I understand.' Hear hear! I agreed with every word, then and now.

CHAPTER 22

A Lucky Escape

Ten days after my reconstructive surgery Lola and I head back to Santa Monica and I'm soon baring the top half for Dr Bob, who frowns and informs me that I have tons of fluid around my huge swollen breast and it must be drained immediately. A giant horse needle is produced while he says it's crystal clear that I've been doing too much. I protest vehemently. Alas, my disloyal daughter tells him that I'm a shocking liar and that I'd spent hours in the garage the day before heaving boxes and looking for paintings and generally acting like some pumped-up circus strongman.

Dr Bob is deliriously happy to hear that his suspicion is right and he orders me to lay low and start another course of antibiotics. Then my Brutus of a daughter mentions that we are all planning a sortie to Australia the following week and Dr Bob nearly has a conniption. 'Why?' he demands.

'Because I have family and friends there and I booked it eight months ago,' I say. 'And I didn't get to go last year,' I add plaintively.

Two days later, after running round buying Christmas presents, because that's what Aussies visiting relatives in Australia do, I'm back at Dr Bob's, hugely swollen again and he drains it first before getting the magnet to find the matching magnet in my expander so he can pump it up through the port—so as not leave any dead space for more fluid to gather. He says I've obviously been doing too much and going to Australia tomorrow's out of the question.

I go home and collapse on the bed amid the half-packed bags. A vision of the next eighteen days alone, with not even a plan for Christmas Day, flashes before me! I just can't bear the thought of it. And my oldest friend, Mandy, who's had pancreatic cancer which has spread to her liver and lungs, is expecting to see me. I also want to see my favourite uncle, Ab, who's not at all well.

By next morning, after dropping the teen at school, I know that staying will be too wretched for words. I call to see if there are any labs back from yesterday's fluid tests, and blow me down if Dr Bob doesn't call back and say that preliminary results indicate there may not be any infection! But best to wait till Monday so I can come back and be drained again and get the official results. I tell him that it will cost $1700 to change my travel date.

'Well, it's your decision. Up to you,' he announces.

'I can *go*?'

'Double the dose of antibiotics and take them for two weeks—not just one—and jump on a plane and come back if anything starts to look weird.'

Having one breast twice as big as the other is already in the weird department but is clearly not what he means. What *does* he mean? Who cares at this point?

'Thanks so much Dr Bob,' I say—and actually mean it.

By now it's just four hours to go before we must head to the airport. Better get moving! And so follows a few manic hours as I must find passports, both Aussie and American, and do my son's packing. Pretty soon my head is spinning as I try to find something to wear to a New Year's Eve bash but too late—our ride has appeared, and Nick and I are off to the airport via Otis College to pick up Lola. Soon we are delivered safely to LAX, and Lola and I stand idly by as my fabulously strong son heaves bags on and off weighing machines, not letting his mum lift a finger.

As we hit the first passport checkpoint, an immigration officer looks at me, looks at my passport picture and then back at me.

'You looked better with the long blonde hair. You might want to grow it again,' he offers as he snaps it shut and takes up the next passport. I'm shocked. But Lola is incensed and jumping to my defence, immediately piping up with, 'Well you know, it's funny but when someone has chemo and *loses all their hair*, they don't have much choice about their hairstyle for a while!' That's my girl.

The officer's not remotely embarrassed. 'Well I wouldn't know about any of that!' before waving us on and shouting, 'Next!'

'Dickhead,' mutters Lola and Nick sweetly puts his arm around me as we march on with the eight pieces of heavy hand luggage I vow to eliminate each year.

And then, naturally, I'm taken aside to some holding area after the X-ray machines have spotted three expensive protein drinks in one of my bags. The female guard recovers the drinks plus a gorgeous hydrating face spray and holds them up as if it was a cache of heroin and a home-made bomb. 'Well, can I drink them now?' I plead as Lola hisses, 'Jesus, Mum, they've only had this law for about ten years. What is your problem?'

I respond loudly with, 'Well what the fuck do they think will happen? I'll drink them and blow myself up on the spot?' Lola yells back and soon she and Nick and I are all shouting at each other. Another gun-toting dude then tells us all to pipe down or we'll be taken 'to another area'. That shuts us up.

As we wait for the flight, my cousin from Melbourne, Jane, calls me on my mobile to say, without even a hello, 'Well I hope to God you're not coming!' She's just read my latest blog and apparently feels I should get a grip and follow doctor's orders.

'Janey, don't be mean, the doc changed his mind and we're about to get on the plane. Sorry!' She sighs and says she'll be at the airport to meet us.

The flight, in Economy, natch, is even more horrendous than I anticipated and after watching four films in a row, I suddenly realise that both my right leg and arm are completely numb. I manage to stagger up and head back towards the toilet where I shake and rub and suddenly remember cousin Jane's warning that I could get a blood clot after all the surgeries. None of my doctors have ever mentioned such a possibility but I suddenly panic ever so slightly and ask a stewardess, 'What are the symptoms of DVT?'

In minutes I'm surrounded by about five airline folk, my blood pressure, temperature and oxygen levels are taken and a Medevac team in Australia are called for their advice before a nice doctor appears to quiz me. I then excitedly overhear one steward whisper to another, 'Are there free seats in Business or First?' and my spirits momentarily soar as I imagine a good lie-down for the next eight hours. 'No, nothing at all,' comes the reply. Feeling has slowly returned to limbs and I'm ready to go back to my seat. But it's very nice to know that apparently about 95 per cent of the time there's a doctor on board any plane.

So, after watching four films and not a wink of sleep, Bob's your uncle and we've landed in Melbourne. We grab a latte—even the airports in Australia are full of fantastic stores and juice bars, sushi cafes and the best coffee in the world and then out into the stunning fresh Aussie summer air and a ride with dear Janey back to her place in Sandringham, a few minutes from Port Phillip Bay and the beach in hip Melbourne.

Within about ten minutes Nick's off on foot to walk round the corner and look up some of his old schoolmates from the Sandringham primary school, a stone's throw away, that he attended for three years. Five minutes later Lola is sunning herself by the pool in the back yard with my gorgeous eighteen-year-old niece Nikki, who's completely grown up since I last saw her. Already I'm feeling nostalgic as Nick loved Melbourne and the genius aspect of having pals a few blocks away. He would have been very happy to stay and live here. It's my first trip back in the just over two years since Dad died and it's odd not to feel the constant guilt I experienced whenever I wasn't by his side. So we tuck into our favourite charcoal-grilled chicken, salad and fruit that just tastes simply superior.

For some reason the jet lag is almost non-existent and when one does inevitably wake at some ungodly hour there's always the comfort of a glass of chocolate Milo and Vegemite on toast. My brother Geoff kindly lends me back my ancient Ford Falcon station wagon—and since I was safely back in the US while my licence was suspended for twelve months for talking on the phone, I'm free to thunder round again in what my kids called the Moose.

So despite endless pacts not to buy each other Christmas gifts, we maniacally run around buying far too many last-minute gifts. And then it's Christmas Day at my cousin Rick's. This year it's confronting to realise *we* are the grown-ups now. No parents at all. Just me and my three cousins—Jane, Rick and Bun—Rick's wife, Sue, and my brother, Geoff. Who knew we were this old? Why are we even doing this? Cos it's bloody Christmas and that's what you do, and in fact it's a very jolly one with seven kids between fourteen and twenty-six who know how to party and drink champagne and beer like it's going out of style. Nick tries to casually walk away with a beer at one point till I put my foot down and tell him to put it down immediately—no ifs or buts! By 5 pm eighteen of us are finally sitting down to eat our Christmas feast. Very traditional. Turkey, plum pudding, the lot, thanks to our hostess Sue who is ruffled by nothing. I stand up and try to make a toast to missing friends, my dad and Uncle Ab and Aunty Pat, but am immediately in tears and unable to speak. Young Tom, twenty-five, gets to his feet and rescues the moment—with great humour. By 6 pm we're dancing like fools to some great oldies that our fabulous DJ Rick always provides. And by 9 the washing up is almost done and we stagger home. I'm very glad I made the trip.

And I'm so grateful I get to see Mandy, a great journalist and my childhood best friend from our all-girls school who I've had fun with on every trip back home—at least thirty of them, since leaving Australia at twenty. But this trip was very different. Cousin Jane and I visit our old school pal twice in Geelong and after two years of pancreatic cancer, she's very ill. Always a little plump, she's now like a skeleton. Every fibre of my being wishes I had the money and resources to somehow produce the perfect holistic team of acupuncturists, reflexologists, chefs and yoga teachers on her doorstep, easing the need for painkillers and anti-nausea drugs and giving her a life- and immune-enhancing concoction of food, drinks, meditations—and the *strength* to keep fighting.

I'm sure the Aussie oncologists are as good as any in the world—but that means well-meaning folks who are trained to prescribe toxic drugs and nothing else in the way of complementary treatments, nutrition or supplements. No one has ever even mentioned to her the concept of smoking pot or ingesting it to help with the nausea. Her weight is perilously low due to endless vomiting caused by the acute nausea and she should at the very least try some weed with her twenty cigarettes a day! I tell her how I'd been convinced by Melissa Etheridge talking on *Ellen* or *Oprah* about pot helping with it—and Mandy and her dear husband Graham seemed open to it, but in Australia no doctors can prescribe it and she says none of her friends partake of same. It's tough to be a know-it-all bossy boots caretaking type but not live in the same country. As I wave goodbye and give her a huge hug on the second and last trip, I know it's certain I won't see her again. I cry halfway back to town.

Loyalties torn and divided, we sadly leave Melbourne after a fleeting nine days and head to Sydney where there are more lovely friends, warm breezes, cockatoos overhead and the heavenly smells of frangipani trees. Our stunning, generous and wildly energetic hostess, Rachel Ward, decides we should stop on the way back from the airport at the fish market on the harbour and check out the huge whacking great barramundi, gleaming freshly caught snapper and all manner of Aussie seafood—some still alive and kicking, newly arrived here at the wharf. Lola and Nick are thrilled to be seeing the Brown kids, whom they've known all their lives.

Minutes later we're lunching on fantastic sushi and then we buy fresh prawns, oysters and sardines to eat the same night under the Sydney stars in the beautiful old sandstone house right on the harbour that Rachel and Bryan Brown share. I retire to my own little guest-house at the bottom of the garden just feet from the harbour itself and the private jetty for speedy morning getaways in their boat to nearby cafes for more lattes or a swing past the Opera House. It's some sort of extraordinary flexible jetty that sways with the waves made by adorable little tugboats and swanky lit-up cruisers that pass all through the night. My first night in Sydney—a full moon—sees a Southern Hemisphere sky that is ablaze with stars and the softly twinkling lights of the famous Harbour Bridge. I'm with dear, loyal friends and I hear my kids laughing nearby with their pals. Not too shabby.

The next morning is stunning, sunny and clear, and by 11 am Rachel and Lola and I are heading across the Sydney Harbour Bridge to our old friend Nell Campbell's house in Longueville, a North Sydney suburb where Nicole Kidman grew up. We arrive at Nell's new digs—a house she bought on moving back after thirty years in London where she acted and New York where she did cabaret acts and ran restaurants and her own wildly successful nightclub, Nell's. She's returned to her roots, a mile from where she grew up, and embraced a whole new life. The house is a true haven, backing onto gorgeously green bushland and surrounded by a virtual forest of trees and laughing kookaburras and her own pet water dragon, Jimmy, who appears daily for raw carrots and any tasty leftovers.

We also sneak in a visit to the Browns' incredibly beautiful farm, with its stunning lily-strewn lake and undulating landscape, the beach nearby, barbecues at twilight, champagne under the stars and kangaroos jumping in the nearby hills. Not to mention big group cooking sessions, shrieking games of charades, stolen beers in the bunkhouse and long afternoons of Scrabble on the verandah—all to the dulcet tones of dear Bryan Brown screeching that it's not his bloody turn to take the washing off the line 'so somebody better bloody get to it'. I know for a fact that for all three of us, many of our fondest memories are from the farm.

Just a few days later another year is about to bite the dust. The day of New Year's Eve in Sydney is a flurry of activity as the perfect hosts, Bryan and Rachel, are preparing the house for their bash that evening on their huge verandah and back lawn overlooking the harbour and thus we, the guests, are thrilled to help in anticipation of yet another of their famous NYE bashes with the fantastic free view of the amazing fireworks show that Sydney puts on for its inhabitants each year. It's a bloody beauty!

There's a lot to be done … no lolling about reading novels or hitting Bondi Beach today. We drink lattes and as the caffeine kicks in, we rise to the occasion. Suddenly gorgeous Turkish rugs and oversized cushions are being flung onto the lawn, verandahs are swept, bushes are pruned, fabulous throws and Indian quilts are put over outdoor sofas, tables are laid, lanterns and candles placed, incense is lit and within a couple of hours we have 'staged' the joint beautifully. The blokes (Nick and Joe Brown being directed by the hilariously bossy Bryan) have been doing bloke work—carrying boxes of booze all over the place and putting out big bins lined with trash bags to hold copious amounts of beer and wine … and now it's time for some food prep before joining Lola and her best pal Matilda (Bryan and

Aussie blokes preparing to barbecue a big old slab of lamb for our Christmas lunch at the Brown farm. Charles Waterstreet, barrister, columnist and inspiration for the TV series Rake, *tries hard to be blokey and does a passable if somewhat campy rendition of a Real Aussie Fella, whereas Bryan Brown and his brother-in-law John McLean are in fact the real thing.*

Rachel's daughter) for a fun, old-fashioned massive trying-on-of-frocks session. So young and gorgeous as they inspect themselves in a full-length mirror and reject one fantastic outfit after another. I borrow a long arm- and leg-covering dress from Rachel and try to not look in the mirror more than absolutely essential. My mouse-brown hair has begun to grow in, about an inch and a half all over.

As the wind dies down and a perfect warm evening presents itself, we realise we have about three minutes to get dressed as people are already arriving, champagne corks have begun popping and the party has begun against one of the best backdrops in the world. Okay—in the Southern Hemisphere. Lola and Matilda appear looking like the exquisite young things they are, each wearing one of the other's outfits, and it's funny to realise they are no longer awkward or shy but totally confident and charming young women able to make small talk with the best of them.

People in Australia are naturally discreet—and no one has once mentioned the fact that I've been crook for the last year. It's a huge relief and such fun to see old friends … and we get to see Sydney's brilliant fireworks *twice* … there's a 9 pm show for young kids and then again of course at midnight, when a lot of us head down and watch from the jetty as the water reflects the flaming sky. Suddenly lots of the young set—led by an inspired Matilda Brown—jump into the harbour, clothes and all. Yes, my two do it and are extremely pleased with themselves. We oldies mutter to each other about sharks but they're having a blast and certain daughters even have a kiss with a very cute local right there in the harbour as the fireworks explode overhead.

But it's funny how things can change in the space of a few days. One minute I'm thinking how adorable it was to see Nick walking round the block in Melbourne to see the pals he's known from the third grade—reverting to the childhood habits of cruising the neighbourhood on bikes—and then a few days later he's a drunken oaf throwing up like a great big revolting teen who, to my horror, admits as he hangs his head over the toilet for about an hour, that he'd downed *ten* beers—apparently between midnight and 2 am when I saw him heading for bed. I'm shocked to think that had I not gone up to check on him—only to discover him lying in a huge pile of vomit on the pillow—he could have choked to death! It's frightening and I berate myself for not keeping a closer eye on him, but when dozens of beers are lying in bins all over the place waiting to be drunk, what can you do? I truly pray that it has taught him a lesson, and as I watch him like a hawk for the rest of the night—as he sleeps in my bed—remind myself to tell him, about fifty times over the next few months, that shockingly, teens die of alcohol poisoning all the time.

As he happily tucks into bacon and eggs the next day at noon with the rest of us (after Bryan sensibly insisted he drag down the sofa bed he slept on and hose it down) and silly tales are swapped of the first time others got drunk, I know it's a New Year's Eve he'll remember for a long time.

I have a few more days of peace and quiet down at unspoilt Whale Beach (about an hour from Sydney) with Rachel and a dear friend Lydia, and on my last day in Sydney I actually wake up feeling somewhat refreshed and not unlike a human being—but no rest for the wicked. One hour later, after a lightning visit to a fabulous local artist Bruce Goold, I am heading back to pack. Me and my boy wrench ourselves from the sultry Sydney summer back onto the plane and a few hours into the tedious flight back, memories of penguin-watching at twilight and Christmas lunch with all the cousins and the dinner party of oysters and artichoke pasta at Frank's and Vegemite on toast at Janey's are beginning to fade.

By the time we're waiting for our luggage at LAX (why does your life flash before you in such a deeply depressing way as you wait for luggage?), it's hard to believe that we were in another hemisphere and another season this very *same* day (due to the nineteen-hour time difference) with lovely friends we won't see again for a good long spell. Travelling is very weird and I am thrilled that Lola is in fact still there—having decided to stay on for another ten days to go on a road trip to Queensland with her BFF Matilda Brown. I close my eyes and try to pretend I'm still on holidays too.

CHAPTER 23

Back to Reality

THE ALARM GOES off at 7 am after what seems like ten minutes of sleep. Where am I? Ah, back in LA, where the frenzied session of unpacking Nick's bag at 3 am has resulted in a sandy pile of stinky damp clothes on the floor. I stagger to his room to wake the sleeping hulk. He has that science test today and naturally the Xeroxed pages from his science textbook that I optimistically packed have not been perused once by him during the entire vacation. It's tempting to say, 'Go back to sleep, honey, you can skip school and the test today,' and run back to bed myself. But he's already missed a day so, setting a dangerous precedent, I take him Weetabix and hot milk in bed and beg him to sit up and eat.

As we drive to school in the biting cold we're not used to after a spell of summer Down Under, I try to jolly up the sleepy teen with thoughts of how cool his new buzz cut is and how his pals will probably like it. Blow me down if, after two long years of unsuccessful threats mixed with cash bribes if only he would cut his shoulder-length hair, he didn't slip out one morning in Melbourne with cousin Jane, to the same barber my dad used to go to on Hampton Street, and get his hair buzzed within half an inch of his head! Well, the bad news is he failed the science test. The good news is that, yes, his pals dug his haircut and by Friday, not one but *three* of them have followed suit and gone from long flowing locks to short, crisp crew cuts! My son the trend-setter. I even spot Johnny Depp's daughter checking him out as he drums with the school band a couple of days later. I am disproportionately proud of the giant child who grew half an inch over Christmas. He's a great drummer. But trying to keep some perspective, I make him retake the science test and after long nights of jet-lagged study, he gets a C.

On the first day back I am down in Santa Monica seeing Dr Bob at 10 am sharp. He's not thrilled with the amount of fluid he has to drain from my left breast. He tells me to do nothing strenuous before coming back in a week—and when I return, it's the same story. He informs me that not one but *two* more surgeries will be needed to replace the expanders with permanent implants and get it looking halfway decent. Two, if we're lucky. Could be more. Just dandy.

Two more surgeries, an immune system to repair and five more months of eighth-grade homework. I decide to cut my hair even shorter and go white blonde.

It's a rash, somewhat impulsive move but foul, dull hair and an invitation to the 'G'day USA' awards—the big black-tie bash promoting Oz–USA relations in trade and showbiz and whatever else they can think of—the next night calls for tough decisions, and I'm pleased to say I am up for the challenge. I make the call at 11 am Friday and am with my old pal Mario by 4 pm that same day. (Yes, he's the one who did not show up to shave my head when I first started chemo.) By 6.30 pm Saturday night I am heading off to join some Aussie pals at the awards—to honour my friend Simon Baker along with Toni Colette and Greg Norman, the golfer.

And shallow tart that I am, I gotta say I feel a hell of a lot more attractive as a blonde than as Ms Mouse Brown. It's an attempt to recapture my youth when, decades ago, I cut my hair and dyed it blonde as I zipped around the Fox lot in pre-production for a studio movie, looking, I must say, pretty darn cool. But my kids both approve wholeheartedly and as I head off to the Hollywood & Highland Center to celebrate the Aussies, I feel like I've made the appropriate effort. And it's a 'bloody good night', with the very sweet and mighty cute Simon Baker introduced by his old friend Nicole Kidman, who clearly feels comfortable surrounded by fellow countrymen like Bryan Brown. She proceeds to tell us all that she took pride in being the one who had convinced the young jack-of-all trades but generally unemployed Simon and his wife to come over to LA about fifteen years ago and 'give it a go'. They followed her advice and some good parts followed. Several years ago, they felt it was time to head home to Sydney and they sold up here and bought a house there. But six months later they were all homesick for LA—and they headed back with three kids in tow to LA, at which point the again-unemployed actor looked for work and was forced to take parts not necessarily suited to his good self, notably when he took a role in the historical drama *The Affair of the Necklace*. Hilary Swank was an orphaned aristocrat in pre-revolutionary France and Simon, in ruffles, breeches and powdered wig, was a well-connected gigolo! Not his finest moment—but he was not alone. The film was a dud, though Simon was still his fun-loving and charming self when we visited during the shoot. But Simon totally hit the jackpot with a new gig as the lead on the top-rating show *The Mentalist*.

Nic and hubby Keith Urban then serenade Simon with a fabulous version of Men At Work's 'Down Under', singing witty new lyrics of their own all about Simon and his wonderful wife, Rebecca, and their three kids. It's a revelation to see Nicole shedding her usually controlled public facade and kicking off her shoes in gay abandon as she dances around behind her hubby. Simon blushes adorably—as does Rebecca when the lyrics turn to her—but it is an amazing tribute and I am thrilled to be there among the fun-loving Aussies like Ben Mendelsohn, who is so wickedly funny and irreverent, till I look up and see myself on the two giant screens televising it all. At first I truly think, 'Who is that sheila smiling goonishly behind Simon with a very shiny forehead and something resembling a wig hat on her head?' before realising it is me. I then try to hide behind Simon but keep dodging in the wrong direction. Mortifying. Though by the time I wake up the next day there are some nice emails from Australian friends saying they had seen it all on Channel 9 in Oz and how much they like the new 'do'. It's a small world!

Well, just as my hair needed a lift, I decide my spiritual side really is in dire need of a makeover. I feel all out of whack and while I want to be a good, kind person, my empathy levels need to be ratcheted down a notch or two. I need some balance. I find myself identifying with any sad soul I see—like the man who sleeps on the sidewalk in a big mess of duvets outside the Papa John's Pizzeria on Beverly Boulevard and who, upon waking, then sits all morning in a camp chair staring into space. I wave every morning and buy him a coffee or give him a couple of bucks but can't help imagining I *am* him and what it would be like to bathe in public restrooms and sleep outside in winter. And if I believed in reincarnation, I'd suspect I've come back as Paul Robeson as I find myself driving round moaning that old spiritual, 'I get weary and sick of crying, 'fraid of livin', but scared of dyin' … but Old Man River just keeps rollin' along.' I spend long periods in the car alone. Who's to know?

So, feeling a tad 'uncentred', I take myself off to the La Brea Showcase Theater, where Marianne Williamson is once again, after a long absence, lecturing on the Course in Miracles every Tuesday evening. I hadn't seen the New Age guru first time around so I am keen to check out her 'spiritual' evenings, which are half lecture, half Q&A with the audience, plus two prayers and a quick 'imagine you are bathed in golden light' meditation.

Meditation, Marianne tells the packed-out crowd, is the key to everything. She says that a mere five minutes of meditation in the mornings is enough to raise your thought patterns to a higher vibrational level to put 'your thought forms in the care of God' for the entire day. How hard can that be? And if it's really that easy, why the hell have I never been able to focus for five measly minutes in order to meditate? It's a tragic indictment of that dark, scary swamp known as my mind. I go from feeling elated to a loser in an ADHD flash.

But wait—it gets even easier and more seductive. While meditation is the way people listen to God, prayer is the way they talk to God. Williamson says that 'prayer is the medium of miracles'. She explains that there is no order of difficulty in miracles. All people have to do in order to receive a miracle is be willing to *ask*.

Not very hard. Just ask. I plan, from here on out, to meditate and pray, though I may have the two words tattooed on my arm since I don't really trust myself to remember.

No, wait. A third word might have to be added. Love. 'Love is to fear what light is to darkness,' she explains. 'Let the love in and fear disappears.' I am up for that. But then Marianne swings into question time and somehow love flies out the window. She's very crabby and wildly impatient with anyone who asks a dopey, annoying or long-winded question. 'What are you asking?' 'Get to the point!' or 'Do you actually have a question?' are snapped at dull folk with her rapid-fire delivery.

She's been talking about career on this one particular night and has managed to lull us all into some mass feeling of bliss as she explains that our careers are really to act with love and all will follow from that. If only we love, the gig will follow. 'And when God is your employer, you can't get fired!' Yes, but what if you didn't get hired in the first place? I wanted to ask.

A jolly-faced blonde of about twenty-five suddenly stands, is swiftly handed a mike by one of the scurrying nervous assistants and beams at Marianne as she says, with a strong Aussie twang, 'Hi Marianne, since you're talking about career, I thought I'd ask you for a job. I'm a singer and I'd like to join you on tour. I've got a tape I'd like to give you.' She gives another big, expectant smile and a nervous laugh. Well, let me tell you—our guru is not amused. She immediately launches into a very put-upon moan about not having enough time to listen to tapes and how she's not even *on* tour.

But our intrepid gal is not put off and with the smile at high-beam, she says, 'Well let me just sing you two lines,' and astutely not waiting for permission, she begins to sing with enormous gusto—in a truly stunning, soaring voice that sends shivers down the spine. I adore it and could listen for another hour. But she politely sticks to the two lines and then sits to raucous cheers and applause. But does Marianne even acknowledge the girl and her lovely voice with a, 'Well done— great pipes. If there's anyone here who is in music, perhaps you could give her some advice'?

Nope, no acknowledgement whatsoever. Marianne turns on her heel and heads up the aisle with her mike and picks on—sorry, picks— the next questioner. But having now dished about the 'cranky mean bitch' side of Ms Williamson, let me just say that she's very entertaining, smart as a whip and let's not forget, as my pal Brooke reminds me on the way home, it's the message not the messenger that counts here. I'm an atheist but I could sure use reminders to meditate and let the love in—especially if it does send the fear packing. I need a cheap life coach, even if it is a group session with eight hundred others.

So in an effort to put it into practice and *show* the love, I decide that despite a torrential downpour, I must show up at the soggy ceremony for my dear friend Anjelica Huston as she is given a much-deserved Star on the Hollywood Walk of Fame. I do so and am glad. It's not every day a pal gets a star. A far, far cry from the long-gone days when she and I would hang out in the spa in Gstaad having hydrotherapy as she talked of her career frustration and how desperate she was to work. But wrangling Jack—and all that entailed—seemed like such an overwhelming, full-time job. It's very, very wet but we feel intrepid and rather fabulous as we stand listening to speeches by Danny Huston, Wes Anderson and Anjelica under a tiny dripping tarp. Unfortunately, the love comes back to me in the form of a foul cold or flu that descends a day later and lingers a week, right through another breast-draining session with Dr Bob, who still won't agree to schedule the next surgery due to this fluid build-up!

I end up having the next step of reconstruction surgery where the temporary expander is removed and replaced with a permanent implant. Apparently it goes smoothly but I am somewhat horrified by what happens post-surgery. There I am, regaining consciousness and entering that netherworld state that, for a little while, resembles a bad trip with nausea, dizziness and just plain terror, when a cranky, business-like nurse appears and asks, as if she's just finished my leg wax and now has another client waiting, 'Is somebody picking you up? Your daughter is listed to call but I'm not getting any answer.'

What? I look about and notice that I am not in a nice hospital room of my own but on the factory floor-like recovery room.

I try to focus. 'My daughter's in Bali. Why would you call her?' I ask but the penny's starting to drop. I'm being hustled the hell out of Dodge—good old Dr Bob has outdone himself and somehow forgotten or not bothered to sort out whatever the hell needs to be sorted out with my insurers, Anthem Blue Cross. Because the bastards at the preposterously profitable Anthem, who, what a *shock*, have just seen fit to raise my monthly premium by 40 per cent due to my unfortunate cancer episode, don't let double mastectomy reconstruction patients stay for several nights in hospital, as is de rigueur in civilised joints like England and Australia, it means Dr Bob is meant to put in a request. At some point on the day of the operation he just tells them I need to stay. Seriously, that's how it works.

So when he finally appears that morning, prior to starting to carve me up with his permanent marker, I very sweetly ask him once more if I will be having a sleepover at St John's. It takes him a good thirty seconds of concentrated staring to decide where the middle of my torso is before starting to draw from my collarbone on down. It seems I'm asymmetrical. 'Yes, yes, you can stay,' he finally says, in a monotone faintly reminiscent of Yul Brynner in *The King and I* (as in, 'I am a surgeon, I am God. You may stay.').

And yet, here I am, nearly five hours after being knocked out and I'm trying to think of someone to call. By the time the security guard shows up with my belongings, I grab my phone and call the first person I can think of ... and she's getting dressed to go out to dinner ... and then I call another friend and it goes to voicemail—and so, I call a third friend, Andrew, who foolishly answers the phone and very sweetly agrees to drive me home.

I wake the next day at 8 am and any semblance of numbing medicine has gone from my system, leaving me in *searing* pain. Had I still been in hospital I would have still been hooked up to an IV and I would have simply squeezed a button, thus releasing pain medicine into my system for a day or two. But no, I must find pills (and even harder, manage to open those wretched childproof caps). I walk like a snail to the kitchen to start guzzling both painkillers and the dreaded antibiotics, realising that to avoid nausea one should eat something.

And then it hits me. Despite being quite convinced that I am of reasonable intelligence, it seems I am wrong. Because only a complete and utter half-witted moron would deem it a nifty idea to choose *this* precise day, after yet more traumatic surgery, to start a cleanse … a juice fast that contains no actual food, for the next five days!

Why would I deprive myself of grub the day after surgery? Now, in my own defence, it did seem smart to do this (a gift from my generous friend Brooke Adams, who had signed up for fourteen days but gave up after nine—thus passing on the five-day credit to me) with both kids away. And God knows, someone who's had the ludicrous toxic load I've had could do with a nice healing cleanse. But the day after surgery?

I stagger to the front door where a cooler of liquids should await me. I pray they've screwed up and nothing is there. I open the front door. I'm outta luck—it's right where it should be. The black cooler that weighs a ton and must now be gotten to the kitchen somehow. I manage to inch myself down to get the strap and then drag it behind me, feeling like an ancient wench dragging a rock to Stonehenge. Me and the cooler make it to the kitchen, but it's still on the friggin' floor and I have to get it to the bench. Wishing I'd paid more attention to Nick's current science studies about inclines and levers, I try to think what could help to raise it four feet. But I'm hardly up to devising a cunning lifting apparatus in my state and so I pick the bastard up and heave it onto kitchen bench and unzip it. There's an annoying letter welcoming me to this crappy cleanse and I see that it gives you the order in which to ingest your ten bottles of liquid. It starts off with a half jar of ANU water. Not even a freakin' juice. Just some really hearty hyper-mineralised water. Does the fun ever stop?

Please believe me when I say this water tastes bad. I spit it out and check what's next on the list. My least favourite thing in the world, super green juice. I despise green juices. They annoy me almost as much as people who don't drink coffee. Time for a Xanax and a nap. I wake around two and wonder what the Juice Feast (I swear—they call it a feast!) has in store for me now. Could it be that a genie will suddenly slip out of one of the bottles and whip up some steaming hot raisin toast slathered in butter? Or will it be a chicken pot pie with a crisp flaky crust?

Or … it could be a Chinese herb tea called Activate that enhances metabolism by way of 'tonifying the spleen'. Bitter, acrid and stinky. The directions say I could actually heat it, ideally by putting it outside to 'catch the blessed rays of the sun'—but like that would make a difference! I force myself to swallow at least half the bottle, and even if it can purify my aura and metabolise my digestive system, how do you control the urge to shoot yourself—or at least shuffle one block to the scarily close 7-Eleven for cigs, a couple of the new dark-chocolate Snickers bars and an iced coffee from the refrigerated section. Will I last the five-day distance? Wildly unlikely! Like a mad junkie, I open three more juices, drink some of each and slip back to bed, a broken woman.

Some people thrive on the discipline of diets and fasts. They actually see results and have something to feel proud about. Smug bastards. Then there are those of us—and I personally blame the Aussie convict gene—who are shocking scofflaws. Natural-born cheaters. Which makes it all the more moronic that I thought I could handle five food-less days.

On night two after surgery, as I stagger to the kitchen like a poor old Pavlovian dog for my usual late-night snack, I find myself popping salty chocolate almonds before I even remember that I'm meant to be cleansing my temple of a body. I could spit them out and pretend I didn't swallow two already but what a waste. So it's decided then and there … this will be a semi, or half-assed, cleanse. That night, it's great gobs of peanut butter … which I desperately need to take my mind off the fact that my skin has started to itch and burn like crazy!

I rip off the stretchy bandages, and with them great big patches of blistery skin peel off too, leaving gaping areas of red raw epidermis. Time for more painkillers, which leave me completely stoned within minutes, and that in turn leads to some slightly impulsive emails to my good pal Dr Bob. I temporarily forget I am supposed to suck up to the almighty surgeon no matter what, and I tell him I'm in agony, ask for an apology for hurling me out of hospital on the same day and generally try to convey how traumatised and upset I am with the last two years. This does not go down well.

Popular surgeons do not appreciate constructive criticism. Dr Bob leaps into email action talking utter nonsense about his wanting to save me money as Anthem consider major reconstructive surgery an outpatient procedure. He says if he had kept me overnight at St John's they might have objected and charged me a quick $20,000. But that's not what happened the last three times he operated on me! The recovery room nurses confirmed he could have easily organised for me to stay. And just how much more could St John's charge? I just saw the bill—$58,000 for the whole procedure with a mere $24,000 for the pharmacy bill. For what, some Propofol? That's it. I paid for my own Vicodin and antibiotics. Dr Bob is talking utter bullshit and I really wish St John's pharmacy would try to charge a smidge less! Plus, for fifty-eight grand the least St Johns could do was let me stay overnight! The whole thing is too infuriating for words. No wonder America spends more on healthcare than any other country. Thinking about healthcare could make one very ill.

I'm a tad anxious the next day when I visit Dr Bob since I now sense unfriendly vibes after I committed medical treason and questioned my standard of care. Sure enough, a frosty atmosphere. He says I've had an allergic reaction to the adhesive bandage and after I'm inspected and rewrapped, he launches into a seemingly rehearsed defence, once again, of his actions. I point out that he told me that I would be staying overnight about ten minutes before the operation and he denies it. But why would I want to wake up in recovery and have no one there to take me home? I swear on my children that he told me I'd be staying and even let him off the hook by saying, 'Perhaps you were just very focused on the surgery and didn't remember what you said ...' Silence. This is where you need the trusty husband who could back you up and insist that *we* were told I would be staying overnight. He orders me to stay on antibiotics for *twice* as long as originally planned.

Twenty-four hours later it's time to put on my happy face and my Uggs to pick up my gorgeous big teen of a son, who's been staying with friends and seems to have grown a good inch in the last five days. I'm so happy to see him that I try to ignore several facts.

1. It looks like he may be wearing the same t-shirt I last saw him in.
2. I've already had emails from two teachers about missing homework.
3. His teeth look a lovely shade of yellow under the braces and it's funny how I noticed his electric toothbrush still in his bathroom.
4. He left his novel at home and clearly is now even further behind with reading.

I take him to his favourite Cactus Taqueria on Vine and get him two fish tacos and a huge bulging burrito. He wolfs it all down before we're even home. Once in his bedroom, I sweetly suggest that he get down to homework soon since Mum needs to drink a foul protein drink on her cleanse and then take a nap. He promises faithfully that he will. Everything is hunky dory. I vow not to fight with him all week.

I wake up over two hours later and he's under the shower. He takes showers that last forever. What do teenage boys do under the shower for that long? Exactly! Let's not dwell on it. And there's his huge school bag on his bed, yet to be unpacked. That means *zero* homework has been done during my two-hour nap. He is not to be trusted! I take the *Playboy*s from their hiding place in his third drawer and chuck them as punishment. And the yelling begins.

But the bathroom door can be locked and he hides in there for hours with his computer and mobile phone and knows I can do nought about it—not until late at night when I stealthily creep into his room, take his computer and hide it in my room. But the truth is he's way sneakier and smarter than me and should seriously consider a career as a spy. He senses missing items and before I know what's happening, has crept up behind me and stolen *my* mobile phone, and refuses to give it back till I tell him where his computer is. You can perhaps sense what exceptional control and authority I have with my teenage son—but you try it. They're relentless, stubborn and always up for a good battle, and these mad chases round the apartment are oft before we've even left for school.

As the shower drones on, I drag a chair into the kitchen to search the top cupboard where I sometimes throw the American Spirits in disgust. Eureka! I find them, and light up a lovely stale fag and open the freezer for the vodka. Well, it is meant to be the purest of alcohols so that fits right into my purifying cleanse. Then I take half a Xanax in a noble attempt to stay calm and not fight with the teen. And since I'm such a cautious soul, drinking on an empty stomach is unthinkable and thus it's time for my version of cooking—opening a can of sardines and the making of some toast. And voila—the juice fast is over!

So I've eaten, I've smoked, I've drunk and still the shower is running. It's almost enough to make me forget my fucking surgery saga!

CHAPTER 24

Ups and Downs

IT'S TEN DAYS after the surgery and I have very cunningly booked tickets for myself and Nick to go on a skiing holiday in Italy, leaving in three days. I would have preferred it to be a week or two later but it's now or never, since Spring Break begins in five days, and Nick has been wanting to go back to my best friend Gael's stunning log cabin–style ski chalet in the Italian Alps since he was six when he first learnt to snowboard. His giant snowboard bag has been packed for a week with the multitude of long johns and snazzy ski boots plus the precious virgin snowboard that he's painted pink and green.

Of course I have no intention of hitting the slopes. My plan is to chill inside, read books and spend time with dear Gael, whom I see so rarely these days. But I'm still so very, very tired. I have to lie down at least twice a day and the thought of packing and economy travel via Chicago to London fills me with such dread that I come to my senses and realise perhaps he can go alone. When I deliver the sad news that I may not be coming, his obvious joy and excitement are downright unseemly. Not a whit of disappointment. He's deliriously happy and I hear him telling a friend, 'It's so stressful travelling with Mum. It's gonna be great going on my own.'

By the time we've made it to the departure lounge, he's livid that I'm trying to sneak bananas and cough drops into his backpack! Needing a distraction I whip out my iPhone and start to take photos. He turns and gives me one of his goofy, adorable grins. That's all it takes. I'm now in floods of tears and Nick, used to his sentimental slob of a mother weeping at the drop of a hat, is merely amused. Just as he tells me he's starving and dying for a Double Whopper from the nearby Burger King, there's an announcement demanding that unaccompanied minors who are being sent off alone by their callous, uncaring mothers must board the plane immediately. I'm allowed to bring him right on board the plane, which he keeps insisting is *not* necessary, but I see him to his seat, try to hug him about five times— and finally, weeping again, take my leave. But as I'm working my way through cranky passengers all heading in the opposite direction, I hear an announcement that cash is no longer accepted on international flights and that meals can be purchased only with credit cards. What?

My poor son, the only child travelling without a parent on this flight, has no credit card. He will starve to death. I have no choice. I make a mad dash to the Burger King and order a Double Whopper burger—which upsets me a great deal having just seen the documentary *Food, Inc.*—but a starving, credit card–less teen must be served and soon, holding the burger, fries and a massive Coke that could strike diabetes into a giant, I'm dodging cranky travellers in a mad sprint back to the gate, terrified it will have closed and I'll be forced to consume it all myself.

The woman punching in the boarding cards is very busy and so I run on through, down the tunnel and up to the plane door. Unbelievable. I could be a terrorist. No one tries to stop me. The stewardess at the plane door sniffs enviously at the fries and sweetly offers to deliver them but a pilot appears and she's immediately distracted. I don't want the lad to get cold fries and so off I dash, past folks stowing bags in the overhead bins, past lots of jokers asking if I have spare grub for them, and finally I spot my boy.

I pause a few feet away and hold up the burger and drink in triumph. Several passengers break into a spontaneous cheer but Nick's expression is one of utter horror. Did I change my mind? Is his mother now coming with him? Reddening with humiliation, he whips iPod wires out of his ears and gives me a beady-eyed stare that in an ideal world would make me invisible, but luckily, the smell of fries and burger reaches his nose in the nick of time and he manages a small smile as I hand it all over and reassure him, 'Just delivering, honey. Don't worry, I'm not staying.' He manages a, 'Thanks, Mum. Love you. Bye,' before popping in his iPod and starting to inhale the food.

I make it out of the terminal before breaking down weeping as I realise that, yet again, cancer has won out. It's robbing me not only of a long-anticipated holiday with my best friend but of precious time with a son who'll soon resist even the idea of holidays together. It's robbed me of memories that can't be repeated. It's also taught me that airport security is pretty darn slack and that one sure-fire way to annoy a teenager is to appear on a plane with food when he thinks he's already escaped his mother for two weeks.

Two days later I'm told there is no sign of bone cancer. I had experienced a lot of back pain for several days and, panicked, I told Dr Glaspy, who sent me in for an MRI. Hooray. I'm a happy camper. I try to decide who I should call with the fabulous news that the cancer hasn't spread to my bones. Ah, no one. Funny thing about being single. There's no significant other to care whether the cancer has returned or not.

Well, time flies and it sure looks like something close to a man walking out in the airport lounge as my boy, not yet fifteen, appears back on American soil after his sixteen-day trip to London and Italy. I'm thrilled to have him back. We're back to routine again.

And suddenly, like a bolt out of the blue, I realise that it's been weeks and weeks since I called Mandy, my oldest friend who's been desperately ill with pancreatic cancer for two years. Her husband, Graham, answers with panic in his voice. 'So you've heard?'

'Heard what?' I ask as my stomach lurches violently and I wish to God I wasn't such a selfish bitch who'd forgotten to call.

'She's not good. She's back in hospital and she doesn't know anyone. The doctor took me aside today and said, "Well, this is it. Brace yourself,"' he confides, his voice breaking. I want to scream. I feel like I've been punched in the stomach but utter the usual platitudes about how deeply sorry I am to this man—who has said, in the past, that if she dies he'll go off somewhere and never be seen again, ending it all. They had no kids, just two divine dogs, a dachshund and a labrador, and after falling in love in their early twenties, they rekindled their affair twenty years later and have been together every day for almost two decades since.

I call Graham the next day, much earlier. He answers quickly again. 'Hi Lindy, have you heard?' he asks, his voice quite calm. My hopes suddenly soar. Perhaps the antibiotics have cleared up her lung infection, she's snapped out of it and soon I'll be having a good ol' natter with Mandy again.

'She died at 4 am this morning. It was very peaceful. I talked to her all night. The doctor said that hearing is the last thing to go.' It's just too much to bear. My oldest friend, the girl I met in the first grade and have been so close to for fifty years, is gone. With pancreatic cancer that spread to her liver and lungs, it's not surprising, but it's utterly devastating.

This is Monday and the funeral will be held on Friday at St Andrew's church in Middle Brighton. As I'm researching flights, I realise that it would mean missing Lola's final art show and graduation from Otis College. I feel utterly wretched and torn but I just can't do it. I must be at her graduation. Heavy-hearted, I decide to write something that will be read by our mutual friend Meredith:

Nine two seven double six oh. I know those numbers as well as I know my own birth date. It was the number I called every morning at about 8.30. Just two rings and then I hung up, ran out the door and jumped into the old grey Vanguard with Mum at the wheel. Off we shot, usually late, Mum driving like a bat out of hell, to the top of Grosvenor Street to pick up my best friend who, almost certainly, would *not* be waiting there as planned. Mum would toot the horn, and then finally the wildly witty, whip-smart whirlwind that was Mandy Zachariah would fly out the door, usually held open by her frowning dad, Harry Zach, the vice principal of Brighton Grammar, and run to the car. In her hand, freshly ironed green hair ribbons—as was de rigueur Firbank dress code—that she would tie around her plaits as we headed to school. Sometimes, if I begged, she would put her hair into a single plait and give one to me, her ribbon-less pal.

In later years, if we had time, we'd head straight to the toilets next to the tuck shop and light up a quick Alpine as we'd suck on a Steamroller to hide the smell and chuckle at the thought of her big sister Sue, the school sports mistress, catching us in the act. Bizarrely, we never got caught. But we did get caught for many other misdeeds that generally involved the passing of notes and us laughing so hard and hysterically that we were in danger of exploding and we would be sent out of Assembly, or out of Divinity Class—or pretty much out of any class you can think of—on a fairly regular basis. We were easily amused but it's not a bad habit to have. We were part of a jolly and—I'm afraid I must boast—a *very* cool gang of seven or eight naughty girls …

When I didn't have to stay at school for athletics training, Mand and I would walk home after school to her place where her mum Joan would feed us huge thick slabs of fresh white bread slathered with butter, sliced bananas and white sugar which energised us sufficiently for a strenuous, shoeless dance session in the living room. Mand, *always* a great dancer, was desperate to get on the TV show *Kommotion* and so she'd pop on a 45 and we'd get down. Mand had a lot of great moves that left me for dead. The 'Swim' and I think something with a lot of head tossing called the 'Pony'. We were pretty even when it came to Chubby Checker and

'The Twist'—though we'd often collapse with a stitch after our massive snack.

Friday nights Mand often made a beeline for our place as she was very partial to the delicious Pine Burgers and chips that Dad would bring back from the joint on St Kilda Street opposite the yacht club. He'd often bring Minties and Jaffas too. We'd lie back, eat our Pine Burgers, watch black and white TV—happy as clams. Then we'd go and practice our Twiggy-like eye makeup. Big black crease lines, white highlighter under the brow and for Mandy, who already had those great big brown eyes, painted-on lashes underneath. And very pale pink or white lips. I told you—we were cool.

Then on Saturdays, Mand often joined Mum and me on trips to Church Street in Brighton to look in the shops. At thirteen, she already had her first pair of heels, in gorgeous white patent leather—and I was now on a desperate mission for heels too. A year younger, I was still twelve—but I needed heels! Mand had spotted a pair in brown with teeny-tiny one inch heels and a very cute bow. They were called Teena Dolls. They fitted to perfection and would match, as Mand pointed out, my itchy brown wool dress for Dancing Class next week. We found Mum and dragged her in but she was underwhelmed and refused to buy them. All the way home I whined on and on about the Teena Dolls and even the loyal Mand tried to convince Mum that the Teena Dolls were a must. But with Mand in mid-sentence, Mum suddenly lost it, took the Peter Stuyvesant out of her mouth, turned round and screamed, 'I'll give you girls a Teena Doll!' Well Mandy thought that was one of the funniest things she'd ever heard and started to shriek with laughter, turning the disappointment into hilarity. Even Mum, who adored Mandy, was soon hooting with laughter too.

Now, it's a silly little anecdote but it pretty much sums Mandy up for me. She had the most brilliant, infectious sense of humour, with a wonderful appreciation of the absurd and for the next forty years, on many different continents, she would suddenly, out of *nowhere*, shout very loudly 'I'll give you a Teena Doll!' and we'd laugh and laugh and laugh.

… and so it went on. Mand was one of the great 'good time' girls and the fact I can no longer call her for a fabulous chat is deeply sad.

My cousin Jane calls at 3 am on Friday morning to tell me about the funeral. A huge turnout, lots of laughs and a tremendous tribute to a darling girl. All the clichés in the world flood my brain as I sit up in bed, crying yet again and talking to my cousin. *Seize the moment. Try to find the joy.* It's all over soon enough.

Twelve hours later it's time to get ready for Lola's final art show down near the airport at Otis. I haven't seen her this excited since … well, maybe Nick's arrival. For weeks she and her fellow graduates have been slogging away till the wee small hours cleaning up their

Most years, as winter descended on London with a vengeance, I would excitedly look forward to the almost annual Christmas trip back home. The highlight—and what I would give to have it all happen again now—was opening a bottle of bubbly with my nearest and dearest. Here, my mum, my cousin Jane and I are visiting my best friend from school, Mandy, in her new apartment.

grubby, chaotic studios, repainting them and turning an entire floor of the building into pristine, professionally snow-white galleries to show their work. Now she runs round the apartment getting dolled up and, without warning, trying on her cap and gown for me to see. I hadn't known she even had the outfit here and as she spots tears springing to my eyes, she quickly whips it off and tells me to 'get a grip' before proceeding to work on her outfit for the evening, which invariably means trying all manner of cute, glam, sexy outfits before opting for her much-preferred laid-back look.

These days, it takes me three minutes to get ready. Black pants, a jacket from twenty-five years ago and a hat.

We're soon hurtling in witty Friday evening traffic with our dear friend and her recently anointed godfather Tim Curry to this place of learning where my darling has been closeted for years. And I'm as happy as I've been in a long time. We arrive at Otis College and rush from art-filled room to room. Lola's pointing out her work with a giant grin on her face, greeting people and being charming, and standing in front of her work for her deeply annoying camera-happy mother. I'm not getting the clear shots I want but it's okay and she's gone and we're trailing behind as she points out the three gorgeous watercolours … and then there's the truly beautiful installation she's done of stunning crystals that won the Juror's Prize last night, and next, three giant drawings of sumo wrestlers that are so fine and beautiful my heart is just bursting.

Oh my goodness, here's the infamous and electrifying knife installation—all manner of shiny, luminous, sparkling knives—and right at this moment her father appears and, ever the joker, loudly insists they're all his missing knives and makes to start pulling them out … and so it goes with friends and *all* her extended family appearing, which includes one mother plus her two stepmothers, her dad, her half-brother and sister, and even her brother Nick and a school friend are soon seen casually strolling in, having just arrived back from a school trip to Washington DC. It's a great night and I truly love her work.

On Sunday morning we're back at Otis as my girl is totally rocking the glam/professorial look in cap and gown, dark red lipstick and a stunning gold sash that signifies she is graduating with Honours— a minor detail she incredibly modestly just happened to tell her mother last night. It's the picture-perfect graduation you see in American movies, the first I've ever been to and which lives up to the build-up with a fabulous procession of faculty and students, rousing speeches and all the appropriate pomp and circumstance. I'm in a muck sweat, standing on my chair trying to work out whether I should use my new Canon, bought specially for the occasion, to just photograph or video the moment her name is called and she walks on stage.

My darling girl graduates with honours from Otis College of Art and Design. She had done her first year in Chicago at the Art Institute, but transferred to Otis so she could work as an assistant to her beloved mentor, artist and sculptor Robert Graham, in Venice—as well as attend college. Her father Chris and I were so, so proud.

At the last minute I opt for video and run halfway down the aisle, fighting my way through a throng of similarly crazed parents so I can really capture the Kodak moment. It doesn't disappoint. She glows and I'm the proudest mum ever.

Moments later, as caps are actually flung into the air—just like in the movies—I realise I've done something right. I have an outstanding, wonderful, kind, clever and talented daughter. Her beloved mentor— one of the best sculptors in America—the late Robert Graham (who was married to my dear pal Anjelica Huston), whom she took a year off college to work for, transferring from the Chicago Art Institute to Otis to be close to Bob's studio in Venice, would have been so utterly delighted and proud of her too.

And the graduation gift from her mum? Not very thrilling. Not a groovy vintage 'woody' Le Baron car. She bought one herself a few weeks ago. Not a stunning new wardrobe from Barneys or a trip to Italy. Nope. A two-month Kaplan course to study for the LSATS— so she can go to Law School next year. 'No dough in art,' I keep telling her in stunningly philistine fashion. 'Get a law degree, baby!' A mother can dream.

CHAPTER 25

A Hot Valentine's Day

Many months later, I'm sprawled on my massive bed. There's heavy breathing and a little gentle moaning. My hair's in disarray. I'm hot and bothered, beads of sweat forming. I hate to be immodest but this cashmere has to come off now. And the t-shirt. I can't wait any longer. Time for a dramatic gesture.

I stagger up like a drunken sailor and head to the kitchen where I grab the giant scissors. I grasp two layers of fabric with one hand and start hacking away, right up the middle of my gorgeous navy v-neck cashmere and my black t-shirt. I try to pull the left side off but with that arm hanging limp and useless, it's not easy. I pull too hard and the blinding rush of pain is excruciating. I scream in agony, burst into floods of tears and collapse back into the bedroom with the destroyed cashmere flapping open to reveal that post-mastectomy bra—flat on one side as I don't even have the energy to stuff it with an old sock these days.

Why am I in such pain? Because four days ago I blacked out at 6.30 am, broke my bloody collarbone and gashed my big fat head as I caught the sharp metal corner of a chest on the way down to the icy bathroom tiles. The pain really is brutal and since then I have not been able to remove the aforementioned t-shirt and sweater. The clothes I went down in have not left my person since. That's how it is for single mothers. I've been too unwell to mind and the one bit of good news about an unruly, hormone-raging, mood-swinging teen is that they really couldn't care less if you wore a sack for a year. A couple of times over the long, lonely weekend, I tried to work out how to disrobe, but the concussion kept me too dizzy to even stand for very long. And yet the balmy heat this Valentine's Day is suddenly suffocating and I must shed these garments now!

Why *did* I black out that morning?

The simple ghastly truth? Because one breast started to 'collapse' and Dr Bob performs more reconstructive surgery in mid-December. Please note that it's wildly inadvisable to ever have surgery, if it can be possibly avoided, a couple of weeks either side of Christmas. Surgeons have lives and wives and families and they even take vacations, often to far-flung expensive places!

You may howl with derision at the repetitive nature of what I now must admit, but during the first follow-up visit three days after surgery I say, 'My left breast looks really red.'

Dr Bob says, 'Just a little inflamed. Nothing to worry about.'

I say, 'But it's really red. I am worried.'

He walks out of the room. (Yes, he actually does this without answering me!)

At the next follow-up visit, I try to keep a lid on my anger when I'm told Dr Bob has left the country for a vacation. He doesn't tell me he's leaving town or leave me in the care of any other doctor. When I say to his assistant, 'It's looking even redder,' she smiles and walks out of the room. This kind of anger is truly not good for a human.

It's 21 December. Panicked, I run from a vitamin IV treatment to a hyperbaric chamber to an insane Russian who waves wands of electricity over my body and gives me 'acid' water to drink for two weeks. That's how far a desperate woman will go. The infectious-disease doctor is also on holidays and so eventually, on Boxing Day, I wearily take myself, alone on a windy, cold grey evening, to the emergency room at St John's and explain the situation to a tired ER doc who sympathetically hooks me up to an IV, pronto.

Dr Bob, on the other side of the planet, finally emails me back. I email some photos of the flaming redness from yet another staph infection, he returns to LA on 2 January and the next morning, I'm being wheeled in for emergency surgery for the removal of the left implant, thus leaving me a mono tit once again.

Of course, being extra careful once the damage is done, good ol' Dr Bob then orders six weeks of IV antibiotics followed by two weeks of oral antibiotics. But that course does not prevent me from getting a terrible case of flu, which leads to the night when I truly can't face any more painful hacking so I down an Ambien. When I wake up an hour later coughing so hard my ribs hurt, I pop half a Vicodin and, okay, two hours later, still coughing, I polish off the other half.

So that's what does it. I'm a drug lightweight. I am preparing the morning bowl of three Weetabix, sliced bananas and honey for the sleeping teen but as I pour the organic milk, I start to feel amazingly nauseous and light-headed. Thinking I can just deliver the cereal before hitting the bathroom, I hurry to Nick's room but the cereal bowl slips through my fingers onto the wooden floor, and I scream out, 'Sorry—I'm feeling sick!' as I lurch into the bathroom. That's all I remember till I wake up a few seconds later unable to move, with the teen looking utterly horrified and deeply traumatised by his prone, bleeding mum.

It's a first. I've never fainted in my life. Frankly, I think it's a pretty lame thing to do. As I regain consciousness, Nick hovers and does as I ask. I haven't had such rapt attention from my big lovable lug of a kid for—well, a really long time. He puts towels over me. I try to get up but as I do, searing pain sends me back down. Now, Nick's a pretty cool customer and not squeamish like his old mum but I can tell by his wide-eyed staring at my forehead that some damage has been sustained. He plays it down though and quickly comes up with the huge bin containing our first-aid supplies. He tries to swab me with disinfectant stuff and then he deftly finds a big bandage to put over the wound—ordering me very firmly, 'Just don't look at it, Mum.' After several attempts, he finally manages to help me to my feet and back to bed, but this pain is scary. I feel as if I have dislocated my shoulder. The room spins around a bit and suddenly, even though I hate Nick growing up, I wish he was older and had a licence. I ask him to call his sister, who could perhaps get him to school, but she doesn't answer.

There is nothing else to be done. 'Help me on with my Uggs,' I plead. Nick has two finals starting in about twenty-five minutes. I have to get him to school. Steering one-handed I drive all the way to Hamilton High near Venice on Robertson. 'Just don't look at your head,' Nick begs me again as he hopped out of the car. I promise and instead of sensibly taking myself to an emergency room I head home—feeling weak, woozy and tearful with pain.

And here's the bad part. I have no mobile phone. The night before I'd driven Nick to his weekly therapy appointment, and on the way back, we stopped at McDonald's for grub and I idiotically left my phone there.

So, no longer knowing anyone's number, it takes me another five hours to rustle up a friend to arrive. It is one of the few numbers I remember and by some miracle the number's owner, my dear pal Brooke, has just arrived back from New York and so I am finally rescued. She takes me to her Toluca Lake chiropractor for X-rays, which show a fractured collarbone. With a sling and limited movement, I am told it will heal in six to eight weeks. Then it's off to my family doctor to get ten stitches in the gaping hole in my forehead.

Rather worryingly, the lovely Dr Kipper keeps asking, 'Don't you want your plastic surgeon to take care of this?' but it is now 4.30 pm and I'd been given the complete cold shoulder by Dr Bob. I've called both his cell and the office asking if he, one of the best in the land, or a colleague, could repair my face. Treating me like a stranger, the office tells me to 'go to an emergency room'.

So after about four numbing injections to my forehead, my good pal Dr Kipper does a decent job of stitching me up, and we head home—whereupon my darling son has never treated me so sweetly and divinely.

He tells his sister that the scene of my collapsing to the floor via the corner of the cabinet, which produced a sickening thud he 'imitates' for us, has replayed in his head throughout the day. He was too far away to stop me falling and he clearly felt impotent and, more than that, scared stiff. And so by the time I go to bed at eight, Nick is hovering like a hawk. I ask him to pass the hand cream. He squeezes it out and gives me a hand massage. I ask for a pillow and he brings six of them. I ask for a glass of water and he brings it in with slices of lemon. He gives a demonstration as to how I should sleep on the one side I am permitted to and keeps asking—maybe five or six times—if I feel okay. 'Do you think you might faint again?' and when I stagger up to pee, he follows and stays outside the door, listening for a tell-tale thump. Is there anything more touching than a heavenly display of love from a terrified teen?

A week later I manage to turn the nasty collarbone fracture into a massive break. I am late to get to the bank and as I tear up Laurel Canyon, swerving wildly to the right at Mount Olympus for a short-cut, I feel it 'go'—a snapping sound that is loud and unmistakable. To distract myself from the pain I pretend I'm in a movie and that I must drive like a one-armed gunslinger to save the day ... I swerve back onto Laurel Canyon and down to Studio City to the bank, painfully slither out of the car with minutes to spare before closing time, and as I sit down opposite my friendly banker, my iPhone beeps, alerting me to a text from my landlord saying that she'd gotten me mixed up with another tenant, my rent cheque had *not* bounced and no eviction was imminent!

Grisly X-rays two days later confirm this nasty break. One half of my collarbone is now lying an inch under the other half and thus it is physically impossible for the bottom half to travel upwards and to the right to knit together naturally. So says an excellent guy at the Santa Monica Orthopedic Group called Dr Modabber, who is offering sympathy for the pain I must be going through and is booking an emergency surgery for the following morning. 'This can't wait,' he says matter-of-factly. This is despite the fact that, the day before, another top orthopedic surgeon at Cedars-Sinai had told me to return in two weeks to see how it was 'coming along'. To me, the layman, it did not seem right in any way, shape or form, and thus I got a second opinion. It was a harsh reminder of how fucking fallible doctors can be. One has to take charge to a certain degree and be one's own advocate—often to a preposterous extent!

By 8 am the next day, I've dropped Nick at school thirty minutes early and am lying on yet another gurney so that yet another part of my top left anatomy can be sliced open. At least this time nothing will be removed. A seven-inch titanium plate will be *added*, screwed into place along the collarbone thus securing the two pieces together. With many people, the metal plate protrudes once the swelling subsides, making you look like 'an alien', and so most patients undergo another surgery a year later to have the plate removed.

I couldn't care less about a protruding plate but I would like another tit. Call me picky, but I really just want a pair and won't rest till I get 'em. To that end I have yet another appointment with Dr Bob coming up. I've been seeing both Dr Bob and a new female infectious-disease doc ever since the emergency and very unceremonious removal of my left tit in January.

Please believe me when I say I tried to leave him! I've been to see many other surgeons hoping someone would rescue me and whisk me away to a magical operating room where promises of restoration would be made—and come true. But instead, grisly ten-hour 'flap' surgeries are suggested by all these surgeons, including Dr Bob. A lengthy recovery time, loss of muscle strength and potential infection follow.

I decide, with encouragement from my new, more evolved and compassionate infectious-disease doc, Dr Sue, that I should persuade Dr Bob to forget the possibly safer but nightmarish, disfiguring flap surgery and agree to do the exact same surgery we've tried twice before—cutting me open to insert an expander and then three months later cutting me open again to remove the expander and put in the implant. *If the right precautions are taken and IV antibiotics are given during and after surgery*, as they should have been by Dr Bob, there's no reason it shouldn't bloody work.

He is finally convinced and agrees to proceed with the same surgery—for a *third* time—and a date is set. But the long-submerged anger I have towards Dr Bob can no longer be contained. It has a mind of its own and I wake up one morning in a white-hot rage, realising that I cannot let him slice me open for a *seventh* time. I call up and cancel the surgery. I'm polite and give no reasons. I simply say that I can't proceed right now.

As I put the phone down I realise I have no idea what to do or how to proceed. But isn't there an old saying—shut one door and another opens?

A few days later I'm given some brand-new information that is riveting. I go to see my holistic gynaecologist, Dr Cynthia Watson, to go over blood work. She mentions that she recently went to a seminar in San Diego hosted by Dr Steven Cohen, where he introduced doctors from Brazil, Israel and Japan who presented photos and videos of some lucky pioneering women waking up, after liposuction with gorgeous new breasts containing no expanders or implants—just their very own fat, which has been gently injected in tiny amounts at dozens of points all over their breasts. Amazing. No repeated surgeries to insert uncomfortable expanders and then implants that rupture, shift, get lumpy or otherwise cause untold horrors and grief. A two-for-one. Wake up with new breasts *and* slimmer thighs or a flat stomach.

It sounds so ridiculously simple but miraculous. I'm stunned. Apparently a couple of surgeons have been doing this one-step magical 'mastectomy and immediate fat grafting' operation for a year or two. Had I known, this whole saga could have been put to bed over two years ago and I could be living happily ever after with Mr Right as I type.

I burn the midnight oil researching it all. I visit a couple of doctors who know about it and are thinking of doing it but don't feel like starting with me.

A few days later, I trudge off to Beverly Hills to see a female surgeon, Dr Betty, who knows all about it. Blow me down if, within thirty seconds flat, she's not talking about everything I've been researching—fat grafting, the Brava suction domes you wear to prepare your skin for it, and how this could be the answer! She's even just begun to do a breast augmentation using the patient's own fat, and since her website focuses largely on the liposuction she does, it makes sense that she'd be interested in recycling the fat that was once thrown away. Once or twice she refers to a doctor—I think she says Dr Cory—who's had great success with fat grafting. But on my third visit Dr Betty says she doesn't feel confident proceeding with me.

Next move? I hit the internet again, looking for surgeons who are doing fat transfers using the Brava technique and finally—duh!—I come across the inventor of the whole darn thing, Dr Roger Khouri. This is the surgeon that Dr Betty had mentioned twice … and I'd been typing in 'Dr Cory' all these weeks. I feel like I've discovered the Holy Grail.

The website is inspiring. I call up and schedule an appointment in Miami for four weeks hence. Hallelujah. But then I put it off for another two weeks as I realise I may be overestimating my energy levels.

Since Lola moved out recently, I no longer need a three-bedroom apartment. I find a cute apartment with no double garage to store the furniture and hundred-odd boxes that have been happily living there. Thus, I make a valiant attempt to acquaint myself with eBay and Craigslist to flog some furniture. I have some success but seem to spend more money buying bubble wrap to protect the bookcases and coffee tables prior to shipping than the dough received from the actual transaction.

There are five weeks of gruelling days packing, selling, shipping before a grim move day and by 7 pm one sweltering Saturday in June, Nick and I have moved into a pretty cool mid-century Hollywood apartment, one block from Runyon Canyon, that Sylvester Stallone lived in—and as the Craigslist ad boasted shamelessly and relentlessly, the very hallowed sanctum in which he wrote *Rocky*. I'd imagined they were lying about this being the actual apartment he lived in till I meet Michael, the oldest tenant in the complex, who lives next door to me. He's been here for thirty-nine years and tells me, 'The owners hate my guts, they want me out—I'm still only paying $900 a month for two bedrooms and a balcony.' Yes, he insists without my asking, 'Sylvester lived in your place. I never liked him!' Michael then confides that he even has a Beta copy of Sly's porno movie *The Italian Stallion* on one of his bookshelves. He points to the apartment ten yards from ours. 'Liz Taylor and Shelley Winters shared that one. They used to entertain a very cute Mexican in there,' he chortles with a wink. 'And Sonny and Cher lived down below. Always fighting. Boy, could she bellow!' It's a tiny slice of Hollywood history.

Ten days after the move, I wake up one Monday morning wondering if I can possibly make the noon plane to Miami to see Dr Khouri. There are still forty boxes in the living room. Alas, it's a non-refundable ticket. I struggle to find clothes and pack in the chaos. But when I smell cigarette smoke coming from the bathroom, I start to shriek and Nick and I have a big fight. Nick barricades himself in the bedroom. I have unscrewed his doorknob and hidden it so now he heaves a sofa in front of the door. We've been fighting a lot. I found a stash of weed and cigarettes a few days ago and threw it right out. In retaliation, he's been leaving the apartment at odd hours, not answering his mobile phone and acting like a lout.

He will *not* answer me now. I plead and beg, 'Nick, I have to get this plane. Please come out now!' No answer. I call a friend to come and take me to the airport and then return to cajole Nick out of his lair and take him to my friends' place where he will stay. Exhausting stuff.

I hit Miami and its suffocating heat at 8 pm, spend the night in a B&B and take a cab to Dr Khouri's offices in what looks like an industrial park the next morning. When the rotund, bow tie–wearing doc enters in a flurry he takes one look at me and says, 'Yes, no problem, I can help you.' He grabs hold of the right breast with the implant and mutters, 'barbaric'. He truly does. And he agrees that it should be taken out and filled with fat too. I'm about to ask if he really thinks I have enough fat but the doc rudely darts out of the room and never returns. A three-minute consultation after I've flown across the country.

I call his office the next day to book surgery and give my insurance details at which point I'm told that Dr Khouri himself takes my insurance but his surgery centre does not! It's a tiny detail they forgot to mention on any of the many calls before I flew out. It will cost $10,000 plus the cost of three trips to Miami and accommodation for the five days I must stay each time.

I then go online and find a website devoted to Dr Khouri and the Brava device he invented to prepare the skin, and several people are complaining about poor results. I suddenly realise I didn't even ask if he actually thinks there's a good chance that the Brava can get the 'superglued' skin on my chest unstuck?

I call several times leaving messages for him to please call. *Nada.* I email politely three times over the next three weeks. *Nada.* I finally send one last email with four questions and the next morning I get a devastating email back where he fires me. He says that there are no guarantees and since it's a long way to come, why don't I find a doctor in my local area who does it and takes my insurance?

Just one problem. There is no such doctor and he knows it.

Stunned and guilt-ridden, I write back three utterly pathetic, begging emails, saying that I'm truly not a 'difficult patient', and that after this excruciatingly long saga where I didn't do all my home-work, I felt I had to check it out thoroughly. I apologise profusely for 'annoying him with questions'. (I wanted to write in caps, 'Sorry for committing the heinous crime of daring to ask a doctor actual questions.' Asshole.)

Meantime, I discuss my plight with four different surgeons. One I visit is all the way in San Diego but he does take my insurance. Two more don't take my insurance.

And then, I have to confess that, almost inexplicably given our history—but out of sheer desperation—I even call Dr Bob, convinced that he must be somehow invested in me and my disfigured state, which I owe to him, and I tell him about this whole new world of fat.

Well, he immediately pooh-poohs it, stating categorically that 'it would not work' for me. I give him chapter and verse as to why I must disagree with him and he calls back six days later, having clearly looked into it and raves about 'the exciting possibilities with fat. Come in and we'll talk.' So I'm suckered into driving again to Santa Monica only to be told, 'I'm going to Miami to watch Dr Khouri work in October. I can do you in November.' Months go by and I'm too tired to do anything.

A few months later, having been to Miami to watch Dr Khouri work, he calls me in to say, 'Let's go.' I agree. I'm ready. One tiny thing he forgets to mention is that he has stopped taking my insurance. On my way out after our meeting, the girl in billing hands me a quote for $22,000. I can't even talk I'm crying so much. I mumble 'sorry' and flee the building.

I email Dr Bob and ask if he can possibly lower the price. Ten days later his receptionist offers a $5000 discount. It's still out of my reach. I email Dr Bob once more and ask if there is any way humanly possible that I could pay it off over time … but I don't hear back. Although insulted, hurt and angry at this man's lack of any decency after such negligence I try not to dwell in a state of 'bitter'. The cancer therapist I saw who strongly urged me to see a lawyer to discuss suing Dr Bob happens to email me a few days later and insists I should think about proceeding—but I'm far too weary to think about it. Case closed with him.

I must press on. I couldn't care less about vanity and looks but just can't bear to have gone through so much and not have the results I should have—or at least a semblance of success. Over the next twelve months, I schlep on a train to the doc in San Diego and book in for surgery, which is a logistical nightmare, but there you go. After liposuction of stomach and thighs, that fat is put into my left breast. I have several deeply tedious follow-up visits, after more lonely long train trips, with this cold, unappealing man. So I end up returning to

Dr McDreamy in Beverly Hills, who takes another couple of cracks at this fat grafting. But it becomes crystal clear that I'm an absolute guinea pig and this whole concept of using your own fat instead of implants should be planned from the get-go—otherwise its chances are massively diminished. My 'situation' is very compromised, I don't have tons of fat and horrifyingly, must finally, *finally* concede that I have just had three surgeries that turned out to be flops. I tried to be a pioneer and it will work for others but I found out about it too late. With much soul-searching despair I must face facts and accept the upsetting truth that I will in fact need implants to create two half-way decent-looking breasts.

I plead with Dr McDreamy for the tiniest ones possible for my frame and we look at different sizes and fix on a size—or so I think. I wake up after my umpteenth surgery with whopping great tits about three sizes bigger than we had discussed. I'm disgusted that these surgeons don't listen. Finally, I get the pleasant and honest Dr Betty to put in small ones. They're just okay. She would like to continue adding bits of my own fat to enhance the look, but I'm done.

CHAPTER 26

The Unsinkable Molly Brown

D ETERMINED TO BE positive and not dwell in dark places, I've started chanting with a wonderful old friend who's been a practising Buddhist for 25 years. Endlessly repeating *nam myoho renge kho* so quickly that the words become nonsense in a stylish Hancock Park living room is gruelling but great discipline, and I'm ready to do anything it takes to change my life and patterns, stay open to hopeful scenarios and emerge from the vile medical horror story of the last few years. (Though so far it's only proved that I'm a shallow flibbertigibbet who can spend an entire chanting session sneaking looks at the pair of stunning mid-century sofas my pal inherited from her mother and fantasising about how their ultra-suede upholstery needs to be ripped off immediately and replaced with a stylish *Mad Men* orangey tweed.)

So what have I learnt during my time as a girl from Oz?

Looking back on my earlier years with Michael White, I realise it was quite simply a magical, blessed decade for the most part—with so much fun and laughter, stimulation and travel, and extravagant good times that now seem impossibly wonderful and joyous. I made so many friends who I can happily claim I still adore and who still adore me. The downside is that most of them are in London and I just wish I had the means to go there so much more often and hang with dear

304

friends like Gael and Francesco and their family. They are like family. Indeed, I oft wished I still lived there. But it's hard to replicate the highs of one's youth. And London is not cheap. It's also good not to dwell in the past. Everyone has one and I'm lucky enough to have had a brilliantly exciting one. I still love Michael and keep in close touch. He's slowed down considerably after a stroke but is so ridiculously stoic and never complains about getting round now on two sticks.

On my last visit to London, I organised for Kate Moss to show up at the Olivier Awards as the surprise presenter who gave Michael his lifetime achievement award! He was thrilled—he's always adored Kate. He was wheeled onto the stage by his three proud children—Liberty, Joshua and Sasha (now a QC—top-class lawyer—in London)—and Sasha read the speech that Michael had written. The Royal Opera House audience was very moved and Michael grinned

With my dear best girlfriend Gael and her lovely, smart, handsome Italian tycoon hubby Francesco Boglione. They are without doubt the kindest, most generous and hospitable true friends a girl could wish for … I'm so lucky to have them in my life, though I don't see them as often as I would like.

so sweetly as they cheered his hugely impressive and innovative body of work in theatre, films and TV. I then organised a lunch for him at the Soho Club. It was touching and sad and I tried to make a toast and got choked up like the sentimental slob I am, and he was gruff and barely thanked me but it's okay. I owe him a lot and every day try to take a leaf out of his book. Don't look back. Have a good time and just get on with it.

This aforementioned trip was to see the darling, utterly superb woman—and my dear friend—Candida Lycett Green, who I met in the first couple of months dating Michael and who, along with her wonderful husband, Rupert, became two of my all-time favourite people. The daughter of the former British poet laureate Sir John Betjeman, Cand was a columnist and the writer of many books, a fantastic cook and hostess and mother of five, an ardent conservationist of all things British, from old churches to riding trails and seaside cottages, a horsewoman and as one of Prince Charles's good friends, she was the royal go-between for Al and me. But Cand was told just four months earlier that her breast cancer had returned— now in both her liver and pancreas, a double whammy that is almost impossible to beat. She started with chemo—which seemed to me a crazy waste of time. Though I said not a word, of course. And indeed, at a certain point, it was clearly not helping and she stopped. She took a thrice daily tincture of CBD—a compound in cannabis that does not get you stoned but has healing, medicinal effects and is being used widely now to treat cancers, MS, Crohn's Disease and epilepsy, to name just a few, and her last few months were as pleasant as they could be.

This is from her last email to me and it has become my 'guiding light'—the piece of wisdom that I think about whenever self-pity or nostalgia for the good old 'high life' days comes knocking:

I feel completely at peace and never so happy. When I decided not to try the hell of an even more violent chemo (just to buy an extra couple of months) I felt a whoosh of calm. I do not fear death in any way—only the possible torture chamber at the end but I am hoping the CBD will continue to dull any pain which it sure is doing now (plus tramadol and anti-sickness tabs.) These last six months have been golden and a blessing privilege to have with my kids and grandkids wrapped around me with love and our wonderful garden wrapped round them …

It went on to say:

Over the decades I have told you again and again and again that you are the kindest, most caring, wonderful girl in the world but you don't want to believe it. Not all RICH HOLIDAY-ING PEOPLE ARE HAPPY and you fucking well know it.

Now I am where I am in my life, will you please listen to me. Facing mortality I know this … That LOVE is the only important thing (LAUGHING AND DANCING A CLOSE SECOND!) YOU HAVE IT WITH MY DARLING LOLA AND NAUGHTY NICK but you also ladle it out to others in such extraordinary dollops (Look at you with your dad—moving beyond compare to an outsider). It's hard/tough to have known the high life of buying what you wanted etc. But of course you know that underneath it's not the point of life. You just have to compromise and downsize your tastes. When Rupert and I lost everything we came out of it feeling far, far better, having plumbed the depths of friendships which we would never have plumbed otherwise. Your close friends are an extraordinarily wonderful bunch so quit complaining about anything. Lyndall, I cherish and love you and will love you forever.

From your good chum, Candy.

What else is there to say? They are the sweetest and most touching words anyone has ever written to me. A tad self-serving to include it—but what a gift it was and is to remember now and always that

For my first visit to Royal Ascot, we all assembled at our house at Egerton Crescent beforehand. The gang included Albert Finney, Diana Quick, Gael, Rupert and, here, the very wonderful, incredibly enchanting woman who would become a truly special friend: the late Candida Lycett Green, who encouraged me to get my snap of Her Majesty the Queen.

happiness is not down to your bank account. *So totally true.* I have *nothing* to complain about. Candy died just over two weeks after sending that email. The invitation to her memorial service arrived, and to my surprise, the cover featured a wonderful photo I took of her in Egerton Crescent one day back in the '70s as we headed off to Ascot. Part of her email was read out at the service to give comfort to others. I loved her so much. It is so fucking tough to lose friends.

What other wisdom have I gained?

Well, a few days ago I found out that my suspicion that stuffing a cell phone in to my bra for the four years I was in Australia may have caused the cancerous tumour could perhaps be right. With a sickening rush of guilt, I just read about it in an article about Devra Davis PhD, author of the book *The Secret History of the War on Cancer*. Dr Davis, who also discusses all the carcinogenic environmental toxins dumped around us (especially in poor areas), writes that doctors have been noticing that many women with breast tumours—and no other cancer risk factors or family history—are also women who stuff their mobile phones in their bras! Look closely at the fine print when you buy your next iPhone and you'll see the dire warnings that it should not be worn really close to your body in your pocket or bra. I talked to friends about my bra theory well over three years ago, convinced that the positioning of my phone and the tiny tumour were too close to be coincidental.

Despite its reputation as the gold-standard cancer treatment, many oncologists, research scientists and patients are questioning just how successful chemo really is—given that everyone's cancer situation is different and thus individuals should not be treated in the cookie cutter way they are now.

For certain types of cancer, when an oncologist says that chemo is 'effective'—they are often referring to statistics such as a 50 per cent shrinkage of a tumour for twenty-eight days, or patient survival being *one* month longer than they might have had without the drugs. But that might mean a month, or perhaps two, where the patient is so ill and depleted that quality of life is virtually non-existent. When the cancer patient hears the doctor say 'effective', he or she thinks, and logically so, that 'effective' means it cures cancer. But it may not, and you should always ask exactly what the doctor means by 'effective'.

For some people it makes sense to have chemo. For others, like me, it does *not*. And it will all but destroy your immune system for a year or two or more.

But most oncologists are very reluctant to skip chemo. Some fear lawsuits if the cancer returns and chemo has not been given. It's easier for doctors to give it and tell their patients they've been super-aggressive even though some studies have shown that the most common chemo drug, Taxol (which is usually given along with another chemo drug Cytoxan and is the combo I was given), may help far fewer patients than has previously been believed. As Dr Glaspy suggested, I almost certainly would have been better off skipping chemo and going straight to radiation. But what did I know?

In short, the standard of care is unsatisfactory. As Julian Whitaker MD states in the foreword to Suzanne Somers's excellent book *Knockout*, 'conventional medicine's approach to cancer prevention and treatment is a debilitating, often deadly fraud'.

For the most part, it's very much about money. Cancer is big business. It truly is about cookie-cutter treatment and maximising profits. In America the pharmaceutical companies actually fund a lot of the medical schools where the oncologists are trained to give these drugs and have devoted years to reach a high level of expertise in the knowledge of poisonous, deadly compounds. The doctors are in a bind because they went into oncology to help the cancer patient and yet the tools they've been given don't always work well. And they see what happens to doctors who step out of line and treat cancer with alternative means. Armed raids, loss of licences, professional smearing and ostracism are some of the consequences.

Pharmaceutical companies are arguably the most profitable on the planet, making three times the profits of the average Fortune 500 Company. The only way to sustain these profits is by flogging the same old toxic drugs whose patents have yet to run out along with introducing new freshly patented drugs that will eventually replace the old ones. But some of the new cancer drugs are approved way too quickly before—whoops—some nasty side effects are discovered. A fairly new drug, Avastin, had its approval for breast cancer treatment rescinded as it did nothing to prolong life—but not until the drug company concerned had made a few billion.

In England right now they're trying to pass a bill that could help everyone with a 'rare' cancer. It seeks to provide legal protection for doctors with terminally ill patients where there is no trial for which they are eligible, giving the doctor the freedom to legally 'innovate' and give them new drugs. Now 'rare' is pretty much everything that is not in the 'big four' cancers (breast, bowel, lung and prostate). Because the big four are more common, they dominate fundraising, research and trials. But less common cancers account for more than half of all British cancer deaths. However, and here's the problem, the lack of trials—which are hugely expensive and affordable only to big companies—means that doctors who want to cure their patients, rather than just manage their deaths, are caught in a hideous catch 22. If there's no evidence that a new treatment will work, it's against the law to use it to find out if it does work. The proposed Medical Innovation Bill would allow doctors to try new treatments on dying patients.

So what I would like to stress is that if cancer comes knocking, try to remember in the chaos and fear that follows diagnosis, chemo is *not* necessarily the answer. And just because so many doctors and hospitals and specialists say to do it, doesn't make it right. There are tests available now that can tell if you'll benefit from chemo at all! Ask for them. There are also supplements that can help counteract the effects of chemo.

Too many doctors prescribe too many drugs that are toxic and we need to be informed. Keep asking questions till something resonates and truly feels right. *Doctors are not gods and recent studies show that many doctors, when asked if they would take chemo if they had a cancer diagnosis, admit that they would definitely hesitate and think hard before undergoing chemo treatment!*

It's too late for me but not for others.

Life took one of its brutal turns on June 26, 2015. On the eve of a career comeback, the unthinkable happened to Lola's dad and my ex-husband, Chris Thompson. He'd been in a major career slump for years and was broke, when suddenly he got a call out of the blue from one of the most powerful men in LA, uber-agent Ari Emanuel, who said, 'Chris, I've got an Israeli TV show for you and you're the only guy in town who can write this and set it in America!'

The call led to meetings and Skype sessions, and Chris got the job! 'I killed it,' he told me after his biggest test. He was always 'good in the room' and started to write great episode ideas, finally energised and enthusiastic after many years in comedy writing jail.

We'd been seeing Chris a lot in recent weeks—at birthdays and family gatherings—with Lola cooking her beloved dad a wonderful Father's Day dinner that Nick and her half-brother and half-sister,

Richard and Taylor, attended. It was lovely and intimate and that night Chris talked about the very last meeting coming up, where he would simply give Amazon, who had already agreed to make the pilot, a verbal outline. 'I think I'm about to become relevant again,' he told me that evening.

Just four days later, on the Friday night, I got a call from the police. Chris was dead. He had accidentally overdosed, probably on heroin. It was never fully explained to us.

I had to go and wake Lola at midnight and tell her that her father had died and then take her and Nick over to where the police kept watch over his body. One of the most gruesome nights of all time. Lola and Nick are heartbroken—as are we all. It's a tragedy. But he had an illness, a disease, and he had it bad. He was a real die-hard addict, unable to control his addiction till it killed him.

Lola organised a beautiful memorial evening for her extremely talented dad—and it was a huge turnout. He'd helped and inspired countless people in his career and the many who spoke all raved about his outsized wit, humor and charisma, and how he lit up a room. Even the reclusive Penny Marshall from *Laverne and Shirley* showed up for Chris and reminisced about the good ol' days with the clever, larger-than-life showrunner Mr Thompson. He is truly, deeply missed.

I know some folk might want to know what actually happened with me and Al. Well, that's hard to say. But we had some issues and just as I was outspoken and not terribly tolerant, so Al could be spoilt, difficult and not terribly sensitive. He claimed recently that I hadn't 'handled' him well. We were great when it was just the two of us. And once in a while I miss the things we did on our own … the silly, simple things. A game of paddle tennis, playing Uno together, always holding hands in the movies. Ordering French fries and ice-cream from room service in hotels in foreign spots at 3 am as we watched old black and white movies or listening to books on tapes in the car. We often played word games in the car, and I was the one who was a champion speller with the great vocabulary, but Al was annoyingly good at them and always won. Go figure.

During our seven years as a couple, we saw a grand total of twelve therapists together and I can honestly say that not one of them helped us a jot! It's hilarious in retrospect but was desperately infuriating at the time, when almost all of them were so utterly and completely in awe of Al—so sycophantic and preposterously on his side—that we would leave the sessions with Al feeling utterly justified, vindicated and pleased with himself while I fumed and felt alone and helpless! It was unfair and led, of course, to more arguments. But that's showbiz, folks. Things sometimes work out—and sometimes they don't and it doesn't necessarily mean the love has gone. I do think that perhaps two famous people together works better than one.

I've now learnt, having joined the dating site OkCupid, that a decent age-appropriate man with any sense of grammar is *not* to be found in sunny Los Angeles. I managed, after about six months of futile attempts, to scrounge up a couple of reasonable photos (having tried umpteen tragic selfies and then demanding that Nick or Lola take a pic every time I put on makeup and thought I looked halfway decent)—and now the vast majority of the messages that trickle in at the rate of about two or three a week seem to come from illiterate men under thirty who actually like the look of my severe black glasses, tight pencil skirt and some ancient red patent-leather Manolo Blahnik heels. It's the glam but bossy schoolteacher look and they write compelling messages like, 'I know your (sic) too old for me—but just wanted to say YUR hot in those heels' or, 'I work late but if you still up at 3 am, I will be ready to know you better!' or, 'I'm only 5'6" but I got plenty where it counts baby!'

And just today, I got this irresistible message from a 'post office dude' on OkCupid: 'I am looking for a woman. Not just any woman. But a woman who would be very open to the possibility of joining my girlfriend and I in a casual relationship or even a triad.' I think you get the picture here. This twerp did not even customise the message for me, just a 'copy and paste' sent to dozens in the wild hopes that someone will bite. Call me an old prude, but *really*? On what planet does this kind of thing happen? So yes, dating seems to be in the category of 'difficult to nigh on impossible'—unless one wants casual sex, which has never been something I cared about. But in my new gung-ho mode, perhaps I should *try* to stop being a picky, judgmental, snobbish bitch, check out a new dating site and try to be open— threesomes *excluded*—to what comes along. And pigs might fly! But seriously, I'm going to try.

I definitely know that, whatever else happens, you can't stop making an effort. If perhaps you're thinking, 'Hey, I'm getting older, maybe I should ease down a bit,' *fuggedaboutit*! We have to go to the gym and work out even harder than before to get those poor flagging muscles to do their thing. Stretching, cardio, weight resistance, yoga—you've gotta do it all just so you can get out of bed in the morning. Or rescue a dog! I did—in what I thought was a cunning plot to get Nick out of his smoky room and up the fantastic Runyon Canyon, literally two minutes from our apartment, with the new Australian cattle-dog mix, Sooky, who alarmingly closely resembles a dingo! (Runyon is a series of wild hiking trails moments from Hollywood Boulevard. It's one of the amazing things about LA—different canyon trails for humans, dogs and horses all over town in the middle of the city.) Alas, Nick did it twice before handing Sooky right over to Mum. But it's fine. I adore our evening hikes, have lost a few kilos and am very fit.

And if you think you can get away with easing up on making an effort to have a social life, no way. Now's when you really have to crank it up and make a huge effort to widen that circle of friends. Have a dinner party. Organise a birthday soiree for a friend. Try and lift your game socially. That's my plan. When I feel a little grim I try to remember that everyone's ageing at exactly the same rate as me. Madonna and Tom Stoppard and Diane Sawyer and I are all getting older at *exactly* the same rate. I truly do know that just having access to fresh water and a soft cosy bed are things not to be taken lightly and that even the richest and most glamorous amongst us can get deathly ill or have car accidents and it's all over in an instant. (Having said that I do loathe travelling economy and must confess to getting a teensy bit bitter as I board a plane and head right instead of the old days when I turned left. Thus I always try to watch a lot of films and read books and worthy articles and feel I've accomplished a huge amount as opposed to those sloths flat on their backs in business or first.)

Nick says I need to stop 'micromanaging' his life. About eighteen months ago I finally escaped LA for the first time in three years and spent about six weeks in London with my darling friend Gael. It was divine, and although Nick was reluctant and in a staggeringly grumpy mood a lot of the time, he and I made it to Paris for three days and did the sights. Naturally, we missed the plane back to London and had to stay an extra wildly expensive night in Paris and then buy one-way train tickets across the Chunnel back to Blighty! We had tears and drama but I know that he will remember our frenzied, chaotic jaunt for a very long time. I saw tons of the many friends I still have in London and I then sent Nick off on his own to be the stage manager for a mini opera at the Edinburgh Festival. It was fantastic, invaluable experience for the lad and not a hint of micromanaging from me for five weeks. He's sweet, sensitive and clever. Affectionate and generous. A great drummer. A fantastic cook! An unusual and truly insightful lad. I adore him. He's now home schooling himself to finish high school before going to college. Trying to find his way in the world and would probably prefer I say not another word.

My darling girl Lola is just a delight, a witty, sweet and adorable girl, and I'm so proud of the work she's doing. Instead of going on to study law after her fine-arts degree—as I'd encouraged her to do in a rather transparent attempt to produce a breadwinner and hedge against possible future complaints that I hadn't guided her well—my extremely charismatic and highly intelligent daughter has gone into full 'starving artist' mode living in her cute apartment in Macarthur Park.

After enthusiastically taking two acting classes for several months and showing amazing promise, she gravitated back to her first love of art when a friend of mine suggested she apply to be a contestant on a Bravo TV show called *Work Of Art: The Next Great Artist*. She applied and was finally chosen, out of thousands of applicants, to compete.

'A Gift from the Euro Zone to the Greek Finance Minister'. One of my favorites of Lola's recent paintings. Oil on panel. Absolutely beautiful. She's very talented and this one had people—including Tim Curry and Al Pacino—fighting over it at a recent Hollywood art show. Tim swiftly moved to the back, spotted the gallery owner and claimed it first. Many were disappointed but she's since been commissioned to do more like this one.

It turned out she was the youngest one on it and the only one who'd never even exhibited her work. It was gripping television, she looked gorgeous, could not have been more watchable or charming on TV— and indeed was featured heavily, if not too heavily, every episode. As artists were eliminated each week following a challenge, the tension rose. Brilliantly, she was not eliminated till almost the very end. I could not believe how any of them dealt with the stress of producing brand-new work that had to fit in a chosen theme, in just a couple of days at most. It was disappointing that she didn't win but a stunning performance with so much original, highly praised art that blew me away.

And it's spurred her on into the rather frightening world of having to get up and create on a daily basis, which she does with great discipline. She's been in three group shows and is producing some beautiful paintings that impress me—and some of my more art-savvy friends—no end. She is so talented and I'm in awe. As I write she is preparing for her very first solo show in Hollywood.

But more to the point, she's loving and compassionate and so incredibly kind. (She tells me she loves me all the time and I just wish my generation had told their parents they loved them more often. Or at all. Sadly, I don't recall saying it to my folks—though they didn't say it to me either. The modern trend to make frequent declarations to one's nearest and dearest is very wonderful.) Lola recently nursed her dying granny for weeks and weeks on end (having looked after me so well for many years) and towards the end she would sleep on the floor next to her bed through the night. Indeed, Lola was right there with her alone one night when she died. She is so good and motherly and sweet to Nick and his friends. Right now Nick and his pal, who got

One very memorable summer, my parents flew to London via Crete and Athens for a trip that I'd been planning for months. It included jaunts up to Scotland and Paris, and then a stay at the magical place I'd been writing to them about for the two previous summers: Le Nid du Duc, near St Tropez. They had a ball!

kicked out of home, are sleeping in Lola's bedroom. She's like Wendy to the Lost Boys. I am preposterously lucky to have them both.

So, do I feel more feminine and appealing? No I do not. I probably need to take some mind-altering drug and try to learn to love my battered body again. But all I want to do now is get creative and back to work. Bugger men. A year ago I sat down and wrote a TV pilot called *Hollywood Mom* and even persuaded Ellen Barkin, Christopher Lloyd (Doc Emmett Brown in *Back to the Future*) and Holland Taylor (the mother in *Two and a Half Men*), among others, to be in it.

I spent months preparing a pitch video for the Indiegogo crowd-funding website. A pitch video? Yes—a horrifying experience where one humbly asks friends, acquaintances and strangers for money for the shoot, complete with visual aids, cast photos and perks for donors. The first attempt did not cut it, and I decided it must be shot a second time in more confident, upbeat fashion. Begging one's poor,

My big babies enjoying Christmas morning at the farm, one of their favourite places on the planet for what it signifies in terms of friendship, love, a sense of belonging and fabulous, kookaburra-chirping Aussieness. They are both so proud to be Australian citizens!

unsuspecting pals and bombarding them with emails in the thirty-day fundraising period is excruciating. But I did it. Shockingly and miraculously it worked. Friends were wonderfully generous and we shot a full pilot several months ago. Pilots can cost upwards of a million dollars if made the traditional studio way, but I did it for US$25,000 at Melanie Griffith's stunning Spanish house in Hancock Park over a chaotic and crazed two days. I have just spent several months editing it, working somewhat painstakingly at 9 o'clock at night once every couple of weeks, when my editor could find time away from her crazed schedule on *NCIS* at Paramount Studios. The hope is to get it going as a TV series, or just as a new reel to reboot my directing career and perhaps even get an agent after a long hiatus.

It's pretty good, and after some colour correction and a sound mix, I will attempt to flog it and get it out there … but it's not going to be easy. None of it. Both ageism and sexism will mean it's going to be tough to even get an agent. And not just for me—for any female director it's a gruelling slog. Not so long ago, there was a story plastered all over the front page of the *Los Angeles Times*: 'Female directors are on the outside looking in'. It went on to report that the American Civil Liberties Union were calling for an investigation into what so many in Hollywood 'have lamented for years—alleging discriminatory hiring' by both film and TV studios. The numbers speak for themselves: just 4.6 per cent of films released by the six major studios were directed by women last year. And just 14 per cent of TV shows were directed by women. It has been talked about for decades—but absolutely bugger all has really changed, and in fact the numbers have gone *down* of late!

Still, despite everything … I'm being optimistic. What choice do I have? I know that whatever happens next, I will soldier on, because I have two kids who I adore utterly and that's who I am and that's what you do. Some friends recently referred to me as the Unsinkable Molly Brown. I thought it was rather patronising and annoying at first, but now, trying hard to be a good 'Aussie battler', I'm rather proud of it.

136

Acknowledgements

There are so many, many good pals whose friendship, loyalty and support have kept me going throughout some tricky times in recent years … I owe them so much.

They include Gael and Francesco Boglione, Rachel and Bryan Brown, Candida and Rupert Lycett Green, Brooke Adams, Bob Ackerman, Robert Fox, Jeremy and Eski Thomas, Andrew Bergman, Sheila Jaffe, Charlotte Barnes, Richard Baskin, Carol Kane, Norma Moriceau, Lorraine Kirke and cousin Jane.

I would also like to truly thank the two very smart sheilas from Hardie Grant: Julie Pinkham, who believed in the book and got the ball rolling, and my editor, Rihana Ries, for her untiring efforts and excellent suggestions. I'm also extremely grateful for the energy and smarts of my superb agent Fran Moore.

Morgan Entrekin was very encouraging to me when I sent him an early draft of the book and my good pals Fiona Lewis, Tracy Tynan and Sharman Forman have encouraged me to keep writing all the way. My dear friend Ken Sylk has been so utterly loyal, supportive and loving throughout these last seven years. Our fabulous phone calls have been a lifesaver. A big shout-out to the talented Ellen Barkin and Holland Taylor for agreeing to be in my TV pilot, and to Melanie Griffith for coming on board as executive producer. My dear, kind and talented brother Geoffrey gave me some great details about my dad that I had forgotten. My neighbourhood gang of James Foley, Evelyn Purcell, Diantha Lebenzon and Scott Zimmerman have been my fun dining pals. And, of course, my two heavenly children, Lola and Nick, are a constant source of comfort, love and inspiration.